GER

The Transformation of

TWAYNE'S INTERNATIONAL HISTORY SERIES

Akira Iriye, editor
Harvard University

GERMANY AND THE UNITED STATES

The Transformation of the German Question
since 1945, Updated Edition

Frank A. Ninkovich

St. John's University

TWAYNE PUBLISHERS • NEW YORK
MAXWELL MACMILLAN CANADA • TORONTO
MAXWELL MACMILLAN INTERNATIONAL • NEW YORK OXFORD SINGAPORE SYDNEY

Twayne Publishers
Macmillan Publishing Company
866 Third Avenue
New York, New York 10022

Maxwell Macmillan Canada, Inc.
1200 Eglinton Avenue East
Suite 200
Don Mills, Ontario M3C 3N1

Twayne's International History Series, No. 2

Library of Congress Cataloging-in-Publication Data

Ninkovich, Frank A., 1944–
    Germany and the United States : the transformation of the German
question since 1945 / by Frank Ninkovich.—Updated ed.
        p. cm.—(Twayne's international history series ; no. 2)
    Includes bibliographical references and index.
    ISBN 0-8057-7928-0 (cloth).—ISBN 0-8057-9223-6 (pbk.)
    1. German reunification question (1949–1990) 2. Germany—Foreign
relations—United States.   3. United States—Foreign relations—
Germany.   I. Title.   II. Series.
    DD257.25.N55   1994
    327.73043'09'045—dc20   1994
                                                                 CIP

The paper used in this publication meets the minimum requirements of American National Standard for Information Sciences—Permanence of Paper for Printed Library Materials, ANSI Z39.48-1984. ∞

10 9 8 7 6 5 4 3 2 1 (alk. paper)
10 9 8 7 6 5 4 3 2 1 (pbk.: alk. paper)

Printed and bound in the United States of America.

To Akira Iriye
friend and teacher

CONTENTS

ILLUSTRATIONS

FOREWORD

Twayne's International History Series seeks to publish reliable and readable accounts of post–World War II international affairs. Today, nearly 50 years after the end of the war, the time seems opportune to undertake a critical assessment of world affairs in the second half of the twentieth century. What themes and trends have characterized international relations since 1945? How have they evolved and changed? What connections have developed between international and domestic affairs? How have states and peoples defined and pursued their objectives and what have they contributed to the world at large? How have conceptions of warfare and visions of peace changed?

These questions must be addressed if one is to arrive at an understanding of the contemporary world that is both international—with an awareness of the linkages among different parts of the world—and historical—with a keen sense of what the immediate past has brought to human civilization. Hence Twayne's International History Series. It is to be hoped that the volumes in this series will help the reader to explore important events and decisions since 1945 and to develop a global awareness and historical sensitivity with which to confront today's problems.

The first volumes in the series examine the United States' relations with other countries, groups of countries, or regions. The focus on the United States is justified in part because of the nation's predominant positions in postwar international relations, and also because far more extensive documentation is available on American foreign affairs than is the case with other countries. The series addresses not only those interested in international relations but also those studying America's and other countries' histories, who will find here useful guides and fresh insights into the recent past. Now more than ever it is imperative to understand the complex ties between national and international history.

When this volume was first published in 1988, it was hailed as a reliable, up-to-date survey of postwar U.S.–German relations. Since then cataclysmic changes have taken place in international affairs, beginning with the fall of the Berlin Wall and the collapse of communist regimes in East Germany and elsewhere in Eastern Europe. Two Germanies were united, the Cold War ended, and the Soviet Union ceased to exist. Professor Ninkovich has revised the last chapters of his book and added new ones, to describe these and other developments that have altered the nature of the bilateral relationship. And yet "the German problem" still remains as a key to European stability and the Atlantic alliance in the post–Cold War period. The book, in the updated edition, offers penetrating observations on the last half-century of U.S.–German relations that should serve as a guide to understanding world affairs at the end of the twentieth century.

Akira Iriye

PREFACE TO THE UPDATED EDITION

As the ever unpredictable historical process would have it, the unification of Germany in 1990 and the end of the cold war occurred not long after the first edition of this survey went to press. These events have given me an opportunity to extend my story and to provide it with a sense of an ending, a luxury that chroniclers of contemporary history caught up in confusing and inconclusive swirls of events typically are forced to do without. Although the dramatic events surrounding reunification came as a complete surprise to me (and to most everyone else), in this case history did not swerve off, as it does on occasion, in a completely unexpected direction. The details of diplomacy were unpredictable, of course, but the basic scenario conformed pretty much to the historical and ideological plot sketched by American policymakers in the first decade of the cold war. I know enough about writing at the border between the present and the future to realize that this continuity was more a matter of good fortune than of any prescience on my part. As a result, I have not been forced to undertake the humbling task of changing the interpretation of German-American relations that informed the original volume. Apart from a reorganization of chapter six and the inclusion of a new concluding chapter to reflect the events of the 1980s and early 1990s, the work stands pretty much unchanged. A number of factual errors have been corrected, and in a few instances I have, for the sake of clarity, added quotations or a few additional lines of explanation. The result, I hope, is an improved edition that retains the virtues of the original. As always, any errors of fact or interpretation are mine alone.

PREFACE TO THE FIRST EDITION

In offering an explanation of why I wrote this volume, I find myself in the position of Woodrow Wilson, who once confessed that he wrote a history of the United States "not to instruct anybody else, but to instruct myself."[1] When Akira Iriye first asked me to try my hand at writing the volume on Germany for the Twayne series, my lack of qualifications led me to decline. Though I was born in Germany at the end of the Second World War, I had long since forgotten the language only to have to relearn it—and poorly at that. Despite my training in U.S. diplomatic history, I knew relatively little about U.S.-German relations, but I did know enough to realize that a mastery of the complex issues and dense literature would require more time, effort, and skill than I could hope to command. Besides, my primary interests lay elsewhere, and other projects weighed on my mind.

Nevertheless, Akira's persistence caused me to change my mind. Apart from the sheer cowardice involved in being unable to say no to my mentor, my change of heart was prompted by a growing belief that I might indeed have something to contribute to a field of study that already contained a large number of fine works. Since this is contemporary history, so close to us as to be confusing and of uncertain meaning, and my talents, such as they are, lie in the analysis of conceptual frameworks, I thought that I might be able to put the important developments in U.S.-German relations into some sort of larger perspective. Happily, this broad interpretive approach was exactly what the originators of the Twayne series wished to encourage.

Therefore, while this is a diplomatic history, it does not pretend to be a microhistory, a book of record, or a detailed, insider's account of diplomatic transactions. Instead of tracing shifts in the diplomatic weather, it offers an interpretation of the long-term changes in the climate of foreign policy. Although it tries to explain dramatic and sudden changes, it emphasizes a long historical arc within whose broad compass German-American relations to the present can consistently be understood—all this, I hope, while doing justice to the chronological presentation of facts required of a survey.

The tactics of interpretation took longer to work out and occupied much of the writing of the book. Throughout I have emphasized the impact of long-term ideological considerations on policy decisions, doing so in the full realization that I have set myself up for criticism from so-called "realists." More often than not, ideology is viewed as something that grows out of the facts—it reflects them, rationalizes them, conceals them, does everything but explain them. Especially in the case of German-American relations, the logic of power seems to present an open-and-shut case that rules out the need for further interpretation. If one were utterly serious about it, as some people are, one could simply say that the division of Germany following World War II reflected the balance of power at war's end and leave it at that. The positions of the armies tell all, making superfluous any further investigation except for the sake of satisfying idle curiosity. By such a definition, this book would be unnecessary.

This wholly inadequate view—admittedly a caricature, but still a good likeness—is what I call "power determinism." I do not mean to argue that power did not matter; it did, and immensely so. But in some situations, such as in America's decisions to fight Germany in the two wars, I believe that power cannot explain developments except in the crudest fashion. In fact, much of the diplomacy of the postwar years makes more sense if viewed as a failure to come to grips with power. And even if realpolitik had been directly applied, the fact that the logic of power operates through men's minds would still have left room for an ideological explanation.

Why did it take so long to solve the German problem? And if it was in fact solved, why do so many people feel that it still remains? Power does not answer such questions. Power may explain the rearmament of Germany in a rudimentary way, but only by taking into account cold war beliefs and the historically conditioned need to contain Germany can we understand the psychological peculiarities, the ironies, and the paradoxes of the rearmament process. Power may describe the division of Germany, but only the Soviet-American ideological confrontation explains the agonizing and protracted way in which the reunification issue evolved. Power may summarize the eventual outcome, but it does not explain frightening events like the Berlin crises, which loom so large in this history, nor does it explain the process of gradual resignation to the facts of life on the part of Germans and Americans and their continuing determination to do away with them. In brief, power, with its mechanistic images of "vacuums" and the like, simplifies the patterns of these past fifty years by a process of metaphorical reduction. History is no stranger to metaphor, but the business of history is not simplification.

As I hope this book demonstrates, facts and situations are indeterminate and puzzling. People, even those diplomats and statesmen who claim to use power formulas the way engineers use equations, find the kaleidoscope of events messy and difficult to understand. Finding themselves in need of further assistance in ordering reality, they inevitably bring to bear their ideological and cultural predispositions. I do not wish to intimate that ideology explains all, because clearly it does not. This reliance on belief systems, while it may provide the comfort of familiar thought patterns, is often of little practical help in solving problems. Despite the seeming comprehensiveness of ideologies, and despite the fact that important decisions are often made because of them, they too fail to wrap up reality in a neat package. I hope that this volume helps to illustrate the complicated dialectic between the structure of events, their interpretation, and their transformation.

In writing this book, I have consciously stayed away from second-guessing the protagonists and have forgone the opportunity to play the game of "lost opportunities." If I have to speculate historically, I find it preferable to speculate about why things turned out the way they did, which seems to me more difficult and more rewarding than playing the counterfactual game of "what if," for whatever motives. In some quarters that approach may appear to give this work a conservative bias, but that would be a rash conclusion. On the other hand, the book may seem revisionist to others, especially portions of Chapter 1. In my defense, all I can say is that I belong to no school except the one that feels every historian worth his salt is a revisionist.

A final word on conceptualization. The book's details focus on the U.S. and West Germany, but it is really about the U.S. and the idea of Germany and its place in international history. This, I hope, justifies the broader implications of the title.

This is contemporary history, but most of the details are already familiar to scholars. While I have relied on some primary sources and archival materials as indicated in the notes, the bulk of the work is derived from a reading of other people's works—that, and my interpretation of them. I have also tried to hold down the scholarly apparatus of this book by keeping footnotes to a minimum and by not citing well-known quotations frequently encountered. I have borrowed freely the ideas of others and have tried to acknowledge them as best I can, but I owe far more to other scholars than I can ever hope to repay. Though one strives for "scholarly originality," we historians know that the phrase is self-contradictory. For those who see themselves in these pages, my hope is that they will take my borrowings as a compliment.

Divided Germany. *Courtesy of the Germany Information Center*

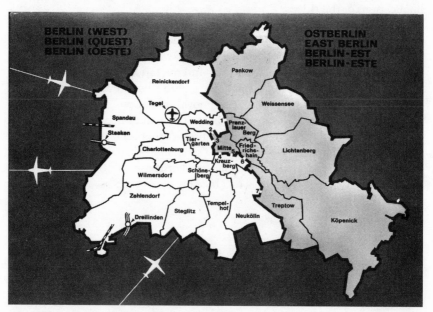

Map of West and East Berlin showing air corridors. *Courtesy of the Germany Information Center*

Germany united. *Courtesy of the Germany Information Center*

Cologne Cathedral and razed city, 1945. *Courtesy of the Germany Information Center*

Cologne rebuilt. *Courtesy of the Germany Information Center*

chapter 1

TWO WARS

The history of international relations is filled with sudden reversals of alliances and unpredictable twists of fate, but few nations have experienced such swift and dramatic swings of fortune as modern Germany. In the case of the United States and Germany, the steep, angular slopes of their relationship remind one of a jagged mountain range or a cardiograph run amok. Twice in this century, in the most terrible wars known to humankind, the United States has fought Germany as the embodiment of evil, only to abandon its hostility shortly after war's end. The sharp turnabout from foe to friend, then ally, following World War II was especially abrupt, unexpected, and puzzling.

In the case of Germany's relationship with its European neighbors, this wild ride on the roller coaster of war and peace is readily understandable from the brute facts of power, the constraints of geography, and the point of view of a history in which Germany was cast as a hereditary enemy. But these kinds of limiting factors do not apply to the United States. The sharp contrasts in America's relationship with Germany have not been produced by realism of the hard-headed kind displayed by France or Russia, but by how Germany fits America's image of the world. Though Germany had much to say about it, the key to understanding this fluctuating relationship has been Germany's changing role in America's liberal historical imagination. Indeed the United States, the home of pragmatism, has behaved almost as if it were following the German philosopher Arthur Schopenhauer's dictum: "the world is my idea."

In the beginning, Germany stood out handsomely in America's group portrait of the family of nations. During the American War of Independence, the exploits of Baron von Steuben were written into the permanent mythology of German-American friendship. Contributing to this favorable first impression were the actions of his sovereign, Frederick the Great of Prussia, who refused to allow Hessian mercenaries, hired by England to suppress the rebellion, to cross Prussian territory on their way to the American colonies. Prussia's enlightened attitude seemed further confirmed when Frederick signed a commercial treaty with the United States that for the first time acknowledged the principle of "free ships, free goods," a doctrine of commercial internationalism that many Americans believed would revolutionize international relations. The treaty failed to realize utopia, but it did prepare the ground for a long and mutually profitable trade relationship.

The middle of the nineteenth century brought developments no less pleasing to Americans. During the Civil War, Prussia once again ingratiated herself by purchasing Union bonds and by refusing to fall in with a Franco-British flirtation with the Confederacy. Friendly feelings were reciprocated during the Franco-Prussian War of 1870–71, when many Americans assumed that the North German Confederation and its successor, the German Empire, were retracing the pattern of American federalism. America's minister to Berlin at the time, the historian George Bancroft, believed that German-American friendship was rooted "in history and nature," because "German institutions and ours most nearly resemble each other, and because so many millions of Germans have become our countrymen."[1] The dramatic transformation of the North German Confederation into the German Reich in 1871 seemed, in American eyes, the harbinger of Europe's march down the road to federal republicanism.

As both nations entered a phase of overseas expansion, points of friction began to emerge. In Samoa, which was useful as a coaling station, a dispute over control of the islands was heating up into a naval confrontation in the 1880s, until a hurricane literally threw cold water on fiery national tempers and allowed time for a diplomatic compromise in which the islands were divided up. In the same decade, the protectionist policies of both countries were irritating enough to foment a brief but lively tariff war over the issue of pork exports to Germany. But these were only minor annoyances. Bismarckian Germany was preoccupied with continental diplomacy, while the United States was hard-pressed even to tend its own hemispheric garden. To seek portents in these events would be to create significance where none existed at the time.

Actually, nineteenth-century diplomatic relations were only a minor subplot in a story whose main theme was commercial and cultural interaction. The German immigrants who flooded into the United States, especially following the revolutions of 1848, contributed significantly to the settlement of the vast American hinterland. More than 200,000 native-born Germans demonstrated the depth of their new national commitment by joining the Union Army during the Civil War. By 1900, the number of Americans of German extraction in the total population numbered an imposing 27 percent, and their concentration made them a potent political force in certain regions, especially in portions of the Midwest.

German high culture was increasingly influential in the decades that followed the Civil War. The prestigious German universities attracted growing numbers of talented Americans interested in advanced study, many of whom would draw upon their overseas training to establish an American university system. By 1895, one-half of the historians in the United States had received part of their training at German schools. German administrative techniques were widely admired by Americans interested in rational governmental reforms during a time of widespread political corruption, and German music, under the spell of Richard Wagner's hypnotic genius, held almost exclusive sway for a time in American (as well as Continental) opera houses.

Nevertheless, when compared with the growing influence of the transatlantic Anglo-American community, these extensive cultural shoots failed to blossom into like-mindedness and produced only a small body of Germanophile opinion in the United States. As German historical thought veered off in an egocentric absorption with German *Kultur*, nationalism, and pan-Germanism, the British and American elites were formulating a vision of a global civilization centered on Anglo-Saxon values. This image was supported by a shared view of the civilizing function of imperialism, by the emergence of a transatlantic society made possible by improved communications, and by a growing sense of a shared destiny that judged the progress of humankind in terms of Anglo-Saxon standards of achievement. Divided by the past, Americans and the English were increasingly drawn back together by their perception of the future.

The German problem began to emerge in the late nineteenth century as a looming cloud over this sunny Anglo-American landscape. Largely as a result of the impression produced by the realpolitik of Otto von Bismarck, Germany seemed to veer away from the benignly civilized paths marked out by its high culture. Gradually Americans began to see in Germany a semifeudal nation of arrogant warlords, governed by a military ethic and less devoted to progress than obsessed by primal dreams of military conquest. Especially with the emergence of the vainglorious and blustering young kaiser, Wilhelm II, who after 1890 embarked on an ambitious program to make Germany a world power, the German image in America went rapidly downhill. Wondering what limits, if any, there were to this new global ambition, the *Washington Post* asked whether it was "possible for Germany to treat any civilized country on equal terms."

A number of episodes, minor in themselves, lent substance to this impressionistic view of the *Reich*. As Commodore George Dewey's squadron quickly finished off the woefully overmatched Spanish naval force at Manila Bay in 1898, the German flotilla of Admiral Otto von Diederichs seemed to hover malevolently in the background, and it continued to linger long afterwards in the back of American minds. German participation in the multinational expedition sent to Peking in 1900 to rescue the besieged diplomatic community from the Boxer rebels also disturbed American sensibilities. When the kaiser exhorted his troops to behave like ruthless "Huns," a military invasion rationalized by chaste arguments on behalf of civilization lost its ideological purity. So disgusted with German behavior was American secretary of state John Hay that he privately declared that he would "rather be the dupe of China, than the drum of the Kaiser." Ominously, "Hun" soon became the everyday journalistic metaphor for describing Germany.

In this atmosphere, policymakers in both countries at the turn of the century began privately to entertain thoughts of a possible military confrontation. Determined to make good on his ambition of achieving unchallenged American hegemony in the western hemisphere, President Theodore Roosevelt fretted for a time about German designs on the Monroe Doctrine. "The only power which may be a menace to us in anything like the immediate future is Germany," he wrote to his friend Henry Cabot Lodge. The German Imperial Navy, for its part, drew up a series of detailed and ambitious contingency plans for a naval assault against the United States, but they were soon discarded because they totally disregarded the geopolitical fact of Germany's exposed continental position. Running on a later schedule than German military thinkers, the Americans devised a complementary war plan that projected a defensive strategy against a hypothetical German assault. Code-named Black, this plan was completed only after the German plan was scrapped.

In both countries, military imagination outran political reality. The political absurdity of a war between the two countries over Caribbean issues became evident in the Venezuela debt collection controversy of 1903. Long after the fact, Roosevelt claimed that he had secretly threatened naval intervention and prevented the Germans from forcibly coercing the delinquent Venezuelans to pay up, thereby preserving the Monroe Doctrine. Though it is still a subject of historical controversy, the most telling aspect of this curious incident is the absence of supporting documentation on both sides. If the confrontation did in fact occur, it could easily have been exaggerated for jingoistic purposes. But its consignment instead to oblivion—probably to prevent embarrassing future relations—indicated a mutual recognition that, from the standpoint of national interests, coldly considered, it was better that it should be treated as not having happened. It was not the only occasion in which Roosevelt intervened quietly to spare the kaiser from the consequences of his indiscretions.

Even though Germany posed no direct danger to American interests, her militarism was increasingly perceived as a threat to the peaceful norms of modern civilization. Roosevelt was an admirer of German culture, and one of his closest friends was the German ambassador to the United States, but in his private correspondence he referred contemptuously to the out-of-date German attitude toward war—"the Bismarck attitude"—and mocked the kaiser's pomposity. The American role in negotiating an end to the first Morocco crisis at the Algeciras Conference of 1906 put this wide gap between interests and sympathies to work. Without becoming directly involved in the issues, Roosevelt used diplomatic finesse to prevent a settlement harmful to France.

This sharp distinction between image and interests is central to an understanding of American policy at the outset of World War I. Even though public opinion in the United States from the beginning favored the Entente cause, in 1914 no German-American showdown was in sight. While there was some talk of a "German menace" and while a few knowledgeable diplomats like Lewis Einstein correctly foresaw that the war would have many adverse consequences for American interests, the tangled European roots of the war seemed so tightly balled that they would not touch on American concerns. One of the few advocates of intervention, ironically, was Theodore Roosevelt, who formerly had been so careful to safeguard German-American relations. Significantly, he took his stand on idealistic ground, seeking to punish Germany for her brutal violation of Belgian neutrality.

Had not the submarine weapon emerged to confound the gentlemanly rules of cruiser warfare that provided for the safety of ships' crews and passengers, it is unlikely that a conflict would have developed. But a number of incidents on the high seas quickly produced a deterioration of relations. The torpedoing of the British passenger liner *Lusitania* in May 1915, which caused the deaths of 128 American men, women, and children, was one of those earth-shaking pieces of news that remain indelibly engraved in popular memory. This violation of international law, notwithstanding the fact that the ship was carrying ammunition, produced great public outrage and stern diplomatic messages from President Woodrow Wilson, who sought to hold Germany strictly accountable for her illegal actions.

The storm blew over following Germany's expression of willingness to make amends, but the sinking of the channel steamer *Sussex* early in 1916 took German-American disagreement one step further. Though the carefully qualified German pledge to end attacks on merchantmen temporarily smoothed matters over, Wilson's promise to sever relations if submarine warfare were resumed put the future of relations in the hands of the German High Command. At this point, Germany was still reluctant to provoke the United States, for fear that she would enter the war and tip the scales in favor of the Entente. But when a sense of desperation took hold at the end of 1916, the cautious Chancellor Theobald von Bethmann-Hollweg lost the policy debate to the military hotspurs. An all-or-nothing gamble for a quick knockout blow was taken, in the hope that England would be starved into submission before American power could become a telling factor.

Superficially the dilemmas of neutrality resembled the whirlpool of events that had sucked the United States into the War of 1812. Then, America's survival as a sovereign republic had depended on its ability and willingness to defend itself from being whipsawed by the belligerents. History appeared to be repeating itself, as both the Central Powers and the Entente were intruding on America's neutral rights: the Germans, with a submarine policy that prevented Americans from enjoying neutral commerce and the right to travel safely on passenger ships; the British, with their high-handed and illegal administration of their naval blockade of the Continent. If it were a matter simply of defending national interests, there would have been little to choose between German predation and British arrogance.

Nevertheless, war against England was highly unlikely. President Wilson was culturally an Anglophile who, in his days as a scholar, had been a keen admirer of British political institutions. Not surprisingly, Wilson's analysis of the War of 1812 was that the United States had fought on the wrong side.[2] The United States' comparatively mild reaction to the British blockade, which from a legalistic standpoint was just as illegal as the German submarine tactics, was an arguable indication of a pro-Allied slant; the skewed neutrality represented by the never-implemented House-Grey memorandum of 1916, in which the United States secretly agreed to intervene against Germany should she refuse to attend a peace conference called by the Americans and the Allies, was proof positive of where Wilson's sympathies lay.

World War I was set apart from earlier European struggles not only by the emergence of submarine warfare, but also by a new sense of history that envisioned a distinct threat to civilization. In 1812, Americans had seen only their young republic as being in peril, whereas now American concerns had expanded to global dimensions. From the beginning, highly placed Americans judged the European conflict by its likely effect on the continued evolution of liberal institutions. The invasion of Belgium and the maltreatment of that country's population, justified by the Germans as a military necessity, deeply wounded the sensibilities of cosmopolitan liberals who assumed that treaty obligations, the basis of international law, were more than the meaningless scraps of paper Bethmann-Hollweg made them out to be. The lineup of liberty versus despotism thus seemed obvious to many prominent Americans. Secretary of State Robert Lansing was typical of many who advocated American intervention because Germany was "utterly hostile to all nations with democratic institutions."[3]

Although President Wilson was aware from the beginning that a German victory would be a blow to democracy, he never defined the larger ideological issues arising from the war in such simple partisan terms. Despite his natural affinity for the Entente, he refused to view the Allies in a wholly virtuous light and disassociated himself from the chauvinist ambitions embodied in their war aims. The attractiveness of Britain and France was further dimmed by their eager adherence to undemocratic diplomatic practices. In addition, Wilson was less concerned with the possibility of a German triumph, which seemed unlikely given the stalemate on the Western Front, than with any victory that would leave the diplomacy of power unchanged in all its ugly essentials. When he looked at the war with a scholar's analytical eye, "from the point of view of the rest of the world,"[4] the real culprit in his view was more the flawed and outdated system of international relations than either of the warring parties.

It was not long before Wilson came to the conviction that this was not a traditional European war, even though it had started out that way. When he spoke of the world being "on fire," with tinder everywhere, he was referring to the difficulty of maintaining neutrality in the modern era.[5] "The effects of war can no longer be confined to the areas of battle," he said in 1916.[6] If the flames of war were leaping over the Atlantic firebreak, so too were American concerns. Americans were no longer provincials but a cosmopolitan people, Wilson insisted. Groping to find some larger meaning in overseas events for his nation, he scoffed at the possibility of an invasion of American territory, expressing instead his concern for the integrity of the hemisphere as "something intangible and visionary."[7]

In one respect, Wilson's policy of neutrality was quite traditional, as he committed American prestige almost instinctively to the defense of neutral rights. But insofar as America's right to do business undisturbed by the war resembled the same selfish nationalist values that had started the war, a stand based narrowly on neutral rights, understandably enough, was unpalatable to a president who sought larger meanings for his policies. Wilson was no pacifist, but he was reluctant to use force unless it contributed to some sort of moral improvement. "I am interested in neutrality because there is something so much greater to do than fight," he said, implying the existence of some higher purpose. Consequently, by 1916 he had pushed neutral rights as an expression of national interest to one side. Hoping now to mediate the conflict, Wilson unveiled a new notion of neutrality, one that envisioned the United States as the agent not of traditional international law, but of a new international morality.

Despite Wilson's sublime articulation of a "peace without victory," this exalted view of neutrality turned out to be incompatible with his worldly policy of defending neutral rights. Once the German High Command announced its decision in January 1917 to resume unrestricted submarine warfare, Wilson's dream of mediating a millennial peace was shattered. Now full-scale participation in the war remained the only way to vindicate America's national honor and to fulfill his grander ambitions. Fortunately, the comic German attempt to buy Mexican participation against the United States, revealed in the so-called Zimmermann telegram, combined with an active campaign of sabotage conducted on American soil by German agents, made the decision for war a little easier to swallow.

With America a belligerent, Wilson's rationale for American participation underwent a momentous change. Just as neutral rights were inadequate to justify neutrality, the defense of American commercial interests was an unworthy motive for full-blooded participation. Having first exalted neutrality, only to have his hand forced, Wilson needed to do the same for the war, so he began to insist that American intervention had been inevitable.[8] By 1917, Wilson was arguing an early version of the domino theory, whose specter of unlimited expansionism would figure heavily in the next war against Germany. Formerly, it had been the war's indirect consequences that had caused him concern; now the danger was military aggression itself.

According to Wilson, the German leadership was seeking a power base, extending from central Europe through central Asia, from which to control the world. "The object of this war," he argued, "is to deliver the free peoples of the world from the menace and the actual power of a vast military establishment controlled by an irresponsible government which, having secretly planned to dominate the world, proceeded to carry the plan out . . . and now stands balked but not defeated, the enemy of four-fifths of the world."[9] Complaining that Germany's enviable intellectual and economic achievements "did not satisfy the German government," he contended that "all the while, there was lying behind its thought and in its dreams of the future a political control which would enable it in the long run to dominate the labor and the industry of the world."[10]

The war and the new Wilsonian rationale so completely broke with traditional political assumptions that American military planners were taken unawares. The decision to send an American expeditionary force to France was emblematic of the rapid shift in outlook. The American military had long been clamoring for a modernized defense structure to prepare for modern warfare, but it was indicative of the army and navy's old-fashioned hemispheric mentality that planning focused on the highly improbable contingency of defense against invasion from overseas. Thus, it was not until after war was declared that the bureaucracy began to think about sending an expeditionary force to fight on French soil.

A crucial manpower shortage on the Western Front certainly helped in the decision to field an independent army, but so did what was admittedly "an instinctive judgment of the matter."[11] The force would probably have been sent in any case, but the internationalist vision of American troops providing the knockout blow on the Western Front and thus validating the nation's credentials for establishing a new world order provided a great incentive in itself. Internationalist war aims dictated a forward military strategy, because the war's end, for Wilson, was only the beginning; it was not the war, but the peace treaty that would make the world "safe for democracy."

Despite domestic anti-German feeling that verged on hysteria, Wilson's intentions for Germany were not punitive. He urged the public time and again to maintain its self-possession and not to get carried away by wartime emotion. He also took pains to distinguish the behavior of Germany's ruling class from the desires of its citizens—the United States was fighting "not people, but a system"[12]—thereby implying that a restructured, democratic

Germany would be punishment enough for the Prussian warlords, though at times he was reluctant to push his reforming zeal even that far.

On the basis of the armistice agreements, the Germans expected a moderate peace based on Wilson's liberal Fourteen Points, a peace to which they felt all the more entitled, since the ambiguous way in which the war ended did not really make clear Germany's desperate military condition (thus was born the "stab-in-the-back" legend, that Germany had been sold out, not defeated). But from the French and British standpoints, the lessons of the past and the prospect of continuing conflicts of interest with Germany seemed to justify the harsh peace that they promoted at the Paris Peace Conference. As for Wilson, he drew different historical conclusions. Seeking neither reparations nor territory, he sought as far as possible to play the role of impartial umpire at Versailles, in an effort to dampen extremist nationalism.

Faced with adamant demands from the Allies for their pound of flesh, Wilson was forced to compromise more than he would have liked in order to obtain his cherished League of Nations. There is some evidence, too, that his attitude toward Germany hardened as the negotiations progressed. Nevertheless, despite the unsatisfactory nature of the territorial and reparations settlements, he expected the League to more than compensate in the long run for the emotional excesses of the moment. Unfortunately, the refusal of the U.S. Senate to approve American entry into the League left the newborn Weimar Republic, whose domestic legitimacy was already undermined for having signed the treaty, to deal with an unrestrained France and Britain alone, each of which was, at the time, driven by narrower motives in its relations with Germany.

The result was continued economic stagnation and political bitterness. While the loss of territory in the east furnished long-term grievances for the Germans, the reparations settlement provided the more immediate shock. Germany's failure to make satisfactory payments toward the total bill of 132 billion gold marks, or 33 billion dollars, led to the Ruhr crisis of 1923, in which French and Belgian troops occupied the industrial Ruhr Valley in an attempt to extract by force reparations from the region's factories and mines. The invasion was met by passive resistance, as the German government urged the workers to go on strike rather than aid the occupiers. The nonworkers of the Ruhr were supported by the uncontrolled printing of currency, which led inexorably to the traumatic hyperinflation of 1923, in which the money turned out to be worthless.

At this point, the United States reentered the European scene, for a number of reasons. The United States had changed from a debtor to a creditor nation in the course of the war and now had a surplus of capital that needed to be reinvested. And while Americans' political internationalism may have died in 1920, many leading businessmen were aware of the interdependence of the global economy and were disposed to lend a helping hand. They were further encouraged to do so by the cult of business and private scientific management that dominated Jazz Age America. Confident of America's managerial expertise and convinced that sound economic structures would eliminate any need for undesirable political entanglement abroad, the Republican administrations of the 1920s relied on a progressive faith in the ability of big business to stabilize the global economy on a sound basis.

The problem was, in broad conceptual terms, simple enough: world prosperity was impossible without a European recovery, which hinged on a German recovery, which depended in turn on a resolution of the thorny reparations question. The United States obliged with a "practical, businesslike solution" to the reparations imbroglio in the Dawes Plan of 1924. In return for American investors' providing dollars to Germany through bond purchases, annual reparations payments were scaled down, the interest reduced, and the burdensome requirement for payment in gold suspended. The initial Dawes loan was only the first in a series of transfusions that kept the German economy alive during the 1920s. The healthier atmosphere produced by the Dawes Plan also made possible the signing of the Locarno Treaties in 1925, which improved relations between Germany, Britain, and France and settled the issue of Germany's western frontiers.

During the 1920s, Germany and the United States seemed more than ever before to have common interests. Fully aware of the crucial financial role of the United States, the German government took pains to tailor its policies to Washington's specifications. Germany agreed to an American proposal for a mixed claims commission, dominated by American interests, to settle outstanding economic differences between the two nations. Still an outcast among nations, in 1923 Germany hastily agreed to a commercial treaty with the United States as a means of raising its international status. The United States, according to one German consul general, was "not only the best friend but actually the only friend which the *Reich* has in international society."

But their agreement on means masked a more important latent difference on objectives. The United States approached German policy from a global framework, while the German perspective remained steadfastly nationalistic. Because German politicians of all shades were determined to erase the injustices of the Versailles Treaty and restore Germany to great power status, German dependence on the United States was necessary as a transitional measure. Ironically, to the degree that the United States succeeded in strengthening Germany, it was contributing not only to the eventual disruption of the Versailles system but also to the undermining of its vision of an "open world" free of traditional nationalism.

Whatever chance existed that continuing prosperity might smooth away these potential differences was swept away by the worldwide depression that began in America in 1929. Although President Herbert Hoover made a few tentative attempts to bring the economic situation under control, most notably with his suggestion of a one-year moratorium on intergovernmental debts, the world economy spun out of control, crashed, and broke up into national and regional pieces. With business expertise disgraced and a prevailing international morality of sauve qui peut, the two nations' policies began to diverge with respect to both means and ends.

After Adolf Hitler's Nazi regime and Franklin D. Roosevelt's New Deal administration came to power in 1933, the good relations of the previous decade were quickly submerged under a flood of disagreements. In its economic policy, the Hitler regime practiced an aggressive bilateral diplomacy that sinned against Secretary of State Cordell Hull's abiding faith in free trade. In short order, the German government defaulted on the interest owed to American bondholders, purchased the bonds at depreciated prices, and then resold them at par to Germans, pocketing the difference and using the American proceeds for foreign exchange to purchase arms. As a result of this economic sleight of hand, not only was the United States financing reparations, it was also financing German rearmament!

In its tariff policy, Hitler's Germany discriminated against American products and denounced the commercial treaty in order to get out from under its liberal most-favored-nation clause. Rather than give in, the Roosevelt administration refused to negotiate a new pact and by 1936 began to apply countervailing duties in retaliation against German practices. Finally, the claims commissions established in the preceding decade fell apart when it was discovered that the Germans were doctoring evidence to win their cases.

Important, too, were the ideological irritations that developed. The blatant anti-Semitism of the Nazi regime, its widely publicized book burnings, and its campaign against the Christian churches were offensive to American moral standards. So repugnant were the principles of the Nazi regime that from time to time boycott movements against German products erupted. Also touching a sensitive nerve was the formation of vocal Nazi claques in the United States, most notably the German-American Bund headed by Fritz Kuhn, which violated the American belief that immigrants should assimilate and leave their old ideologies behind them. By the end of the decade, crude attempts at organizing the substantial colonies of German immigrants in South America were causing grave concern in the U.S. State Department.

Nevertheless, Hitler was not yet the antichrist he would later become. Public opinion polls in the mid-1930s consistently viewed Josef Stalin, the Soviet strongman, in an even less favorable light, while Benito Mussolini and his Italian experiment in fascism enjoyed a surprisingly good press. Working to Hitler's advantage was a widespread disgust with the Versailles settlement, combined with a lingering sense of guilt for America's contribution to the postwar crisis. In the demonology of the 1930s, the world war was portrayed as a mistake, with American intervention ascribed in lurid terms to "merchants of death," greedy bankers, cynical Allied propaganda, and the machinations of pro-British statesmen.

Beginning in 1935, Congress even tried to legislate against a repetition of history. Successive neutrality acts instituted an arms embargo on warring nations, forbade them loans, and prohibited passenger travel on belligerent countries' ships. Contrary to appearances, the neutrality acts were more a repudiation of nationalism than of internationalism. With the nation renouncing the right to travel immune from marauding submarines, the right to lend money, and the right to unimpeded trade, little of the traditional conception of national interest remained other than the right of self-defense.

This legislation proved to be very important for the subsequent course of German-American relations, but hardly in the way Congress had intended. Far from shutting the door on American involvement in overseas wars, the neutrality laws smoothed the path for a revival of internationalism. If economic interests were presumed to be base, perhaps loftier concerns, once activated, could spur a revival of American concern for Europe's fate. So long as continental affairs resembled traditional power politics, Americans preferred to remain literally disinterested; but if the overcast moral climate of the 1930s should dissipate and the light of a worthy cause once again break through the clouds, and if war itself regained a measure of nobility and righteousness thereby, the seemingly irreducible fortress of isolationism could very easily be bypassed altogether. Thanks to the neutrality acts, "hard" interests would not be a confusing factor in the next German-American war.

Instead of reinforcing isolationist sentiment, the events of the mid-1930s, especially the reoccupation of the Rhineland in 1936, the annexation of Austria (the Anschluss) in March 1938, and the Sudeten crisis later that year, fueled a resurgence of internationalist thinking in the United States. American public opinion was profoundly disturbed by the ominous direction events were taking on the Continent. Especially in Washington, where the New Deal's ship of state was manned by a full complement of true believers in a liberal world order, these events caused deep concern.

The New Deal's isolationism, much like its domestic program, was only of a provisional, emergency character, awaiting the restoration of prosperity before unfurling its internationalist colors. Franklin D. Roosevelt had cut his teeth in foreign affairs as an assistant secretary of the navy under Woodrow Wilson and had run for the vice presidency in 1920 as a strong supporter of the League of Nations. Secretary of the Interior Harold Ickes, Secretary of the Treasury Henry Morgenthau, Secretary of State Cordell Hull, and Under Secretary Sumner Welles were all to varying degrees acolytes of the internationalist faith.

Nevertheless, the appeasement bargain struck at Munich, whereby the German-speaking areas of Czechoslovakia were handed over to Hitler by an accommodating Britain and France, was greeted with a deep sigh of relief in

Washington. As a token of his appreciation for British prime minister Neville Chamberlain's efforts to preserve peace, FDR sent him the two-word "good man" telegram, while Sumner Welles announced shortly afterwards in a radio broadcast that the Munich settlement laid the basis for "a new world order based upon justice and law." Others found different cause for satisfaction. For some officials in the State Department and isolationists who were more anti-Communist than anti-Nazi, the outcome preserved Nazi Germany as the main bulwark against the even more odious Soviet peril.

The Roosevelt administration had little sympathy for Chamberlain's methods, although it cheered his results. This seemingly odd attitude originated not in any hostility to appeasement as a genus, but to its power-political species. More committed to pursuing a liberal antipolitical ideology in international affairs, the administration would have preferred economic appeasement. This idea was embodied in a number of short-lived schemes in 1937 and 1938, incubated by Welles, to organize a World Economic Conference that would guarantee Germany equal access to markets and raw materials. However, these economic nostrums, when coupled with Roosevelt's repeated pleas for peaceful behavior, could hardly be dignified with the term *diplomacy*, which implies bargaining over mutually conflicting interests. The United States did take the symbolic step in 1938 of stopping the sale of helium for zeppelins, but American trade with Germany was declining so rapidly that the government was in no position to lose anything or to give anything away.[13] Nevertheless, these feeble efforts at accommodation and hostility, even though they came to nothing, cleared the decks for what State Department official George Messersmith called "an even more basic clash of ideologies."

Munich was analogous to the rape of Belgium: it shocked sensibilities, but it was insufficient to generate a fighting consensus. It would assume vast symbolic importance only after the fact, as a reflection of a new worldview. More decisive events followed in short order, however. On the heels of the Munich capitulation came the vicious anti-Jewish program known as Kristallnacht, the "night of the broken glass." Using as a pretext the shooting of Ernst vom Rath, the third secretary of the German Embassy in Paris, the Nazi regime incited an anti-Semitic rampage throughout Germany in which thugs broke shop windows and looted synagogues, and followed up with severely punitive economic measures against the Jews. The American ambassador to Germany, Hugh Wilson, was pointedly called home for consultations (never to return), while the president expressed his amazement that such an event could take place in a civilized country.

From this point on it was all downhill, as the German absorption of Bohemia and Moravia in the spring of 1939 and Hitler's pressure on Poland for territorial concessions gave the lie to his claim that, with the creation of a Grossdeutschland, his diplomatic goals had been achieved. With the invasion of Poland in September 1939, the lightning defeat of France the following spring, and what appeared to be an imminent Nazi invasion of the British Isles, the image of unlimited and ruthless German ambition was in place.

Today, Pearl Harbor and the Holocaust stand at either end of World War II as powerful moral beacons legitimating America's passage through the war. Before these events, however, the German problem was the subject of an enormous but inconclusive debate, which was cut short by the Japanese attack on Pearl Harbor and Hitler's decision four days later to declare war on the United States. These events produced an overwhelming American consensus on the rightness of joining in the Second World War, but they also obscured the motives behind America's confrontation with Germany, which to this day remain murky. For this reason, and also for a better understanding of subsequent U.S. foreign policy, we should have a better idea than we do of what that debate was about.

The basic threat, as articulated by administration officials from 1939 onward and repeated ever afterwards in popular mythology, was clear enough: world conquest. Because Hitler's expansionist lust was thought to be insatiable, it was believed that the defeat of Great Britain and Germany's consolidation of control over the Eurasian land mass would lead inevitably to a contest for control of the Atlantic and a struggle to maintain the security of the Americas.

Indeed, Hitler was no lover of things American. As a fanatical believer in Aryan racial purity, America's racial and ethnic melting pot appeared to him as a mongrelized racial mixture in which "the scum floated naturally to the top."[14] Though at one time he was respectful of America's great productive capacity, by the 1930s Hitler had come to view the United States as a decaying nation, "half Judaized half negrified with everything built on the dollar." Even though German diplomats took care to inform their führer of America's potentially enormous power and warned of the possibility of a swift change of national mood, Hitler preferred to judge the United States on the basis of delusory evaluations provided by some of his ignorant Nazi favorites.

There is considerable debate among historians as to whether Hitler was Europe-oriented or motivated by a desire for world mastery, but there is little question that, in contrast to his European program, Hitler's plans for the United States were vague, decidedly long-range, and visionary. In *Mein Kampf* he had elaborated a two-stage process by which his revitalized Reich would attain world power, first by consolidating a continental empire through the conquest of living space (*lebensraum*) in the east, after which he envisioned his successors, following his death, waging a final conflict for world supremacy with the United States.[15] On a more concrete level, there were on-again, off-again plans to build a formidable high-seas navy, which might have presented a serious threat to the United States at some time in the future. Following his early successes in Russia, Hitler accelerated his naval preparations a bit, but by the fall of 1941 unexpectedly strong Soviet resistance led him to revert to his initial "timetable." Of the struggle with America, he told an associate in October 1941: "I will not live to see it."[16]

Roosevelt was generally aware of these grandiose ideas, but his problem was what to make of them. Even when amplified by ideology, Hitler's world-view, which was clearly limited by the Eurocentric tradition of pan-Germanism, remained hopelessly provincial. Loose talk among the Nazi elite of a possible conflict with America, perhaps some thirty to fifty years in the future, was not the stuff of diplomacy but of historical speculation, hot-air balloons floated without any political ballast to bring them down to earth. Looking at the matter only in the most glancing and hypothetical manner, the Nazis professed to have no idea of how America might be defeated and focused on more immediate continental objectives.

Whatever the status of Nazi intentions, whether realistic strategy for world conquest or ideological fantasy, they were filtered through the looking glass of American perceptions, which were in any case concerned more with general trends than immediate dangers. Nazi Germany's subjective tendencies mattered more than solid knowledge of plans or capabilities. According to the prevailing disease metaphor, Germany was but the most frightening symptom of a global contagion of militarism that included the expansionist Japanese empire. Specific military threats were not at issue; more worrisome was the menacing prospect of existence in a world increasingly dominated by expansionist political empires. There was, moreover, a distinct absence of faith in the ability of the balance of power to set things right, a point of view that in the 1950s would be given doctrinal status in the domino theory.

Hitler's megalomania thus struck directly at fundamental historical perceptions of the American leadership. Assistant Secretary of State Adolf Berle's assertion that "the present struggle is distinctly philosophical" came as close as any other remark to suggesting the basis of America's concern over Germany's behavior. This phrase was descriptive of more than the ideological gulf between fascism and democracy. Indeed, the ascendancy of perception over events was so pronounced that internationalist thinking in the late 1930s bore more than a superficial resemblance to the realism of medieval metaphysics, in which, according to the scholastics, universal forms existed anterior to an otherwise meaningless concrete reality.

The German threat was shaped not by hard interests but by perceptions of space and time. When Roosevelt, in a fireside chat delivered in September 1939, argued that "when peace has been broken anywhere, the peace of all countries is in danger," he was not asserting a matter of fact. He was revealing a cultural schema that gave meaning to his construction of geography and history. In this framework, anything and everything was important. Thus, after Munich, he insisted that Czechoslovakia "could very properly be called a link in the American defense against German and Italian aggression in the future,"[17] even if France and Britain, on the front lines, felt differently.

The president's closest adviser, Harry Hopkins, defined the problem in the following way to a reporter: "Suppose that Germany wins the war in the next two months and does on the economic fronts what they have done on the military fronts. What will they do in South America presuming they win, and then, what are we going to do about it?"[18] So intent on driving home this point was Roosevelt that in 1941 he produced a spurious map as proof of Germany's expansionist plans in the hemisphere. Even those within the administration who advocated a policy of hemispheric defense were convinced that it was only a question of when, not whether, the Nazis would attempt to breach the Atlantic barrier.

However unsettling such a prospect was, it did not have the status of a strategic reality, for national security was not threatened in any immediate, objective sense by German behavior. Berle admitted as much when analyzing the implications of the sinking of the German battleship *Bismarck* in May 1941. From this dramatic event he concluded that "even if the Germans conquered Europe, and if they outbuilt us navally and with merchant marine, it would still be a question whether these ships could live long enough to reach the United States."[19]

Even with Hitler's aggressive challenge to the continental balance of power, it was far from certain in 1941 that the British Empire would be defeated or that the Soviet Union would collapse. Lacking the clear and present danger that could trigger an instinctive defensive response, the Roosevelt administration practiced a politics of anticipation based on worst-case assumptions. After describing the whole disastrous sequence of toppling dominoes to Adolf Berle, Roosevelt admitted the indeterminacy of it all. According to Berle, "This he described as possibility only but a possibility no far-sighted statesman could afford to permit. His job was to make sure that that kind of possibility could not happen."[20] Illustrative of the premium placed on an abstract, imaginative construction of events was Secretary of State Cordell Hull's complaint that the isolationists "did not look very far in the future."

The debate between interventionists and isolationists over Germany cannot be judged by comparing the validity of their specific predictions, for both turned out to be wrong in their chosen fields of argument. After World War II, it became rather common to observe that the elimination of Germany had left a power vacuum on the Continent that the USSR obligingly rushed in to fill. Judged purely from this power standpoint, the war was a mistake. But then, on the other hand, what would the world have been like if the isolationist position had been adopted? The Holocaust would have gone unpunished, nuclear weapons would likely have come into German and Japanese hands, Eastern Europe might have been Sovietized in any case, while the Far East would have languished under Japanese control. Moreover the struggle between fascism and communism, which so many observers in the 1930s took to be the climactic moment of modern history, might in fact have become so, leaving democracy irrelevantly on the sidelines, suited up but unable to play.

Measured against these kinds of unanticipated consequences, foreign policy judgments of the 1930s had more in common with tea leaf reading than with the calculated weighing of interests. Instead of looking at the great debate as a confrontation over how to define the American national interest, it makes more sense to view it as a dispute over the meaning of history, over the legitimacy of the perceptual frameworks from which the "far-sighted" predictions were made.

For internationalists, American political isolation had been possible only within a favorable civilizational and historical context that now seemed to be called in question. According to the influential journalist Walter Lippmann, for example, Europe and the United States were united by "a profound web of interest which joins together the western world"; they formed "one community in their deepest needs and their deepest purposes." That is to say, America had meaning only in the larger context of a family relationship with European civilization. The isolation of the nineteenth century, by this logic, was only a historical accident deriving from the temporary superiority of the British navy rather than, as isolationists assumed, an eternal truth of geography and history.

Shorn of such a friendly global environment, American isolation would take on a naked meaning totally different from the warm and comforting associations of the past. America might survive in an Axis-dominated world, but in what form and to what end? According to Ambassador to Great Britain Joseph P. Kennedy, "America, alone in a jealous and hostile world, would find that the cost and effort of maintaining 'splendid isolation' would be such as to bring about the destruction of all those values which the isolation policy had been designed to preserve."[21] According to this point of view, German aggression would not end isolation, but produce it. The United States would undoubtedly survive, but in the fashion of Robinson Crusoe, washed ashore on a bleak island of history, divorced from civilized companionship. As FDR put it, "Civilization, after all, is not national—it is international."[22] In short, the real danger was not involvement, but isolation of a kind never before experienced.

Well before Pearl Harbor, the United States already felt isolated. With the Fascist powers apparently riding the wave of history, the most significant conquests had already been made. To fall back on a defensive posture in the hemisphere would have been to concede the ascendancy of the Fascist definition of the future. Coming at a moment when American self-confidence was profoundly shaken by the Great Depression, and when the New Deal as a nationalist experiment was itself seriously in question, dictatorial success would have provided conclusive proof of America's failure. The strategic dominoes were still standing, but with the liberal historical sensibility in danger of collapse, the Munich crisis and its aftermath set in motion the dominoes in the American historical imagination. When looked at in this way, the fate of the world was, in a profound sense, at stake.

The isolationist position, too, according to historian Manfred Jonas, was "devoid of political, economic and social content."[23] The chief spokesman for isolationism, Charles Lindbergh, also talked about civilization, the future, and the potentially disastrous effects of the war on America's domestic structure, but his point of departure was shaped by a nominalist predisposition that saw no universal pattern to the complex field of particular events. If American civilization was unique, it made sense for the United States to retain its privileged position outside of history. Cultural separation was fortified by geography and technology. Arguing that air power reinforced America's inherent invulnerability, he continued to view the ocean as an impassable defensive barrier.

For Lindbergh, the European war was a traditional power struggle in which the issue of defending civilization was not so cut and dried and the morality of the situation was far from clear. Whatever the outcome, in Lindbergh's forward projection of history, the future would resemble the past, with the postwar world little changed in its essentials from its current sorry state. Since America could not hope to resolve these chronic international problems or reset the course of history, American identity would best be preserved by standing aside. In this view, isolation from European civilization continued to be America's greatest blessing; the false idol of internationalism, her greatest danger.

Beginning with the German invasion of Poland in September 1939, American policy began a slow turn away from the storm cellar isolationism of the mid-1930s. In November, Congress repealed the arms embargo, making munitions available on a "cash and carry" basis. The following year, in the midst of the Battle of Britain and the U.S. presidential election campaign, the administration negotiated a trade of fifty overage destroyers in exchange for the right to garrison strategic British bases in the western hemisphere. In December 1940, the president's "Arsenal of Democracy" speech set into motion what would become, through the Lend-Lease Act, a program of all-out material aid, short of war.

Events further sorted themselves out as a consequence of the Tripartite Pact of September 1940. This treaty between Germany, Italy, and Japan was intended to cow the United States into remaining a nonparticipant, but it backfired by further solidifying the image of a global threat. Meanwhile, Germany's invasion of the Soviet Union on 22 June 1941, "Operation Barbarossa," temporarily laid to rest the troublesome problem of where the USSR fit in. To some observers the invasion appeared to provide realistic grounds for nonintervention, in the hope that the two contestants might wear each other down. But inasmuch as the USSR appeared to be a sure loser, it solidified the domino rationale of a global threat to peace.

To politicians eagerly looking for cues, public opinion was exasperatingly ambivalent. On the one hand, the public viewed Germany as a threat and was inclined pessimistically to the belief that war with Germany was likely to come; on the other, up to the day of the Pearl Harbor attack it opposed military intervention in a European conflict. The president's policies reflected this combination of hostility and caution. Given the absence of any significant economic leverage against Germany, the only sensible policy was to rearm to the extent possible, proceeding particularly with naval rearmament, and to provide as much moral and material support to the democracies as possible.

War was definitely in the air, but it could not be entered into for philosophical reasons. Ambassador to France William Bullitt was correct in 1939 when he predicted to the president that "even though it should seem that France and England were going to be defeated, the American people would not desire to declare war on Germany unless Germany had committed direct acts of aggression against the United States or American citizens."[24] Bullitt believed that such provocations would be forthcoming, but the gap between historical hypothesis and the realities of limited contact and limited frictions made an "overt act" difficult to envision.

The immediate causes of military conflict were as murky as American and German definitions of their world interests. Hitler, too, appeared to have learned the lessons of the past and seemed determined to avoid antagonizing the United States. During 1940, his U-boat commanders were kept on a short leash. Consistent with his ideological purposes, following the Battle of Britain his military attention turned eastward, toward the goal of attaining *lebensraum* in the Soviet Union. American hostility found vent only in provocative actions in the Atlantic such as convoying, in the order to "shoot on sight" following a U-boat incident, and in an increasingly hard-line posture toward Japan.

The tactics of American diplomacy never did conform to military strategy. The get-tough policy against Japan by no means guaranteed involvement with Germany, as the military planners recognized when they consistently urged a go-slow posture in the Pacific. But the antipathy toward Germany, even when Germany was defined as "public enemy number one," was part of a larger global outlook that could not be confined to strategic pigeonholes. And without any firm mooring in strategy, this abstract ideological antagonism was an easy hostage to events, as nervous American military planners were discovering.

Hitler's declaration of war a few days after Pearl Harbor providentially put an end to the confusion between ideology and strategy. The reasons for his decision remain unclear, for hindsight indicates that it would have been far more preferable to have kept the United States tied up with Japan. We know now that Hitler was being egged on by his navy and by party hotheads eager to bring Great Britain to her knees. Beyond that, he may have been assuming a quick knockout of the USSR, after which his mastery of the Eurasian heartland would have made a successful Anglo-American invasion almost unthinkable—all the more so as the United States would likely have had its hands full with Japan in the Far East. From a longer view, perhaps Hitler sensed the inevitability of American participation and decided to throw down the gauntlet at a moment that seemed as good as any. All this may have been carefully thought out, but given the colossal importance of this wrongheadedness, the lack of discussion beforehand and the rash self-assurance with which the decision was made remains breathtaking if not downright puzzling.[25]

In contrast to the peacetime confusion of strategy and diplomacy, Germany's role in the war posed few problems for the United States, at least in principle. The "Europe first" military strategy, in effect since the winter of 1940, meant the defeat of Hitler would have priority. The bulk of U.S. resources would be concentrated against Germany, in Lend-Lease shipments and in logistical preparations for opening as soon as possible a Second Front on the Continent to relieve the pressure against the beleaguered Soviet armies. Though not religiously adhered to, the strategy remained intact until war's end.

The question of what to do with Germany following her defeat was something else again, an infinitely more difficult problem than it had been in World War I. The first major decision was Roosevelt's much-criticized demand, made early in 1942 at his Casablanca meeting with British prime minister Winston Churchill, for "unconditional surrender." This policy was mercilessly raked over the coals by those who argued that it provided Germany with a powerful incentive to fight to the bitter end, but it had much to recommend it.

Though the analogy Roosevelt drew to the Appomattox surrender was meant for home consumption, unconditional surrender was not a simple-minded approach to the war. Among its virtues was the fact that it would put an end, once and for all, to the question of Germany's secession from the civilized community. After all, Germany's ambiguous defeat in World War I had made possible the demagogic "stab in the back" legend that had contributed so greatly to Weimar Germany's weakness. To the extent that war could settle historical issues, unconditional surrender would conclusively put an end to Germany's global ambitions. Coming at a time when the United States and Britain could offer the USSR little else, it also reassured Stalin that no separate peace would be concluded.

In fairness to FDR, what would a negotiated peace have looked like? Before any alternative to unconditional surrender could have been considered, some compelling idea of what was in the cards for the Reich following the war would have been necessary. Besides that, a common policy would have to have been hammered out among the three major allies. The United States came close to neither throughout the war.

It was clear, as a State Department planning committee concluded, that the treatment of Germany would have to "conform to the long-range interests of the American government regarding the world at large," but just what those long-range interests were was a matter of great perplexity. There were, at bottom, three general approaches to the German problem, each of which had broad political implications and each of which assumed a specific postwar role for the Soviet Union.

The first approach was a reflection of the attitude of the president, who considered himself something of an expert on the German national character. Roosevelt was not a Germanophile. (He had had the misfortune in his youth of having been arrested four times in one day by German authorities, for one peccadillo or another, one of which involved the decapitation of a goose that had stuck its neck into the spokes of his bicycle.) In a conversation with Henry Morgenthau, Roosevelt insisted, "We have got to be tough with the German people, not just the Nazis. You either have to castrate the German people or you have got to treat them in such a manner so they can't just go on reproducing people who want to continue the way they have in the past."

Contrary to his reassuring statement at Casablanca that the United States was fighting a philosophy and not the German people, Roosevelt believed in collective guilt. On this score, at least, the views of this notoriously elusive statesman were unambiguous: "Too many people here and in England hold to the view that the German people as a whole are not responsible for what has taken place—that only a few Nazi leaders are responsible. That unfortunately is not based on fact." Convinced that "Germany understands only one kind of language," he saw no common cultural ground on which to reconstruct the German character.[26] In 1944 he advocated harsh treatment, to let the Germans have a taste of their own medicine and to bring home unmistakably the implications of defeat. In addition to dismemberment of the country, he favored breadlines and the abolition of marching bands and the goose step. This stern attitude conformed with public opinion, which throughout 1943 and 1944 was inclined to control Germany rather than reconstruct it.

Roosevelt's talk of "castration" was obviously ridiculous, but his always eager-to-please secretary of the treasury, Henry Morgenthau, came up with a close substitute. Appalled by what he perceived to be the leniency of army occupation planners, who had issued a handbook of occupation procedures based on the traditional military doctrine of not antagonizing the local population, Morgenthau proposed to FDR and Churchill that Germany be permanently deindustrialized—its factories dismantled, its mines flooded—making it, in Churchill's phrasing, "a nation agricultural and pastoral in character."

Morgenthau secured temporary British agreement at the Second Quebec Conference in September 1944 by dangling the lure of postwar aid and by arguing that Britain's foreign trade could not help but benefit from the elimination of her foremost European economic competitor. Here was a program of industrial castration whose effect would be to change the baritone of Germany's international voice into a weak falsetto.

According to Morgenthau's logic, a Carthaginian peace would have the advantage of continuing the alliance with the Soviet Union into the postwar period, a matter of no small concern in wartime Washington. Dismantling of industrial plants would be a source of reparations that would at one and the same time solve the German problem and preserve the Grand Alliance. To Morgenthau, a policy of leniency toward Germany seemed a transparently anti-Russian smokescreen for those who saw a restored Germany as a bulwark against Russia. "We must address ourselves to the German problem and not be shunted off into a whispering orgy of red baiting on how to prepare for war against Russia," he argued.[27] Besides, what else could the Americans and Soviets so readily agree on?

Once the Morgenthau Plan was leaked to the press, a popular outcry forced the president to backpedal and to shift blame to his treasury secretary. "Henry pulled a boner," he said in his charmingly disingenuous way. Nevertheless, the Treasury won a partial victory by having many of its punitive ideas incorporated into the interim occupation directive for Germany that would govern American policy until agreed-upon long-range solutions had emerged.

The Morgenthau Plan had never been fully thought out. Besides failing to address the problems of American public opinion and hopes for a liberal postwar world, it had other impossible defects. Since Germany was not agriculturally self-supporting and depended on exports to feed 20 to 25 million of her people, what would happen to them under a program of deindustrialization? What about the German exports on which the economies of other European nations depended? And what about America's ability or willingness to enforce a permanently despotic occupation? With respect to such important particulars, Morgenthau's biblical vengefulness was an attitude, not a plan.

In any case, it quickly ran afoul of a second, less popular approach—but one with deeper roots in American tradition—in which the war was seen as a struggle of philosophies, not cultures. According to the liberal point of view, which assumed the underlying sameness of human nature, the only permanent solution to the German problem was to reintegrate her eventually into a liberal family of nations. Not only did the prospect of deindustrialization seem barbaric and uncivilized to internationalists like Cordell Hull and Secretary of War Henry Stimson, who opposed "turning such a gift of nature into a dust heap,"[28] the lessons of the past seemed to argue against it as well. Had not the harsh Treaty of Versailles sown the seeds of World War II? However, the problem with this approach was that it presupposed adherence by the USSR to the liberal world economy outlined in the Declaration of the United Nations, and the Soviets showed no signs of wishing to do away with their closed economic system.

The third and last possibility, a partition of Germany into several smaller states, was discussed with enthusiasm by the "Big Three" at their November 1943 meeting in Tehran. Agreement on dismemberment, especially with regard to the amputation of what had formerly been East Prussia, was reached easily enough. At the Yalta Conference in February 1945 a seemingly firm decision to carve the Reich into pieces was reached, but it became evident shortly thereafter that none of the parties had its heart set on such a solution. For reasons that are still not clear, by the time of the Big Three meeting at Potsdam in July 1945, the idea of partition had been abandoned by all.

Even though partition was, in retrospect, the most realistic approach, it was the least seriously considered, probably because it presupposed a breakup of the Grand Alliance. As the Soviet expert George Kennan argued, mainly to himself, "the idea of a Germany run jointly with the Russians is a chimera." According to his view, a resort to partition was necessary not because it was desirable in itself, but because Soviet behavior would offer no other viable alterative. Germany would have to be divided for the foreseeable future into Eastern and Western spheres of control, which in turn meant a division of Europe into spheres of influence.

Though seemingly hard-headed, the partition scheme was freighted with unacceptable implications. It assumed a noncooperative Soviet Union and the impossibility of attaining a liberal world order. It was bound to sow the dragon's teeth of German nationalist sentiment and produce the kind of revanchism that followed World War I. It would also entail building up the western portion of Germany. But even if partition could have been brought off amicably, it looked too much like prewar power politics, and anything smacking of a cold-blooded division of Europe would be taken by Americans as a reversion to the kind of reprehensible behavior that had characterized the discredited Munich bargain. Indeed, for that very reason the Yalta accords would be for four decades heavily criticized as a sellout of Eastern Europe.

By default, then, Germany was to remain united, if shrunken in size, but no one professed to be able to work out in advance the conditions of that unity. Indeed, no one wanted to try. While the past offered many disastrous precedents to be avoided, the ideological confusion of wartime meant that history was of little help in providing positive, practical solutions. Given its enormous importance for postwar developments, American silence on the German question was, in retrospect, more significant than the policies formally considered. The inability, coupled with reluctance, to think the problem through set the pattern for the way in which the German problem would develop after the war.

American reticence had little to do with the oft-cited American taboo against mixing diplomacy and warfare. For FDR, cooperation begat cooperation; the successful conduct of coalition warfare was the precondition of successful postwar diplomacy. Whatever America's preferences might have been, it was clear that Germany's future depended equally on Soviet desires. Since any hard proposals were bound either to shake the Grand Alliance or to rattle public opinion, Roosevelt remained content with the inconclusive discussions and misty understandings of the wartime conferences. German policy would have to be shaped by postwar events and, he hoped, paid for by the Allied goodwill banked during the war. For the moment, it was more important to build that indispensable foundation of trust than to tackle potentially divisive issues in no immediate need of settlement.

This policy was consistent with the president's anti-utopian mentality and with his antitheoretical, pragmatic approach to issues in which the will, rather than precise abstract formulas, determined the way. If his government spoke with many tongues about Germany and seemed to procrastinate, it was because FDR was convinced that no amount of grand planning could frame reality in advance. In any case, with his death on 10 April 1945, Roosevelt left the war as he had entered it: shooting the rapids of history, kept afloat by his improvisational skills, his buoyant spirit, and his unsinkable liberal faith that smoother waters lay ahead.

In this atmosphere of agreed indeterminacy, the best that the Allies could do in negotiations in London was to reach agreement on the terms of surrender and on postwar zones of occupation. After much stalling, the United States agreed to take a zone in the mostly agrarian south and west of Germany, with the enclave of Bremen as a seaport. As the saying at the time went, the Russians received the agriculture, the British the heavy industry, and the Americans the scenery. The zonal arrangement was a kind of mutual insurance policy, taken out against the chance that one of the Allies should overrun Germany before the other's armies could reach it.[29] Though it had the appearance of a spheres-of-influence arrangement, it was intended to form the basis of postwar bargaining over Germany, not to stand as the last word on the issue.

In addition, as a symbol of Allied unity it was agreed that the occupation would be run from Berlin. Even though the Nazi capital lay 110 miles deep in the Soviet zone, each power would administer a sector of the city as its own. The terms of surrender made it clear that the Allies would assume supreme authority in Germany. Since there would remain no German government to deal with, they would act directly on the German people. Apart from these administrative agreements, the hard political decisions with respect to the German problem were left to the war's end.

As the Western Front collapsed in the spring of 1945 and American and British troops advanced into Germany more quickly than anticipated, Churchill suggested that American and British troops not be pulled back to the agreed zonal boundaries until the Russians had demonstrated their good faith on outstanding political issues. But FDR's successor, Harry S Truman, decided to abide by the letter of the agreements, and Allied forces sorted themselves out successfully a few months following the German surrender.

Ironically, then, the remarkably vivid picture of the world that had brought the United States to war against Germany was nearly blank when the war ended. The year 1945 has frequently been described by Germans as "zero hour" (*Stunde null*), the moment in time when history had been obliterated and everything began again from scratch. The situation was, of course, quite different for the American victors, who came out of the war with enormous self-confidence and optimism. Nevertheless, standing triumphant on the charred ruins of the *Reich*, their view of Germany and its role in the world would also have to be built anew.

chapter 2

TWO CULTURES: THE OCCUPATION

When V-E Day arrived on 8 May 1945, the United States had
no conceptual road map, no clear image of Germany's place in the world, no
idée maîtresse with which to plot Germany's future. Indeed, following the fra-
cas kicked up by the Morgenthau Plan, it was all the government could do—
and this only after six months of endless dickering between the State, War,
and Treasury Departments—to draft an occupation directive. Immortalized
by its bureaucratic designation, JCS 1067, this document remained "the
Bible" of the occupation until mid-1947, when a long-range policy finally
began to emerge.

Army jargon quickly reduced this twelve-page document to the "four D's":
demilitarization, denazification, decartelization, and democratization of
Germany. JCS 1067, whose goal was "preventing Germany from becoming
again a threat to the world," was a harsh document that reflected the unfor-
giving state of American public opinion at the close of the war.[1] It called for
such obvious steps as the breaking up of the once formidable Reichswehr, the
abolition of the Nazi party, the annulment of Nazi laws, and the arrest and
trial of war criminals and high-ranking officials of the Third Reich. Besides
treating symptoms, it aimed also at effecting a complete cure through industrial disarmament and the creation of democratic political institutions.

Many observers then and now have treated JCS 1067 as if it were the
Morgenthau Plan in military costume. The Treasury Department, its frontal
attack having been repulsed, had fought tenaciously to smuggle its punitive
views into the occupation directive. And to some extent it had succeeded,
most notably in the prohibition on steps "looking toward the economic rehabilitation of Germany" or any measures "designed to maintain or strengthen
the German economy." This was the way Morgenthau himself saw it, as he

confided with evident satisfaction in his diary his hope that "somebody doesn't recognize it as the Morgenthau Plan."

By magnifying his own preoccupations, Morgenthau failed to see the larger picture. As the four D's suggest, JCS 1067's emphasis on rooting out Nazism was less punitive than reformative in intent. Eschewing punishment as an end in itself, it focused on decriminalization. Moreover, whereas the Morgenthau Plan had outlined a lasting settlement of the German problem, JCS 1067 was from the first a design for treading water until permanent solutions could be worked out.

The U.S. Army was too conscious of its short and inglorious tradition of military government to see itself as building for the ages. Opposed to economic rehabilitation less as a matter of principle than because it did not feel adequate to the task, the army accepted the neo-Morgenthauian features for the sake of administrative convenience, in the expectation that the occupation would soon be handed over to civilian administration.

The man who personified the American occupation was General Lucius DuBignon Clay, a chain-smoking scion of the southern aristocracy who had made his reputation as a desk soldier. Clay was an engineer by training, with an unsurpassed capacity for manipulating facts and figures. Like most officers, he had yearned for a combat command, but it was in the bureaucratic trenches of wartime Washington, where his organizational skills were considered too precious to be wasted on the battlefield, that he distinguished himself. His desk experience having made him an expert in the workings of the government, he was selected for the job of deputy military governor primarily because of his keen understanding of the civilian viewpoint, not because of any special knowledge of Germany.

According to John McCloy, being military governor "was the nearest thing to a Roman proconsulship the modern world afforded. You could turn to your secretary and say, 'Take a law.'" With his piercing eyes, gaunt features, and Roman nose, Clay even looked the part of a Roman patrician. According to some accounts he acted like one, too, but if so, he was not guided by the merciless spirit of Cato the Elder. He took very seriously his mandate to bring democracy to Germany and was wary of the dilemmas involved in forcing a people to freedom. His southern heritage mattered too, for he was determined not to preside over an occupation that would leave memories as bitter as those of Reconstruction in his native Georgia.[2]

Autocratic by nature and by training, Clay was a liberal in ideology who had been deeply impressed by Henry Stimson's portrayal of Germany as a workshop for the world. He agreed with his financial advisor Lewis Douglas's assessment of JCS 1067, that it was "assembled by economic idiots!" Douglas felt that it made "no sense to forbid the most skilled workers in Europe from producing as much as they can for a continent which is desperately short of everything." Reinforcing Clay's attitude was his engineer's ethic, which honored human creation over retributive destruction.

Clay doubted from the very first that JCS 1067 was realistic, but after some quixotic attempts to have it toned down he made his peace with "the Bible's" tenets. As a seasoned bureaucratic warrior, he realized that JCS 1067, like all sacred texts, was subject to a wide range of interpretations. As a loose constructionist, Clay was willing and able to take advantage of his on-the-spot authority by exploiting the document's ambiguities. Experience, not the reopening of bitter theoretical arguments, would provide the impetus to revision.

He agreed, however, that the Germans should be punished. Clay felt that "the Germans should suffer from hunger and cold," an experience that would help them "realize the consequences of a war which they caused." Nevertheless, punishment "should not extend to the point where it results in mass starvation and sickness." Happily for Clay, and fortunately for the Germans, a major loophole in JCS 1067 was its recognition that relief supplies might be needed to prevent "disease and disorder." As it happened, food imports were required from the first under this disease and unrest formula. There was in addition a less humanitarian reason for moderation. Contrary to the intuitive desire to take it out of the hides of the Germans, Clay understood that simple-minded vengeance would in the end only punish the U.S. taxpayer.

The result of these ambiguities was an occupation that was to administration what jazz is to classical music. Without any coherent long-range policy toward Germany, and with JCS 1067's nearsighted philosophy vitiated by the facts, occupational routines were of necessity less orchestrated than improvised. According to Assistant Secretary of State for Occupied Areas John Hilldring, long-range policy would have to "bubble up out of the facts."[3]

Yet just because decisions were taken primarily in the field, at least for the first few years, this did not mean that the military administrators shaped German policy. Clay and his lieutenants enjoyed considerable authority, to be sure, but only as caretakers pending the creation of a new legitimate order. In any case, as we shall see, the success or failure of the occupation vis-à-vis the Germans was not all that important, because the occupation contributed to policy formation only in the sense that its inability to work out an ad hoc system of administration ultimately forced the articulation of a high policy. In the last analysis, Germany's fate depended not on administrators but on the resolution of European difficulties and the working out of a relationship with the USSR. Any fundamental improvement in Germany's chaotic internal situation presupposed some kind of agreement with the Russians on the terms of economic unification. And this in turn depended on policy with respect to the rest of Europe.

At first, however, the absence of a high policy did not seem to matter. In light of the prevailing assumption that the occupation of Germany might last perhaps as long as twenty-five years, there seemed no reason to hurry. As

Clay said at his first press conference: "We have time enough later to consider the long-range terms of Germany and the regeneration of the German people. Our first objective is to smash whatever remaining power Germany may have with which to develop a future war potential." This proved to be entirely too optimistic. The occupation demonstrated that administrative improvisation, even if focused on short-term objectives, was impossible without farsighted guidance.

Besides lack of policy, there were many other obstacles to effective governance of the country. The army had no effective tradition in civil affairs. Even though the military government (OMGUS, in the GI vernacular) reported ultimately to the Civil Affairs Division in the War Department (through the military chain of command), the occupation was largely an army show. An army is an administrative bureaucracy par excellence, but it is as a fighting machine and not a civil affairs body that it excels. Memories of the brief but unhappy post–World War I occupation of Germany underscored the conviction held by many officers that the army was unsuited to sociopolitical tasks.

Yet another difficulty was the low level of competence among occupation personnel. Military government was not administered by specially trained occupation cadres or by combat veterans. The army had begun training occupation troops during the war, but the pell-mell demobilization caused by the universal desire to go home made it extremely difficult to find first-rate administrators willing to serve in a less than edenic environment. The result was that less able men often filled staff positions, while the rank and file often consisted of the dregs of the American army. Since few Americans spoke German, there was a heavy call on the services of émigrés and liberal Germans.

When the U.S. occupation forces first arrived, harshness was the rule. Americans came as conquerors rather than liberators and attempted to behave accordingly. Unlike the French, who billeted themselves among the local inhabitants, the GIs segregated themselves in barbed-wire compounds, causing local wits to ask when they were going to liberate themselves from their concentration camps. ("Hans Crowism," one American called it.) To the great irritation of the Germans, they acted in blithe disregard of local custom. They chlorinated the water supply whether it needed it or not, arrogated hunting and fishing privileges to themselves without regard to property rights, and sought to make the Germans bear the occupation costs to the greatest extent possible.

Higher ranking officials often requisitioned the most desirable German housing stock and land, made generous use of German servants, and left the locals to shift for themselves. Frequently the imperial standard of living so far exceeded that which would have been possible in America that it bordered on the obscene. Disgusted by this ostentatious parasitism, the puritanical George Kennan came away from one visit "with a sense of sheer horror at the spectacle of this horde of my compatriots and their dependents camping in luxury amidst the ruins of a shattered national community."[4]

The U.S. nonfraternization policy—and its failure—was an example of how even the most simple intentions could become complicated beyond measure. This attempt to segregate the country into American Brahmins and German untouchables was designed to bring home to the Germans how their behavior had made them outcasts among their fellow men. Because the Germans were considered "unclean," there existed also the possibility of pollution through contact. Incoming GIs were warned of the sinful implications of friendly behavior: "If in a German town you bow to a pretty girl or pat a blond child . . . you caress the ideology that means death and persecution. Don't fraternize."[5] That was symbolism. Translated into terms GIs could understand, fraternization meant sex.[6] The shortage of German men and the distress of many German women, whose privations GIs were in a position to ameliorate, meant that the law of supply and demand and the laws of human nature went swiftly into operation. Realizing the futility of trying to enforce the narrow official definition of fraternization, Clay tried to put a humorous face on the matter. "I guess it means when you stay for breakfast," he said.[7]

Though a system of fines and controls was imposed to forestall both the patting of children and more sensual contact, the nonfraternization policy, like Prohibition, was universally disregarded, and the army was forced to revoke its ban shortly after it was instituted. Its removal, according to one historian, was "a necessary concession to human nature in a situation where hunger, desire, and compassion were often quite literally bedfellows."[8] Eventually, as relationships flowered to the point that growing numbers of American soldiers were taking German wives, the War Brides Act reflected the army's recognition of human reality.

The haughty attitude would have been difficult to maintain in any case. Hanging on the wall behind the desk of one occupation officer was the declaration "I hate Germans," but it hastened to add that "were it not for them, I would be America's most famous architect." The statement was revealing, for it demonstrated in principle what contact proved in practice: American hatred of Germans was not deeply rooted. To be sure, there was reason enough for enmity, created by the experience of war, propaganda, and the nauseating discovery of the extermination camps. The French attitude was to view all Germans as Nazis, but American hatred was a consequence of the war, not its cause. Lacking any heritage of antipathy between the two peoples, the occupation's early vindictive emphasis was softened by the passage of time, by bureaucratic complications, and ultimately by overarching political and economic calculations.

That revenge and simple-minded repression were alien to the Americans was evident from the Nuremberg trials of the Nazi leadership in 1945 and 1946. The Nazis had been put on notice early in the war, long before the public revelation of their genocidal policies, that they would be held legally accountable for their violation of the laws of war. Despite the farcical outcome of war crimes trials following the First World War, the members of the Grand Alliance chose not to rely on military courts-martial or summary executions. At the Tehran meeting of 1943, Stalin, perhaps recalling his earlier use of the technique against the Poles in the Katyn Forest massacre, proposed shooting at least fifty thousand German officers. Taking offense at this barbaric suggestion, Churchill nevertheless favored drumhead courts-martial and the execution of five or ten of the Nazi elite.

Neither course appealed to the Americans, whose sense of justice and long-standing desire to create an effective system of international law made the alternative of legal prosecution more attractive. Many American liberal internationalists believed trials would bring home the consequences of what appeared to be a criminal disregard for solemn covenants such as the Kellogg-Briand Pact of 1928, which had sought to eliminate war through international agreement. Learning from the mistakes of the past also played a part, as the unresolved question of war guilt had allowed aggressive German nationalism to be rekindled in the 1930s by Nazi propaganda. Additionally, officials like Secretary of War Henry Stimson, seeing in legal punishment of the Nazis a firebreak against Morgenthauism, hoped that harsh judicial treatment would forestall mindless vengeance in the socioeconomic sphere.

The tripartite agreement signed in London in August 1945 was radically internationalist in character. The governing assumption of its charter was that "individuals have international duties which transcend the national obligations of obedience imposed by the individual state."[9] Once the idea of an International Military Tribunal (IMT) was accepted by the British and the Russians, President Harry S Truman appointed Robert Jackson, an associate justice of the Supreme Court, as the prosecutor. As the U.S. judge, he selected Attorney General Francis Biddle.

The London Charter listed three categories of crimes for which defendants could be tried: crimes against peace (aggression was defined as the "supreme crime," in contrast to long-standing international doctrine that justified war if it was found to be in the national interest), war crimes, and crimes against humanity. The charter also made statesmen personally responsible for their policies. Extending this principle down the chain of command, it ruled out a defense based on the plea of following orders from one's superior. Going further, it declared that certain groups were in themselves criminal, the most prominent being the leadership cadre of the Nazi party, Hitler's SS praetorian guard (*Schutzstaffel*), the paramilitary SA storm troopers (*Sturmabteilung*), and the secret police or Gestapo (*Geheimstaatspolizei*). By concentrating attention on these miscreant organizations, the trials would punish Germany judicially, rather than socioeconomically, as had been envisaged under the Morgenthau Plan.

Eventually, twenty-one defendants were arraigned in Nuremberg, a city chosen in part for its ironic symbolism. It seemed only fitting that Nazism should be brought to book in the same location that had hosted the spectacular Nazi party rallies of the 1930s. The most prominent defendants were Hermann Göring, the number two man in the Reich, Rudolf Hess, the führer's deputy, and Joachim von Ribbentrop, the wine merchant turned foreign minister. In addition, industrialists such as the head of the Krupp works, bureaucrats such as Hjalmar Schacht, head of the Reichsbank, and some prominent diplomats were also put in the dock. The trials stretched from November 1945 through August 1946 and resulted in ten death sentences (Göring cheated the hangman by committing suicide in his cell), three sentences of life imprisonment, four lesser sentences, and three acquittals.

The Nuremberg trials were a reflection of their time, as an expression both of the internationalist idealism coming out of the war and of the imperfections and realities that prevented its realization. There were indeed many problems with the Nuremberg system. It did not effectively create international law, and some jurists felt that it actually diminished it. Trying Germans on the basis of ex post facto law and dubious definitions of conspiracy, however satisfying at the moment, seemed to blur moral principles and set an uninspiring example for justice in the future.

That the IMT was not an international court of justice but a victor's tribunal also seemed to raise more questions than it resolved. How could international law be made binding on individuals by military conquerors? If might made right, then the old problem of what constituted aggression was simply being swept under the rug. What would be done in the event of subsequent aggressive behavior by one of the current victors? For some critics, there was no need to look to the future. George Kennan, for example, recoiled at the prospect of making moral judgments in tandem with the Soviets, whose hands seemed just as bloody as those of the Nazis.

From a less narrowly legalistic point of view, however, Nuremberg takes on a different complexion. By ventilating issues and evidence rather than resorting to summary judgment, by providing a vehicle for continued cooperation with the USSR, by raising, however imperfectly, the legal concept of crimes against humanity, and by defining standards of civic morality that even the victors could not meet, the Nuremberg trials furnished an outlet for the expression of civilized ideals in what was, after all, a war for civilization. From hindsight, Nuremberg remains a potent symbol of the reassertion of international morality and idealism. Had stricter legal standards or political expediency won the day, it is hard to see the bar of history agreeing that justice had been done.

Follow-up trials for some of the upper administrative echelons of the Nazi regime were held at Nuremberg under the direction of Brigadier General Telford Taylor. Baron von Weizsäcker of the foreign office and a number of other Nazi cabinet members, diplomats, and economic officials were accused of war crimes. On the assumption that big business had been complicit in the Nazi conspiracy, charges were also brought against the directors of the I. G. Farben, Flick, and Krupp industrial empires. In addition, at the Dachau concentration camp on the outskirts of Munich, the judge advocate general held a series of trials of concentration camp officials who were charged with murder.

Disposing of the lesser offenders turned out to be much more difficult, controversial, and unsatisfying than dealing with the big shots. Following the trial of the alleged SS perpetrators of the Malmédy massacre, for instance, twelve of whom were originally sentenced to death, allegations of brutality, coerced confessions, concealment of evidence, and other legal improprieties reached such a crescendo that a commission of inquiry appointed by the secretary of the army recommended commutation. In an unpopular move, Clay felt he had no choice but to overturn the sentence of Ilse Koch, the so-called "Bitch of Buchenwald," on grounds of insufficient evidence.

Excessive zeal tarnished the occupation in liberal eyes and led to conservative opposition back in the states, where the heating up of cold war hysteria produced a backlash against the occupation and a growing inclination to let bygones be bygones. Right-wing congressman John Rankin (D-Miss.) decried "this saturnalia of persecution," while others like George Dondero and Joseph McCarthy demagogically suggested that a left-wing, conspiratorial, Jewish vendetta was behind what they felt to be these unwarranted prosecutions. Whatever remained of the hard-line anti-Germanism of the Morgenthau Plan disappeared in 1948 following sensational allegations that Morgenthau's principal assistant, Harry Dexter White, was a Communist. Conservative cold warriors were now convinced that the plan was at best a devilishly sly way of maintaining the wartime alliance with the Soviets, and at worst a formula for promoting the Bolshevization of Germany.

The trials also backfired in German public opinion. Though mountains of evidence led to the execution of more than one hundred individuals for committing mass murders, the tales of judicial irregularities were more than enough to excite the sympathies of the German population on behalf of what they considered to be their ill-treated countrymen. If these trials were intended in part to drive home to the Germans an understanding of the heinous crimes of the regime, ironically they often wound up shifting culpability to the shoulders of the accusers.

Some early cold war measures also introduced hidden inconsistencies and moral ambiguities, all the more serious because they were kept secret for many years. As we now know, sections of U.S. Army Intelligence, viewing former Nazis as potential assets in the looming confrontation with the Russians, smuggled out individuals who might otherwise have been tried and convicted as war criminals. Klaus Barbie, the "Butcher of Lyons," was hired by American intelligence; Hitler's intelligence chief, Reinhard Gehlen, was hired by the CIA to conduct intelligence operations against the Soviet Union and eventually became chief of West German intelligence after the occupation; and a number of White Russian Nazi collaborators with intimate knowledge of the USSR, who as members of the SS death squads (*Einsatzgruppen*) were responsible for thousands of executions, were given safe passage to the United States.

Punishing war criminals was only the tip of the iceberg, however. Just below the water line, hidden from public view, sensational journalism, and political demagoguery, there remained the job of tracking down and bringing to justice the members of organizations defined as conspiratorial. Deeper yet, at the base of the iceberg, the occupation faced an awesome task: a program of denazification that amounted to nothing less than an attempted purge of Germany society.

As General John Hilldring, who headed the State Department's Civil Affairs Bureau, argued: "The very essence of our policy in Germany and Japan is to take control of these countries away from the fascist-minded people until democratic ideas and ideals take root in these countries."[10] Unlike the other three zones, denazification in the American zone was so broadly construed that it amounted in effect to a program designed to punish collective guilt. General Dwight Eisenhower's view was representative: "The German people must not be allowed to escape a sense of personal guilt."[11]

The military government—OMGUS—decided to have every adult in the U.S. zone complete a lengthy questionnaire, or *Fragebogen*, whose 131 questions were designed to elicit complete histories of individual political behavior under the Third Reich. As an incentive to compliance, submission of a completed *Fragebogen* was made a condition for obtaining food coupons, travel permits, and employment. Those who had supported or benefitted from the Nazi regime were to be removed from positions of influence or denied employment. As an aid to memory, OMGUS let it be known that it had captured the Nazi regime's copious archives.

At first enforcement was halfhearted, since overburdened army detachments were preoccupied with trying to restore German administrative machinery, but then, on 26 September 1945, Clay lowered the boom with the promulgation of Law Number 8. Applicable to public servants and the private sector alike, this law prohibited any employment above that of common laborer for Nazis and sympathizers. By December, 13 million questionnaires had inundated American offices.

The intent was crystal-clear, but the capacity for effective follow-through was missing. It was too much to expect that a military organization could undertake the job of social purification. Moreover, the determination of guilt was not as self-evident as the criterion of party membership seemed to indicate. The Nazi party was a mass organization whose membership numbered eight million, with some four million others in auxiliary organizations. Membership had been obligatory even for nonideologues, as a condition of holding their jobs.

General George Patton, the swashbuckling hero whose mouth was often more dangerous than his armies, was not entirely wrong when he observed that "it is no more possible for a man to be a civil servant in Germany and not have paid lip service to Nazism than it is possible for a man to be a postmaster in America and not have paid at least lip service to the Democratic Party, or the Republican Party when it is in power."[12] Another remark in this vein cost Patton his job, but it contained a nugget of truth Americans did not care to face at the time. While Patton could be whisked offstage, the embarrassing questions he raised would remain to vex the occupation.

Even if the Americans had been clearer in their minds as to the implications of the denazification program, its administrative application would in any case have posed problems aplenty. What about those Germans who were not party members but who had benefitted from party rule? What about outright lies on the *Fragebogen*? Finally, the era of modern bureaucratic juggernauts notwithstanding, how was an entire society to be judged? Inevitably, as has so often been the case throughout history, the conqueror became dependent on the conquered. Since OMGUS lacked the resources to conduct such a massive purge, in a step that amounted to letting the criminals do the prosecuting, it handed over responsibility to the Germans for "self-cleansing."

Here the Americans ran into difficulties with their own theories. Notwithstanding their denials about imposing punishment for collective guilt, the aim of "complete denazification of Germany" required penetration into the deepest recesses of the society. In the U.S. zone, some 20 percent of the population, or 3.5 million people, were implicated. Predictably, German public opinion, less than gung-ho in the first place about denazification and not holding the same broad view of its criminality, was reluctant to admit the legitimacy of such a far-ranging enterprise.

Local tribunals (*Spruchkammern*) composed of reputable Germans were set up to decide the appeals of those who claimed only nominal party membership. Once denazification was handed over to them in March 1946, the tribunals wound up flooded with appeals, which the Americans had not anticipated. At high tide, the program relied on about 22,000 Germans in the American zone to examine the questionnaires, while more than 500 tribunals processed some 50,000 cases per month. In adjudicating these cases, the panels tended as a rule to be less than scrupulous. The typical panel was characterized by one American military government officer as "inefficient, incompetent, laughable, and corrupt."[13] However, even with their obvious slap-on-the-wrist approach to their jobs, panel members were often ostracized and later denied employment for their complicity in what the Germans saw as an odious American witch-hunt.

The scope of the task demanded further self-defeating shortcuts. Germans were allowed to submit affidavits attesting to their ideological cleanliness, called *Persilscheine* in the vernacular (Persil being a popular detergent), and these turned out often to be fraudulent. OMGUS further reduced its burden by granting amnesty to all those born after 1 January 1919 and by letting off a category of petty offenders, but still the caseload exceeded 900,000. The final count was 9,000 prison sentences, 22,000 people barred from public office, 25,000 who lost their property, and more than 500,000 who were fined. As time went on, sentences tended to become more lenient.

Again, the process was shot through with unintended consequences. The American insistence on legal rather than political forms enabled Germans to point to procedural irregularities and to make accusations of legal terrorism. The effort to instill a sense of guilt in the German civic conscience ended by instead producing resentment, self-justification, and the feeling that denazification was a farce. Worse yet, by shifting the spotlight of culpability from Nazi criminality to American administrative misdeeds, the moral issue disappeared into the shadows. Ironically, the persecution complex generated by this issue inevitably lent to those with a Nazi past the very air of respectability the conquerors wanted so desperately to eradicate.

Denazification also wreaked chaos with the orderly administration of the American zone, for until it was completed Americans could not effectively deal with the longer-range problems of reviving local government, the economy, and basic social services such as education. Widespread circumvention of the spirit of the denazification process meant that the purges did not accomplish their task of rooting out the villains in the German civil service or in industry. As for the big fish who were snared in the porous net, they were reduced to menial work in a modern industrial society badly in need of their expertise. When the period of outright occupation stumbled to its end, German politicians played on the public dislike of denazification, and in 1951 they undid most of its results by legally rehabilitating all Nazis not accused of war crimes.

Not content with punishing Nazism, Americans wished also to uproot the conditions that supported it. A few thoughtful souls like George Kennan may have rejected the view of the German people as "a mass of human monsters, solidly behind Hitler and consumed with a demonic enthusiasm for the ruin and enslavement of Europe." But most Americans familiar with Germany and its history would have agreed that German culture provided a fertile medium for the luxuriant growth of Nazism. An extreme statement of this position, one that would have been shared by Franklin Roosevelt, came in a 1946 OMGUS report: "It happens that the German culture is a bad culture which also represents a menace to orderly world society. . . . The German culture is authoritarian and has made real democracy an impossibility."[14]

The corollary to denazification was reeducation of Germans toward democracy. Public pronouncements by the U.S. government had indicated that the United States had fought Germany on the Rousseauian assumption that war takes place between nations, not peoples, and was not the result of cultural conflict per se. However, the occupation tried for a time to act on the basis of another of Rousseau's assumptions: Germany would be forced to be free.

In an attempt to reorient German historical values, the names of prominent Nazis were removed from street signs, parks, and public buildings. The
same held true for monuments, statues, emblems, and symbols of German
militarism. It did not stop there, however, for the long view held that
Bismarck, Gneisenau, and other historical figures who had contributed to
the rise of Prussian militarism shared responsibility. Sucked into the memory
hole, they, too, became nonpersons.

Clay also ordered the removal of Nazi-issued textbooks from school classrooms and had these replaced with schoolbooks that had been prepared in
advance of the occupation. Only just barely was he dissuaded from ordering
the destruction of all Nazi literature found in the American zone. His logic
was that "After all, we prohibit obscene literature at home and the worst
Nazi poison is certainly as offensive to public morals." To him, the question
was: "Should we hang a Göring and let his works roll merrily along?" As a
concession to freedom of inquiry, the offending texts were segregated in the
libraries, banished from contaminating contact with true literature.

For a few months following V-E day, movies and theaters were closed
until satisfactory German films could be licensed, and a number of
Hollywood products (generally of a mediocre character due to the absence of
profit potential) were hastily assembled for circulation. Although at first the
military government went into the business of publishing German newspapers, it decided that such matters should quickly be handed over to the locals
and shifted instead to licensing them. The staffs were required to be representative of the political spectrum, which meant that even Communists were
included at the beginning.

In the later stages of the occupation, subsidies were provided to encourage
democratically inclined newspapers and journals. In terms of direct publication, OMGUS published magazines patterned after *Life*, *Reader's Digest*, and
the *Atlantic Monthly*. The occupation also translated a number of American
novels into German and opened a series of informal libraries known as
Amerika Haüser, which in addition to their print collections served as focal
points for lectures, movies, and other activities. Radio transmissions were
kept under American control until 1949, when they were turned over to the
Germans.

The most ambitious goal, at least conceptually, was the reform of the
German educational system. Influenced by the widely held belief that wars
began in the minds of men, "cultural reconstruction" was thought to be necessary.[15] According to the reigning progressive pedagogical formulas of John
Dewey, the primary mission of schools was to assure progress and to teach
democratic living. Therefore, imparting a healthy sense of democracy meant
tinkering with the German school system, which, according to one education officer, was "just as dangerous as those war-materials factories." Elitism
could be broken down and replaced with an egalitarian spirit by the rather

simple expedient of reorganizing the German public schools so that they contained students of different socioeconomic and religious backgrounds.

The two-track German tradition as it had developed from the early nineteenth century diverged considerably from the American ideal of a single educational system for all—an ideal that applied only to public education, of course. In Germany, following a brief period in a school where all students followed a common curriculum, a sharp separation took place at the age of ten. At this point, only 10 percent—largely a gifted minority of middle-class status—would enter the secondary school, or gymnasium, as a preparation for professional careers, while the balance would receive vocational training. Despite a few changes during the period of the Weimar Republic and much talk during the Hitler era of reform along National Socialist lines, the German educational system of 1945 was basically that installed in the nineteenth century.[16]

American educational reform consisted of more than lip service, but like denazification, it fell far short of the root and branch change that would have been required to give substance to American ideals. Part of the problem was that robust ambition conflicted with an anemic bureaucratic capability. The shortage of able educational officers was more severe than in other branches of military government. From 1945 through 1947, there were no more than fifty members of the Educational and Religious Affairs (E&RA) staff. Paradoxically, despite the fundamental nature of the educational reform, educational affairs were a low-status activity in the military hierarchy compared with the more prestigious political and economic posts, a situation not unknown in the United States itself.

More important was a conceptual difficulty, a confusion between culture and ideology, which made the task seem easier than it turned out to be. Americans acted as if the two were the same. They seemed to believe that, like tarnish on metal, misconceived educational ideals could easily be buffed off to reveal the shining metallic surface of democratic spirit lying underneath. But the fundamental axiom that educational reform must proceed from the grass roots and be internalized by the Germans collided head-on with cultural reality, as the Germans proved to have a deep attachment to their educational tradition, which they rightfully saw as German rather than Nazi in character.

In practice, denazification and the running of an effective school system proved for a time to be mutually contradictory. In addition to problems with physical plant and the shortage of adequate textbooks, there were vexing political complications. Teachers, like everyone else, had to submit the *Fragebogen*. Regardless of whether or not they were enthusiastic ideologues, schoolteachers had been put under enormous pressure to join the party, and most of them had done so. For the occupation, this meant mandatory removals reaching 80 percent in some areas, appallingly high teacher-student ratios, and often totally unqualified individuals in charge of classrooms.

Structural reforms, which presumably could have come about through a stroke of the pen, proved to be beyond the reach of American idealism. The Mission Report in 1946 recommended the formation of a comprehensive school system as a means of promoting the democratic spirit in education. However, an attempt to install the American system in Bavaria in 1947 encountered tenacious, foot-dragging opposition from German Catholic conservatives "nearing outright sabotage." American threats produced only token modifications of the existing two-track system, and, as a slap in the face, the Bavarians approved the reinstitution of the decidedly nonprogressive practice of corporal punishment (*Prügelstrafe*) in their schools.

Direct orders to the education ministry to toe the line were met with a publicity campaign to mobilize public sentiment against the occupiers, as the Germans, resorting to cultural jujitsu, came to recognize that American values could be used against the occupiers. Moreover, since a considerable degree of local autonomy had already been granted, it was questionable whether the Bavarian legislature, or *Landtag*, would provide the necessary approval. As time went on, it became increasingly clear that the occupation's heart was not in its work. American reformers continued to press forward until the formal end of the occupation, but like Bismarck with his Kulturkampf, they experienced no great success.

The world-renowned German universities, seeking to circumvent the *Fragebogen* system, reopened their doors and relied on in-house committees to conduct internal purges and establish the democratic bona fides of faculty. These committees were responsible for internal appointments and denazification, subject to the approval of a university officer from Educational and Religious Affairs. As in the lower schools, removals were heavy, for higher education had been a Nazi showcase. Consequently, many high academic chairs went unfilled. Students, too, had to submit the despised questionnaires. Again, the mass character of the party meant that the denazification of student bodies would suffer the same dilemmas and inconsistencies experienced elsewhere.

The problem, as one officer reported it, was of "a nationalistic state with a conservative and, in many respects, reactionary tradition in higher education."[17] Goaded by sensationalist reporting from the United States and persistent reports of conspiracies and cabals within the universities, the military government took on the problem by sending denazification teams to the universities and cleaning house according to its own strict standards of "the primacy of political concerns over educational traditions and qualifications." The result was a predictable drop in institutional effectiveness and morale. Even after the political hubbub died down, education did not come easily. If they wished to begin their studies, students, frequently cold and malnourished, often had to form construction brigades to restore the physical plants of their universities. Understandably, at Munich, a graffito on the WC wall read, "Lord, send us the Fifth Reich. The Fourth is just like the Third."

It is not being flippant to say that there were only two stumbling blocks to cultural reform: German culture and American culture. Failing voluntary internalization, the Americans had no taste for forcing a people to be democratic. If the objective was increasingly to win the hearts and minds of Germans in support of the cold war, excessively harsh cultural policies risked alienating one's targets. Finally, education reform fell victim to time. As the occupation dragged on and the Germans sensed their recovery of control, the authority of the military government dwindled to ineffectiveness in the face of masterful German stalling tactics.

When the possibility of directed cultural reeducation waned with the restoration of self-government and the onset of the cold war, American policy shifted in 1948 to its strong suit. Replacing halfhearted authoritarianism was the one-sided, but nevertheless authentically liberal, emphasis on cultural exchanges. This did not imply a scaling down of ambitions, which remained the "moral and spiritual reorientation of the German people." Now, however, these goals would be pursued by sending Germans to the United States, where they would imbibe the spirit of democracy and be able "to contribute to the program of democratic orientation in their native country upon their return."

Only a few hundred Germans came to America in the first few years, but by 1955 about 10,000 had visited. Exchanges were supplemented by a variety of institutional ties between German and American universities and by the activities of American philanthropic organizations—the assistance of the Ford Foundation in helping to establish the Free University of Berlin was perhaps the most dramatic example. Although the effects of these exchanges are impossible to measure, the goal of deeper cultural understanding has remained a constant feature of West German and American policies in the postwar period. If nothing else, the occupation's often misconceived cultural experimentation demonstrated the need for such understanding.

One reason America's grandiose cultural ambitions were not more aggressively pursued, as General Clay recognized, was that democracy "could not be taught or learned on empty stomachs."[18] While denazification and democratization ran into insurmountable cultural barriers, the overwhelming physical and institutional problems of postwar Germany alone presented formidable obstacles to their success.

JCS 1067's harshness was a dead letter from the very beginning, as reality turned out to be more punitive than anything the Americans had imagined. American and British bombing raids had done enormous damage, reducing cities to ugly ruins, cutting railway lines, roads, and bridges. "The country is devastated," General Eisenhower wrote to his wife. "Whole cities are obliterated; and the German population, to say nothing of millions of former slave laborers, is largely homeless."[19] President Truman, riding through Berlin on his way to the meeting at Potsdam, marveled at the desolation of the once meticulously groomed German capital. Berlin in 1945, according to Clay, was "like a city of the dead." Targets of military significance that the Allied bombers happened to have missed, the retreating Germans took care to destroy under Hitler's scorched earth policy. The larger cities were 50 to 75 percent flattened. Flying over a desolate urban moonscape, one American asked: "Where do the people live?"[20] The lack of housing forced many Germans to live like moles in areas that hardly deserved to be called cities. Public utilities were destroyed and public services of all sorts—fire departments, schools, post offices, courts, banks—were not in operation. Trucks were unable to move for lack of gasoline.

Still, as the Strategic Bombing Survey discovered, the effects of saturation bombing had been less devastating than air power advocates had claimed. Indeed, German war production had reached its peak only in the last year of war. Though serious, the purely physical ravages of war had been tackled by specialized units of army engineers, signal units, and so forth.

Clay recognized from the first that "being 'hard' on Germany doesn't call for unnecessary destruction of economy." Within a year, the railway system had been restored to operation, the rivers reopened to navigation, and communications greatly improved. When it came time for economic reform, Clay was able to boast that the infrastructure was well in place, ready to accommodate expansion. Bringing order out of chaos was, after all, the kind of activity on which Clay had made his reputation.

Social disorganization proved less amenable to army engineering. Germany was flooded with refugees from the former eastern territories of the Reich as well as stranded slave laborers who had been abducted from their homelands to service the Nazi industrial machine. Millions of soldiers were still unaccounted for, many having been transported to the Soviet Union to perform labor as reparations.

Adding to the chaos was the de facto partition of the country, temporary but real enough, into four watertight compartments. The natural division of labor and exchange of goods were disrupted by the zonal arrangement and by an inability to reach agreement on treating the German economy as a unit. Nor did Mother Nature cooperate, as a severe drought and the winter of 1946, the coldest in generations, conspired to bring down food production. By condemning some of the country's most highly skilled people to "ordinary labor," denazification contributed to the economic paralysis. In the American zone, where denazification was most pronounced, economic problems were correspondingly magnified. Fifty percent of the doctors, for example, were prohibited from practicing their profession. All this, combined with uncertainty regarding the future, brought economic processes to a virtual standstill.

Most seriously, hunger gnawed at the German people. Because Germany had been 85 percent self-sufficient in foodstuffs prior to the war and had enjoyed the highest living standards in Europe, it seemed feasible at first to set the German diet at a daily level of 2,000 calories, but from the beginning the occupation was forced to import massive quantities of food to avert famine. For nearly two years the daily ration hovered, except for brief periods following harvests, at 1,100 calories, little more than half the daily amount required by inactive persons—indeed, barely more than that allowed concentration camp inmates. Bavarian students protesting their daily ration of 1,550 calories carried signs declaring that "Even a dog needs 1,700 calories." FDR's hardhearted wish had been fulfilled—no planning required.

Another serious problem was the shortage of coal. One of the most vivid memories that many Germans retained of the early occupation period was that of shivering through cold winters. One student, when asked to write an essay entitled "The Most Beautiful Day in My Life," cited the day "when my brother died and I inherited his overcoat, his shoes, and his woolen jacket." The primary centers of coal production were in the British zone, and thus beyond American control. While coal was plentiful as a raw material, the destruction of equipment, inadequate rations for miners, the priority given to coal shipments to Allied nations, and the disappearance of coal stocks into the black market all contributed to making an ordeal of the harsh winter of 1946–47.[21] Not until 1949 did coal production begin to approach 1936 levels.

The nearly complete paralysis of economic activity in Germany soon made it clear that military government could not solve economic difficulties or put an end to the need for American subsidies. Even though the appalling amount of rubble made it appear as if destruction had been nearly total, the fact was that only about 20 percent of German industry had been destroyed. Nevertheless, economic output in the U.S. zone for the first year of occupation averaged only around 20 percent of capacity, with only marginal improvement thereafter.

Much of this lack of productivity among a traditionally industrious people was the result of the disappearance of any incentive to work. The reichsmark (RM) had been inflated by 1,000 percent since 1935, with an even greater increase in the national debt. Having few assets to back it up, it was, according to one historian, "worth little more than the paper it was printed on."[22] With wage and price controls in effect, there were no desirable goods to be found that could be purchased for cash. From the seller's point of view, it seemed pointless to produce or exchange goods for worthless currency when prices were set at artificially low official rates.

Germans, who had the experience of the disastrous inflation and harsh deflation of the 1920s to guide them, chose instead to deal in real property (Sachwerte), the value of which was immune from currency upheavals. The same logic applied to the chronic shortage of foodstuffs. For German farmers who were little inclined to produce for the regulated cash market in the first place, the inefficiency of the U.S. Army in grain collection made the black market a much more lucrative outlet for their products.

At first, goods sold in the black market could fetch amounts 50 to 100 times greater than their official value. For a time, American soldiers were allowed to exchange RMs for dollars, and with the tremendously inflated RM prices they could charge for the scarce coffee, lingerie, cigarettes, and other items readily available from their post exchanges and shipments from home, many profiteering GIs made fortunes by redeeming black market marks for dollars before this practice was made illegal. To take one example: at 1,500 RM per carton of cigarettes, with RMs exchangeable at ten to the dollar, a single carton would bring in $150! Soviet soldiers were reputedly willing to pay exorbitant sums in occupation marks for Mickey Mouse watches. The practice whereby GI profits in effect came from Uncle Sam's coffers was finally ended when the government started paying GIs in chits, an unpopular move that led to the unofficial naming of the new Truman Hall in Berlin as "Truman's Chit House."

With the German currency nearly worthless, there sprang up a primitive barter economy in which the preferred unit of exchange eventually became Lucky Strike cigarettes. By June 1948, a carton of Luckies brought 23,000 reichsmarks on the black market, which figured out to some $2,300 American.[23] Even with strict currency controls and the threat of court-martial as deterrents, the army was unable to eliminate the black market. The impotence of OMGUS, indeed its ill-disguised attitude of benign neglect, combined with the knowledge among Germans that punishments for economic crimes would not be as harsh as those administered by the Russians, led to black market dealings conducted with a casual disregard for American authority.

The problem of too much money chasing too few goods was aggravated by the existence of an uncontrolled supply of Russian-printed marks, for which the Americans had generously provided the engraving presses at the end of the war—not without much soul searching, to be sure. Soviet soldiers were paid with this currency, which rolled freely from the Russian presses. But while the need for some currency reform was recognized early in the occupation, the Soviets would not agree to a reform unless the new currency was printed under their control in Leipzig.

Still another restraint on economic growth was the web of bureaucratic regulations surrounding economic activity, which prevented civilized forms of supply and demand from operating in a money economy. For example, by assuming complete responsibility for all aspects of imports and exports, including the setting of export prices, OMGUS had taken on "the role of a Soviet-type ministry of foreign trade."[24] The sorry results justify the comparison. Because German exporters were paid in reichsmarks, they had no incentive to sell; in the rest of Europe, there was a reluctance to buy German. The net result, as one author beautifully summed it up, was: "the bureaucracy and machinery of administration kept growing, with innumerable decrees, rules, and a bewildering multitude of permits; at the same time, the quantity of goods to administer kept diminishing. In the end, there was nothing left to administer but the lack of things. . . . Everything was at a standstill. Only inflation kept moving forward."[25] By 1948 sweeping action on the economic front was a necessity. Administration can at times change policy, but it cannot succeed without policy.

Demilitarization was the only unqualified success of the four D's, but only because the task had been essentially accomplished by the time the Americans took over their zone. Despite American fears of encountering stubborn guerrilla resistance from die-hard Nazi fanatics (the impressively named "Werewolves") fighting out of Bavarian mountain redoubts, like the Japanese the Germans had no stomach for further combat or resistance. With 2.1 million soldiers dead and another 3 million missing in action, the once-mighty *Wehrmacht* had completely disintegrated by war's end. Under these conditions, an aggressive pursuit of measures looking to demilitarization would have been, as one wag put it, "like undertakers performing an amputation on a corpse."[26]

Demilitarization meant, in effect, industrial disarmament. JCS 1067 had been drawn up partly under the spell of the liberal thesis that industrial concentration leads to war, and that in Hitler's case big business was heavily implicated in his rise to power. Thus the importance of decartelizing the economy. Though there were some ambitious trustbusters in OMGUS, Clay remembered them as "extremists, sincere but determined to break up German industry into small units regardless of their economic sufficiency." As this statement might suggest, the Americans brought to this problem the same degree of enthusiasm with which they pursued it at home, which is to say very little.

A Control Council law drafted at American initiative would have made cartels illegal in all four zones, but it ran into British and Soviet objections. Following that, antitrust action in the American zone amounted to little. I. G. Farben, the mammoth chemical firm, was eventually split into three smaller but still powerful concerns, and desultory efforts were made in banking, coal, and steel. But continuing economic chaos in Germany and the fall from grace of New Deal thinking in 1946 took the steam out of trustbusting attempts. In the later stages of the occupation, the overriding emphasis on productivity and the disinclination of Germans to tamper with a system that they understood and that had worked well for them weakened an already lackadaisical effort.

Contradictory American attitudes also surfaced in the occupation's policy toward labor unions, which Hitler's regime had completely dominated. Labor organizing resumed in late 1945 with the formation of grass-roots works councils, which appeared to have common cause with Americans in their dislike for German cartels. However, the occupation authorities, under the influence of the conservative "bread and butter" unionism of the American Federation of Labor (AFL), soon came to view these councils as too radical.

Conservatives feared that they would sow "utter chaos and confusion on the American side so that the German Communists should be able to take over at the appropriate time." Communist danger or no, the left-wing political demands of the councils, including the socialization of industry and worker co-determination with management of industrial policy, were repugnant enough to officials accustomed to thinking in terms of wages and hours. As a result, the occupation moved in 1946 to promote trade unions dominated by reliable old-guard émigré Social Democrats, to which the works councils would be subordinated.

OMGUS also had to deal with problems of labor radicalism on an interzonal basis. In Berlin, the occupation was faced with a powerful labor federation, the Free German Trade Union League (FDGB), which was largely under the influence of the Communist-dominated Socialist Unity Party. After failing to shift the organization in a pro-Western direction, the Americans organized an opposing faction, the Independent Workers Opposition, which by the time of the Berlin blockade in 1948 had seceded from the FDGB. A similar scenario was played out with the interzonal unification of a national body that would have been tied internationally to the World Federation of Trade Unions, then widely viewed as a Communist front organization.

Another prominent feature of both JCS 1067 and Potsdam was political reconstruction, "to prepare for the eventual reconstruction of German political life on a democratic basis." The Potsdam agreement stated that "all democratic political parties with rights of assembly and discussion shall be allowed and encouraged throughout Germany." An important symbolic step was the elimination by Control Council fiat in 1947 of the state of Prussia, whose territory was amalgamated into the new administrative structures of the four zones.

Here the American occupation enjoyed one of its greatest successes. Pending agreement by the four powers on an all-German government, OMGUS decided very early to build democracy from the local level, with the result that self-government emerged most rapidly in the American zone. There were some disappointments: civil service reform never took root, and attempts at stimulating grass-roots citizen involvement following the New England town meeting model were largely ineffective and discontinued by the Germans once they regained control.

OMGUS licensed anti-Nazi and non-Fascist groups to organize at the village and county levels in the summer of 1945, and allowed expansion to the zonal level early in 1946. The first elections took place in 1946, originally for local assemblies, then for the constituent assemblies in the various states (Länder), and finally, late in the year, for the state parliaments, or Landtage. A Länderrat, or Council of States, consisting of their minister-presidents was created in October 1945. Initially it functioned on an advisory level, but it was gradually assigned greater responsibilities. Further interzonal expansion of responsibilities would have to await agreement among the Allies.

To victors and vanquished alike the occupation was a very confusing period, and it remains confusing still. Over the course of the three years from 1945 to 1948, Americans tried to manage and transform nearly every phase of German life in their zone. What stands out most clearly when one looks back at this period is the gap between ambition and realization, as reflected in the many ironic outcomes of policies gone awry. Denazification made it respectable to have been a Nazi; the attempt to transform German culture was defeated by American cultural values; the intent to punish the vanquished was instantly transformed into the necessity of aiding them; the attempt to impose modern bureaucratic rationality on the economy led to economic primitivism. Judged purely on its own terms, the occupation was a sorry failure.

Yet that is not a final judgment, nor should it be. When viewed from the vantage point of the future, the judgment becomes both puzzling and doubtful. The West German state's ready adoption of democracy proved wrong those many observers who assumed that political democracy was based on cultural individualism. Even George Kennan, normally an acute judge of national character, was "not sure the Germans can ever be democratized within our time."[27] Certainly any visitor to Germany today can find numerous examples of the herd instinct that formerly was thought to lie at the root of the German susceptibility to authoritarianism. But no one today, with the exception of those who naively equate capitalism with fascism, would claim that Germany is a neo-Fascist society.

Of course, this leaves the problem of why, if the occupation was such a disaster, this long-range success came about. Developments after the occupation period had a lot to do with it, but the most important reason, in my view, was the war. Though power has its limits, in this case the war accomplished a good deal. It uprooted in the minds of all but the most fanatical any illusions of Germany's role as a world power and eradicated Nazism's ideological appeal. The complete prostration of Germany and the nation's utter dependence on its conquerors drove home the lessons of Hitler's folly, if not his wickedness, as no program of reeducation could have. In sum, World War II did what World War I should have done.

True, most Germans accepted neither the thesis of collective guilt nor any personal moral responsibility for the death camp atrocities or other evils of the Nazi regime, preferring to shunt the blame to higher-ups. In this sense, denazification was indeed a failure. But Nazism was discredited and destroyed where it most counted, stripped of its aura of historical legitimacy by the disasters it had visited on its country. "Nothing fails like total failure," said one scholar of the German experience.[28] Indeed, by managing the incredible feat of simultaneously alienating ideologies as hostile to one another as those of the United States and Soviet Union, the regime showed conclusively that it was not only inept, but an historical anachronism to boot.

Although a failure in its own time and puzzling when viewed from today's vantage point, the occupation takes on a different look when seen as an extension of the war. Wartime attitudes cannot be turned on and off like a faucet. They are more like an electric motor, which continues to spin for a time when turned off. In its punitive aspects, its utopianism, its disorganization, and its lack of ultimate political goals, the occupation was clearly driven by inertial wartime energies.

But then if the war was successful, the occupation, as a continuation of the war's disasters, was also successful. It is often said that an ideology reflects material conditions, but that holds true for the absence of an ideology as well. In this case, the material conditions for the disappearance of Nazism had been created, to which the occupation made its contribution. Thus it was that the occupation took mistaken aim at German culture, only to hit the bull's-eye of Nazi beliefs. Ironies, after all, can work both ways.

Nevertheless, the true test of American policy lay in its ability to build on wartime achievements. Not only the positive tasks of political and economic reconstruction, but also the creation of a durable peace and the determination of Germany's place in the world were still up in the air. For the solutions to these crucial problems, we must look past the occupation to the international politics of the postwar period.

chapter 3

TWO WORLDS: THE POSTWAR DIVISION OF GERMANY

In *Mein Kampf* Hitler had predicted that "the world shall be German or it will be the end of Germany." Of the führer's many prophecies, this was one of the few to be fulfilled, but he was not around to witness its vindication when President Truman remarked grimly at Potsdam that "Germany no longer exists." For the moment, only the German people existed; whether or not the German state or nation would reappear, or in what form, remained to be decided.

The ambitious U.S. Army occupation may have given a contrary impression, but Germany's future did not rest solely in American hands. Whatever its desires, the United States could not resolve the German problem without the political agreement of its wartime allies. Even as the occupiers drifted into the uncooperative pattern of looking after their own respective zones, they could not continue to do so indefinitely. At some point they would have to face the implications of their actions for their larger European policies and for their mutual relations. Barring the outbreak of a new war, some kind of settlement acceptable to all would have to be reached.

Besides recuperation, Franklin Roosevelt's prescription for the postwar world had been "cooperation," a term that could have any number of meanings. Certainly it applied to Germany, where between 1945 and 1949 the search for a cooperative agreement among the Allied occupiers went through three phases. It began with an attempt to extend the spirit of wartime harmony into postwar German governance, was followed by a period in which liberal ideas regained their ascendancy in American thinking, and culminated in 1949 with their simultaneous fruition and frustration in what turned out to be, by default rather than intention, the only feasible solution to the German problem: the de facto division of Germany. The

United States first attempted to run Germany jointly with its wartime partners on the basis of agreements reached at the Potsdam Conference, which was held at Frederick the Great's palace outside the ravaged city of Berlin from 17 July to 2 August 1945. After a few weeks of hard bargaining, the three Allies, represented by President Truman, Marshal Stalin, and Prime Minister Churchill (later replaced by Clement Attlee, following the Labor Party's victory in national elections), hammered out an accord that defined their joint responsibilities in Germany for the immediate future, pending a final settlement.

Recollections of Potsdam would sour with the passage of years, but at the time, its decisions were greeted with sweet optimism. The four D's of demilitarization, denazification, democratization, and decartelization received everyone's ready agreement. More controversial was the question of Germany's eastern boundary. Though it was agreed during the war that Poland would be awarded some German territory to the west to compensate for sections of prewar Poland that had been annexed by the Russians, the Soviets lopped off more of Prussia than the Western powers would have liked and unilaterally set the new Polish-German border at the Oder-Neisse line. Since the other Allies could do little about the Russian fait accompli but object in principle, the territorial problem was left to hang fire until final terms were set in a peace treaty.

More contentious were the reparations discussions, which one participant described as "endless, tortuous, complicated, and confused."[1] At Yalta six months earlier, Roosevelt had agreed to a figure of 20 billion dollars as a "basis of discussion" for calculating the reparations tab. Of this sum, the Russians claimed the right to extract at least 10 billion dollars in kind to help rebuild their devastated economy. By the time of Potsdam, however, the United States and Britain had shifted course, now insisting that the 20 billion figure was not sacred and arguing strongly for a more modest reparations total.

American opposition to sizable reparations was governed by a variety of factors, the most prominent at the moment being narrow self-interest. Germany, everyone agreed, should be left with a low standard of living, but not so low as to require outside relief. The fear at the time was that if the figure were too large and if reparations removals were excessive, American relief supplies would be necessary to prevent starvation under the "disease and unrest" formula of JCS 1067. With relief being pumped in from one end and factories, which might have been used to make Germany self-supporting, flowing out the other, the United States, in such a situation, would in effect be subsidizing reparations to the Soviets, and the U.S. taxpayer would be left holding the bag. Obviously, then, Germany would have to become self-supporting once again.

Larger considerations also preyed on American minds. The tangled history of German reparations following World War I, which had contributed mightily to the collapse of the international economy and fueled German resentment against the Versailles Treaty, was a potent sanction against repeating the sin of avarice. President Truman, a history buff, was determined not to commit "the same mistake again of exacting reparations and then lending the money to pay for them."[2] Recalling the consequences of the harsh post–World War I terms, Truman felt that "there was no possible way for Germany to pay vast reparations—although morally she should have been made to pay."

The American position hardened as a result of reports that the Russians were stripping their zone bare by removing all the capital equipment that they could lay their hands on. Basically, they treated Germany as a vast junkyard in which they felt free to salvage anything usable, excusing themselves from any accountability by asserting the right to take "war trophies." If continued, it seemed that the Russians might well turn their zone into an industrial wasteland. Secretary of War Henry Stimson called this conduct "oriental," while Ambassador to the Soviet Union W. Averell Harriman pictured the USSR as "a vacuum into which all movable goods would be sucked."[3] To the Americans, the Soviets appeared bent on impoverishing not only their zone, but the western zones as well, making it likely that massive relief to fatten up Germany would be required after a reparations settlement had reduced her to a bag of bones.

Given these contrasting positions, arriving at a reparations agreement was tough going. After a week of fruitless argument, Secretary of States James Byrnes concluded that, for the time being at least, each country should collect reparations from its own zone. From the American perspective, this plan had a number of virtues. First of all, it conformed to the military facts of life in Germany, according to which each power was sovereign in its own zone. Second, it insulated the western zones from the effects of the Soviet vacuum cleaner. And finally, it bought time until a comprehensive reparations accord could be reached.

Had this been the last word on the topic, it would have been true, as one State Department official analyzed the situation, that the plan would "go very far toward a *de facto* partition of Germany," but then the same might have been said of the zonal occupation scheme.[4] However, other aspects of the Potsdam accords held out hope for common policies in Germany. For one thing, it was agreed that Germany would be treated as an economic unit. With the efficiencies resulting from a unified German economy, the reparations take would be proportionately greater than that available from a purely zonal grab-bag arrangement. It was left to the Allied Control Council (ACC), guided by the principle that industrial capacity in excess of the amount needed for subsistence would be left over for reparations, to decide on the size of the German economy. If a satisfactory subsistence level for Germany could be determined, it was assumed that everything else would fall into place.

At the time, there was considerable optimism that such an accord could in fact be negotiated because the reservoir of goodwill toward the Russians was still full. General Eisenhower, who was the first commander of the American zone, felt warmly about the Russians and was a firm believer in the possibilities of Soviet-American harmony. Like FDR, who had seen Germany as a "proving ground" for U.S.-Soviet amity, Eisenhower felt that the Control Council in Berlin would be "an experimental laboratory for the development of international accord."[5] Wartime experience seemed to have shown that agreement could be reached with the Russians by working closely and patiently with them. According to General Clay, "the key to getting along with the Soviets was that you had to give trust to get trust." The logic may have been circular, but given the apparent absence of alternatives to harmonious coexistence in the postwar world, it seemed evident that the overriding determination to agree would produce the necessary agreements, regardless of conflicting interests.

Thus Germany would be the litmus test of cooperation. If the Control Council did not work, Clay felt certain that "we might as well throw the idea of a United Nations out of the window."[6] Passing through Berlin, even as hard-bitten an advocate of a quid pro quo approach to the Russians as Averell Harriman, though he recognized that discussions had yet to address the big issues, could conclude that "the Russians are trying to play ball."[7] Some people were skeptical about Potsdam, to be sure, but not wishing to march out of step, they kept their doubts to themselves and hoped for the best.

The initial labors of the Control Council went smoothly enough, helped along by a deliberate policy of focusing first on noncontroversial issues. In September, Clay reported optimistically of the Russians that "we are making real headway in breaking down their feeling of suspicion and distrust. I am hopeful that by the time conflicting views develop in major issues, we will trust one another sufficiently to deal with the problems objectively and to work out sensible compromises of our views."[8] The representatives managed to agree on the obvious punitive measures and, of great weight to those Americans who saw international relations as being based on friendly people-to-people contacts, the Soviets made efforts to relate warmly on the personal level.

More encouraging yet was the progress being made on a final settlement of the reparations problem. Potsdam, it should be emphasized, was not a liberal document. It is easy to become confused on this point because the positions on reparations and German unity prompted by narrow, dollars-and-cents, national-interest motives coincided with those taken by liberal internationalists who had a larger ideological agenda in mind. But at the time, the former motives were clearly dominant. The final protocol may not have sought to wield Morgenthau's wrecking ball, but it was, as one Treasury policymaker recalled, "a hell of a lot closer to the Morgenthau Plan than it was to the State Department['s]."[9]

The Potsdam protocol entrusted the Control Council with setting a suitable "level of industry" for the German economy. All capital equipment in excess of this agreed minimum needed to sustain the standard of living would be the "surplus" earmarked for reparations. The sixty-four dollar question for American policymakers was: What degree of industrialization would Germany need to sustain herself? For some, the answer was quite a bit, meaning that the reparations take would be meager. The German economy was hemorrhaging so badly from a loss of territory, an increase in population, physical damage, and general demoralization that a transfusion, rather than a further drawing of blood, seemed in order.

The State Department and the military government, however, were more optimistic about Germany's capacity to pay and felt that very large removals were possible from existing German industrial capacity. Furthermore, the State Department believed that large-scale removals would not exercise a fatal drag on European economic recovery. Indeed, Clay was amazed to discover that the State Department thought a steelmaking capacity of 3.5 million tons a year, less than half of what others thought was a bare minimum, would be sufficient. To Clay, this seemed "very close to a 'scorched earth' policy."[10]

Because the subject was incredibly complex and required a good deal of preparation, the level-of-industry negotiations did not begin in earnest until November 1945. A host of economic factors had to be analyzed by the economists and then stitched together in the hope that the result would be a coherent fabric capable of covering both reparations and a self-sustaining economy. Where the calculations of each power's experts were at variance, the differences would have to be negotiated. Since the steel industry was a basic economic component, an agreement on steel was widely agreed to be both symbolically and substantively crucial. Not only would it set the tone for other industries, but the amount of steel capacity allowed would also set strict limits on German industrial capacity generally.

When the ACC talks opened, disagreements had not yet congealed into an East-West pattern. Originally, it was not the Soviets but the British who seemed most resistant to compromise. Initial proposals on steel production disclosed a wide range of opinion, from an expected low Soviet figure of 4.6 million tons to the high of 9.0 million proposed by the British. Rather than cart off or destroy everything but a bare minimum, the British at least hoped to retain some slack capacity. The British delegate insisted that he "could never agree to turning Germany into a wilderness."[11] The Americans tended to be more cold-blooded, taking the attitude that, after all, one couldn't make wine without crushing grapes. If it came down to a choice between the destruction of war potential and the German standard of living, then the German living standards would have to be reduced. Finally the British were placated by an agreement to allow a steel production capacity of 7.5 million tons, with actual production limited to 5.8 million tons annually.

Another crucial issue that produced delays was the question of a common import-export program. Since Germany was not self-sufficient in foodstuffs and raw materials, to be self-sustaining she would need to export finished goods to cover her import costs. Agreement on an overall level of industry was thus not possible until accord was reached on an allowable level of production for the export trade. Agreement on a balancing sum of 3 billion reichsmarks was reached on 15 March 1946.

The plan finally adopted on 27 March was far from lenient. Once put into effect, Germany's industrial capacity would be reduced to about half her 1938 level, and crucial heavy industries would be even more sharply curtailed. Under these conditions, Germany could not hope to resume her former industrial hegemony over Europe. At best, she could hope to become an equal, but even that possibility was far from assured by the terms of the plan.

To this point, what was bad for Germany was good for Allied unity. Russian-American relations on the council had been friendly, and the Soviets appeared to be negotiating in good faith, exhibiting their usual hard bargaining tactics to be sure, but seeming open to compromise. For their part, the Americans had taken the position of mediator between the British and Soviet viewpoints. But this cooperative mood turned out to be simply a hangover from wartime exuberance.

The first serious snag came from the French, who enjoyed a position of power without responsibility. At Churchill's pleading, they had been accorded a share of the occupation at Yalta, but not having been represented at Potsdam, they did not feel bound by the accords. After having suffered three wars with a unified Germany, the French were not eager to invite another through misguided magnanimity. The Quai d'Orsay (the French foreign ministry) quite early on made known its opposition to any measure that would "revive the trend towards a united Germany and to favor the return of a centralized German state."[12] Consequently, the French vetoed any and all measures proposed in the Control Council, aimed at implementing Potsdam's intent to create central administrative agencies for Germany. If continued, French obstructionism could easily prove fatal to the negotiations and, Clay felt, might even lead to the "actual dismemberment of Germany."[13]

It was at this point that larger political considerations began to intrude on purely German issues. Seeking to end the impasse in the Control Council, Clay and others urged the State Department to pressure the French, lest the system of Allied control break down completely. But that was more easily said than done, for success in Germany could result in catastrophe for France. The French postwar governments were so weak that succumbing to American pressures on this issue could conceivably install a leftist regime in power. Fearful that Paris would sneeze and Europe would once again catch cold, the State Department temporized, while the French played adroitly on American fears of communism by arguing that a unified German regime could not help but be dominated by the Russians. "You are mistaken," said

General Charles de Gaulle to the American ambassador in Paris, "if you believe that you can prevent the Russians from dominating a central German government. They have all the useful weapons at hand and they are not over scrupulous as to how they would use them."[14]

The argument's self-serving motivation was transparent, but many Americans were nevertheless susceptible to it. Clay's political advisor, Robert Murphy, had early noted that the Soviets' ability to rapidly create a central administration in their zone would "give them a better bargaining position in the composition of a central government for all Germany." The rapid politicization of the eastern zone would help Russia to "push forward her own already tested candidates" in the event central German ministries were created.

In contrast to Western confusion, Soviet policy appeared to have been well thought out. As early as July 1945 a program of expropriation and land redistribution had begun in the eastern zone. The large *Junker* estates were broken down into smaller peasant holdings, but the new landholders were centrally controlled with respect to production quotas and plantings. In addition, the Soviets quickly installed Communists in regional and local administration, trade unions, and cooperatives, and they executed a sweeping program of social reform in land policy, banking, insurance, and so on. Alarmed, Murphy warned that "within a few months the Soviet zone of Germany will be virtually a centralized state, which will exert great pressure in the direction of similar changes in western Germany."[15]

Adding to American suspicions were Communist leaders' statements, which went under the State Department microscope for analysis. While Walter Ulbricht, leader of the Socialist Unity Party in the eastern zone, called for German unity, French Communist leader Maurice Thorez backed the divisive actions of his government. Instead of writing off these differences to conflicting nationalist motives, Murphy argued that the French Communist view reflected Moscow's own complicated designs. He insisted that "French obstructionism is welcomed by the USSR which may intend to exploit to its own advantage western resistance to a united Germany and emerge later as the champion of a United Reich whose only salvation lies in close affiliation with the Soviet Union." According to this analysis, the French had "played directly into the hands" of the Russians.[16] The kernel of Murphy's argument was the formerly unthinkable idea that a united Germany constituted a political prize, which the Soviets seemed well positioned to snatch for themselves.

This sudden outpouring of negativism with respect to Germany was echoed by American diplomats and statesmen elsewhere. Its root causes lay not in the tangled mass of German problems, but in the rapid deterioration of Soviet-American relations that took place in the first half of 1946. The Sovietization of Eastern Europe behind the "Iron Curtain"; the quarrel over occupational control of Japan; the Nationalist-Communist civil war in

China; disputes in the Korean Control Council; the Soviets' refusal to withdraw from Iran and their diplomatic pressures on Turkey; the ominous
strength of the Communist parties in Italy and France; and most of all, perhaps, a speech delivered by Stalin that emphasized the inevitability of war
between communism and capitalism—all these placed German issues in a
larger context of increasingly contentious relations. It was not surprising,
then, that Americans benignly interpreted French obstructionism as a minor
irritant that ought not divert attention from more serious ailments.

Though the French had proved to be the immediate problem, the existence of deeper East-West divisions among the Allies was confirmed by the
inability to implement the painfully negotiated level-of-industry plan. No
sooner had the ink dried on the agreement than conflicting interpretations
arose as to how it should be carried out. The disagreement centered on the
question of a common import-export policy. The Russians argued that it
ought to go into effect only after the zonal economies were in balance or the
reparations program had been put into effect. From the American point of
view, this was putting the cart before the horse. The entire agreement rested
on the assumption that a successful import-export program was a necessary
prerequisite for a balanced economy and reparations.

Actually, there was sound economic logic to the Russian position. Since
the eastern zone was a surplus area, a common program might for a time
have wound up financing deficits in the western zones. Regardless, the
implications seemed clear enough: the Russians were unwilling to take the
steps toward unity envisioned by Potsdam, except on their own one-sided
terms. As a symbolic countermeasure, Clay immediately ordered a halt to
the dismantling of plants in the U.S. zone that had already been approved
for advance delivery to the Russians. To revive the German economy at
least to the extent of averting economic chaos and political unrest the following winter, Clay called for an immediate merger of the British and
American zones and a pooling of resources. Having pushed the German
boulder slowly uphill in the level-of-industry talks, both the Soviets and
Americans now let go and watched it roll downhill, crushing prior agreements in its path.

By this time, a different kind of logic was beginning to replace the narrow
pocketbook considerations that had been uppermost in American minds at
Potsdam. Under Secretary of State Dean Acheson indicated that the desire
to reduce occupation expenses was now "of secondary importance." Instead,
the United States was "motivated primarily by [the] U.S. interest in preventing [a] permanent division of Germany into two antagonistic halves corresponding to our interest in preventing [a] split of Europe as [a] whole into
irreconcilable blocs and [the] definitive failure of four-power collaboration."
In other words, German unity, formerly desirable as an earnest of collaboration with the Russians, was now being viewed with some urgency as the key
to European unity.

Given the continent's serious economic and political problems, German issues were being gradually merged into a larger geographic and ideological context. With the Iron Curtain already drawn shut to the east, fears for the communization of Western Europe came to be mirrored in the fear of a Soviet takeover in Germany. In addition, American policymakers began gradually to realize that any kind of economic agreement acceptable to the Soviets would likely subvert any chances for European recovery and political stability.

As their larger implications became apparent, from this point German issues, formerly an off-Broadway affair, would be played out in the more prestigious theaters of diplomacy. Although the State Department now seemed prepared to compromise on the dollars-and-cents issues that had dominated negotiations in the Control Council, these issues were rapidly eclipsed by economic considerations more ideological in nature and by high-level political maneuvering. The reparations issue, vexing but not insoluble when viewed close up in a German context, became quite intractable when seen from a wide-angle European perspective.

At a Paris meeting in April 1946 of the Council of Foreign Ministers (CFM), a body established at Potsdam to provide a continuing forum for discussion of issues related to the peace settlement, Byrnes tried to allay Soviet suspicions of American motives by offering a twenty-five-year security treaty and suggesting a special high-level study of the German question. For his pains, he was met by indifferent silence from Soviet foreign minister Vyacheslav Molotov ("Stone-ass," American diplomats called him, not without a measure of respect, for his legendary reserves of diplomatic *Sitzfleisch*).

Molotov did speak a few months later, after the conference had reconvened, but only to launch a diatribe against the Western Allies for their supposed laxity on demilitarization, denazification, and disarmament. He criticized the proposed treaty for ignoring reparations and resurrected the Soviet demand for 10 billion dollars. This about-face blithely ignored all the preceding year's negotiations. So did Molotov's suggestion that reparations be satisfied in the form of goods taken from current production rather than through plant removals. This new demand implied setting a larger level of industry than the one laboriously hammered out by the Control Council.

More ominous yet was his demand that a central German government be established at once. Given his reference to the emergence of "substantial democratic forces" that had "sprung up" within Germany and were "already working with a certain amount of success for the democratic renascence of Germany," he looked to be playing to the grandstands of German public opinion in what was a poorly disguised promotional effort on behalf of a Sovietized Germany.[17] Taking this as a rejection of his treaty offer, Byrnes proposed strictly economic mergers to the other occupying powers, and the British accepted soon afterwards. "We cannot continue to administer Germany as four airtight compartments," he said. The hard-strapped British agreed to this zonal fusion in December, and shortly thereafter the entity popularly known as bizonia was created.

It was obvious that the Kremlin had cleverly shifted its policy on Germany. Besides trying to regain its old reparations demands, it was also beginning to maneuver to larger political effect. Byrnes realized that the Soviet policy statement had all the more impact because it came at a time when American policy, by comparison, "had not been satisfactorily defined." On arriving home from the conference, he reported that "it is no secret that the four-power control of Germany is not working well," while the influential Republican Senator Arthur Vandenberg noted "appalling disagreement" over Germany.

Byrnes countered the Soviet maneuver with a widely publicized address delivered in Stuttgart on 6 September. The speech was notable because it indicated that the United States was prepared to stay in Germany as long as necessary, and because it held out the possibility for Germans to win back their respectability through hard work. The rest was devoted to details. Byrnes did not rule out reparations from current production, so long as the level of industry over and above Germany's minimum needs was increased for this purpose. He denied that the American government had ever envisaged withholding from the Germans the right to manage their internal affairs. Showing that the United States, too, could pluck the strings of German nationalism, he spoke in favor of German retention of the Ruhr and Rhineland and intimated that the United States did not consider the Oder-Neisse frontier to be a closed issue, as the Russians and Poles obviously did.

Like the Molotov speech to which it was a response, this message amounted to little more than a revision of Potsdam rather than a new definition of policy. It spoke to the issues from within the existing framework, without taking into account in more than a tentative manner the larger European issues that had begun to intrude themselves into German discussions. However, a growing number of Americans now believed that Potsdam was out of date. George Kennan had thought so from the day the protocol was signed. He consistently maintained his view that pretenses should be abandoned and that the division of Germany be made the fact on which further policy efforts should be grounded. Rather than allow a central German government that might be open to Soviet influence, Kennan's preferred alternative was to "retain complete control over the Western zones of Germany. . . . I just hope we will follow it to the bitter end. I think it may mean the partition of Germany, and we all admit that is undesirable. . . . I hope we won't shrink from carrying out that partition rather than giving the Russians the chance to dominate the whole country, however."[18] Yet a falling out with the Russians would require a new policy for Germany, something the Americans did not have.

The idea of abandoning four-power cooperation did not come easily, for it also implied the abandonment of Eastern Europe. In late 1946 Clay still assumed that Soviet opposition to the American program rested "primarily on its need and desire for current production as reparations." He, for one, hoped that the United States would explore this avenue, for a Germany functioning successfully under quadripartite control would give the United States "the opportunity to fight for democratic ideals in East Germany and in Eastern Europe." Failure to follow through, he said, would leave "the frontier of Western democracy along the Elbe."[19] For want of anything better, hope remained that solutions could be found to the problem of a German government and to the economic issues.

The turning point came at the Moscow CFM meeting held in March 1947, the first occasion on which the Allies systematically picked through the accumulated pile of German issues. The meeting took place at a time when American foreign policy as a whole was on the brink of a revolutionary change. The president's decision, known as the Truman Doctrine, to provide assistance to Greece and Turkey so that they could resist Communist pressures was a barometer of the American sense of crisis. In the background, Europe's inability to recover economically from the war had produced a serious threat of Communist takeovers, particularly in the vital nations of France and Italy. This, too, was a situation crying out for larger measures.

This radical change of context caused the German problem to assume a different shape. Prompted in equal measure by Europe's economic chaos and the four-power failure, the liberal U.S. State Department thinking on Germany that had been swamped by the Morgenthauism and by the eagerness to get along with the Russians now began to resurface. In the new anti-Soviet climate, a central German government also took on a new aspect. Without a "sound" four-power agreement, Secretary of State George C. Marshall feared "a Germany which will ally herself with one or the other of the four associated powers."[20]

From this point forward economic unity was thought necessary not only to make Germany self-sustaining, but also to help contribute to the recovery of Europe, which would require far more than the crippled German economy contemplated to this point. Former president Herbert Hoover, who was sent to Germany at Truman's instance, concluded that economic unity and a restoration of German industrial production were indispensable, both to lift the burden from the American taxpayer and for the benefit of the rest of Europe. "You can have vengeance, or peace, but you can't have both," he told Truman.[21] Clay was now among the many who realized that "if we left an economic vacuum in Germany, Western Europe could never come back."[22]

Kennan, as usual, put the issue most clearly and starkly. "To talk about the recovery of Europe and to oppose the recovery of Germany is nonsense," he said. "People can have both or they can have neither."[23] President Truman had never been sold on Morgenthauism; indeed, his liberal economic preferences were evident in his proposal, rejected by Stalin at Potsdam, for a free trade area embracing the whole of Europe and connected by a network of internationalized waterways.

The Moscow discussions on Germany got under way as the Truman Doctrine was announced. Six weeks of strenuous pushing by both sides failed to move stalled German positions out of the quagmire. Economic disagreements, still stuck on the complex and contentious reparations problem, were discouraging. According to Charles Kindleberger, "The Molotov economics are of course fantastic. . . . Germany shall be able to pay Russia its reparations, pay reparations in coal to France, balance its export and import trade so that no occupying power has to bear any cost, increase its standard of living and particularly food level, bear internal and external occupation costs, all simultaneously."[24] Still, at least on paper, the economic issues were not beyond salvaging. Clay, for one, believed that an accord on reparations from current production could and should be reached: "The availability of production for this purpose may be the deciding factor in fixing our influence at the Elbe rather than along the Oder-Neisse."[25] Believing that U.S. policy should be more flexible, Clay left the conference in a funk after voicing his disagreement.

Though economic proposals and counterproposals continued to fly back and forth and the parties did not take non-negotiable, irreconcilable positions, the conference mood was dominated by the open emergence of a corrosive suspicion of one another's political motives for Germany as a whole. For the Americans, the Soviet desire for a strong German central government seemed to be motivated, in spirit at least, by Karl Marx's 1850 statement that revolutionary activity in Germany should "emanate in full strength only from the center."[26] Marshall believed that Soviet insistence on a centralized government would make possible "the seizure of absolute control of a country which would be doomed economically through inadequate area and excessive population, and would be mortgaged to turn over a large part of its production as reparations." It would lead to "the inevitable emergence of dictatorship and strife."[27]

The most disheartening episode of the talks was Marshall's private meeting with Stalin, at which the Soviet dictator, doodling his usual wolves' heads, pooh-poohed the Allies' inability to reach agreement. According to Stalin, the situation was not so tragic: "After all, these were only the first skirmishes and brushes of reconnaissance forces on this question. Differences had occurred before on other questions, and as a rule after people had exhausted themselves in dispute they then recognized the necessity of compromise." It was necessary "to have patience and not become depressed."[28]

Though superficially reasonable, Stalin's attitude was interpreted in the most negative possible sense. The Americans felt that they could not afford to wait until the next meeting. According to Kennan, the Soviets "must have expected that in the meantime *their* negotiating position would increase and *ours* would decrease . . . they were confident that by fall fear and

unrest would have increased in Europe to a point where Communist influences would have become dominant . . . and where we would then be compelled either to face a German settlement dictated by Russia or to abandon
the field."[29] This interpretation was summed up in Marshall's famous remark:
"the patient is sinking while the doctors deliberate." The announcement of
the Marshall Plan in June had obvious implications for Germany, for it was
highly unlikely that Western Europe could revive without a simultaneous
German recovery. With Europe sliding into economic despair, the necessity
of economic cooperation in Europe supplanted the desire to cooperate with
the Russians in Germany.

Once the German problem was defined in a Western European context,
once the issue became Germany's relation to Europe, the point of no return
was reached. The Soviet Union's refusal to participate in the Marshall Plan,
or to permit her Eastern European satellites to do so, made it certain that
continued four-power wrangling in Germany would inhibit a general
European economic revival. The only other cooperative option available,
agreeing to an economically weak but united Germany, seemed even less
attractive because it would have added the potential for Sovietization to its
economic drawbacks. Given these grim alternatives, the only sensible course
seemed to lie in the direction of building up the western zones with a view to
promoting Western European recovery.

There was a major potential snag, however, to this logic. The bulk of the
planning was left to the Europeans, who obviously had reservations about
rejuvenating the German economy. In fact, they had a long-range scheme,
the Monnet Plan, which would have built up France at the expense of
Germany. At American urging, this project was shelved in favor of a short-
term emphasis on general European recovery. Not without some grumbling
and foot-dragging from the French, six weeks following the plan's announcement the representatives of fifteen Western European nations agreed that "in
order for European cooperation to be effective, the German economy should
be integrated into the European economy." The three western zones were
then invited to participate in planning for European recovery. Not much was
said about Germany in the congressional hearings on the Marshall Plan, but
what little did come out left no doubt as to Germany's central importance in
the overall scheme of things.

At almost the same time, a new occupation directive, JCS 1779, was
issued, which considerably loosened the occupation's restrictive economic
corset. Reflecting the new liberal logic at work, the directive argued that "an
orderly and prosperous Europe requires the economic contributions of a stable
and productive Germany" and that reparations removals "should not permanently limit Germany's industrial capacity." Shortly thereafter, a revised
level-of-industry plan in Bizonia substantially increased the limits on steel
production capacity. That autumn, restrictions on attacking the Soviets were
lifted from the German press, and the war of words accelerated to full throttle.

Talks with the Soviets would continue, but it was becoming difficult to envisage a joint solution. Another CFM meeting in London at the end of the year was, according to Marshall, only a "dreary repetition of what had been said and resaid at the Moscow conference."[30] Weary of the endless wrangling, Marshall proposed that the council adjourn indefinitely. Until the fundamental economic preconditions for unity were worked out, the Soviet call for the early establishment of an all-German government was "a sham and not a reality." But an economic agreement was clearly out of reach, as the Soviets appeared to desire unity "only on terms which would enslave the German people and retard European recovery."[31]

By this time, the maneuvering was for symbolic advantage only, as Walter Bedell Smith, the U.S. ambassador to the Soviet Union, privately admitted: "In spite of our announced position, we really do not want nor intend to accept German unification in any terms that the Russians might agree to, even though they seemed to meet most of our requirements, since, as they have declared war on European recovery, we know very well from past experience that they would operate to prevent the resources of Germany from contributing." As Smith fully recognized: "this puts us in a somewhat difficult position, and it will require careful maneuvering to avoid the appearance of inconsistency if not hypocrisy." Prophetically, he predicted that "the Russians will make some rather positive moves in the direction of a centralized government, and may at that time want to push us out of Berlin."[32]

The question was, What next? The choice had already been made for a prosperous Western Europe with a divided but recovered Germany, as opposed to a chaotic and politically unstable Continent with a weak Germany, easily susceptible to Communist influence, at its core. The logic was as elegantly simple as it was unpalatable: western unity and prosperity implied a divided Germany.

American statesmen, however, were as yet unwilling to accept the ultimate conclusions of their policy. Thus while Marshall decided to push on with a program for the western zones, he preferred to interpret these steps as "an interim solution."[33] At a series of informal conferences in London between February and June, it was agreed that the three western zones would be integrated into the newly formed Marshall Plan body, the Organization for European Economic Cooperation (OEEC). The Ruhr would be placed under an international authority that would not involve its political separation from Germany, as the French had been advocating.

Most important, the conferees decided that the West Germans should have a government of their own. It was to be "provisional" in character, and under a new occupation statute, the occupying powers would reserve authority to deal only with general issues. Though the statement was careful to insist that the new government was "designed not to split Germany but to provide a basis and starting point for ultimate German unity," it was clear that the era of four-power rule was nearing an end and that the German problem would be transformed as a result.

Before Germany could contribute to European recovery, the economy had to be brought to life by restoring confidence in the currency. The Germans, of course, were justifiably leery of currency tinkering, given the fact that the money economy had collapsed twice in the span of one generation. Clay could sympathize with their fears, for he recalled old family stories about life in the South during the period when Confederate money had become worthless. But economic growth in Germany was clearly not possible without first clearing out the weeds of the barter economy that had sprung up.

A strong application of currency reform would be necessary to enable people to exchange goods for currency and also to save. The medicine prescribed was called Operation Bird Dog, a drastic reform that had secretly been in preparation for two years. Five hundred tons of a new currency, the deutsche mark, had been printed in preparation for the day that the discredited reichsmark would be summarily abolished. However, since a western currency reform clearly would have signalled the end of four-power management of Germany, no action was taken until it became clear that a program of economic cooperation with the Russians was not forthcoming. Only after the Russians protested the London decisions by walking out of the Control Council in Berlin on 20 March was the decision made to go ahead. The Soviets received only short notice before the deutsche mark was put into circulation in all three western zones and in West Berlin, on 20 June 1948.

In an action designed to purge the economy of excess currency, immediately more than 90 percent of the paper wealth of the German people was erased. The old reichsmarks could be exchanged for new deutsche marks at the rate of ten to one, but only within strict limits. As a result, people holding stocks, bonds, mortgages, and other assets denominated in reichsmarks found themselves with virtually worthless assets. The medicine was harsh, but there seemed no other way to get goods back into the stores and to encourage the accumulation of investment capital. As one administrator of the currency reform described the results: "[it] transformed the German scene from one day to the next. On June 21, 1948 goods reappeared in the stores, money resumed its normal function, the black and grey markets reverted to a minor role. . . . The spirit of the country changed overnight. The grey, hungry and dead-looking figures wandering about the streets in their everlasting search for food came to life as, pocketing their 40 D-marks, they went on their first spending spree."

Equally drastic was the sudden removal of the economic controls that had been strangling economic activity. Credit for this step went to the German economic director of bizonia, Ludwig Erhard, who, as fate would have it, owed his position to a cultural misunderstanding (his predecessor had been sacked for calling American donations of sweet corn, which Germans had never eaten but used as animal fodder, "chicken feed"). At odds with the prevailing sentiment in Germany that favored the socialization of industry in a controlled economy, Erhard was a follower of Friedrich von Hayek's beliefs in the free market. There were "too many laws," Erhard complained.

Without any prior authorization, on the day of the currency reform Erhard in one stroke cut through the Gordian knot of tangled economic regulations. Called on the carpet the next day to be reminded that military law prohibited any price changes, he responded cheekily with the disingenuous argument that he had not altered price controls, simply removed them! Fortunately for him, Clay decided to take his side. Although the effects of this bold decision were less immediately apparent than the changes brought about by currency reform, this was the beginning of the *Wirtschaftswunder*, or "economic miracle," that would lift Germany to undreamed of economic heights in a relatively brief period of time.

The introduction of the new deutsche mark into Berlin put the Russians on the spot. To this point in time, the city had gotten along with a single occupation currency. On 23 June, the Soviets introduced an improvised currency of their own into the city, with stamps pasted on the old notes to reflect the new values. If two currencies were circulated freely throughout Berlin and people opted for the deutsche mark, it would prove highly embarrassing to Soviet economic management. Because currency is also a symbol of sovereignty, such a situation would leave little doubt as to the desires of the inhabitants.

Four-power rule in Berlin had been intended to demonstrate Allied unity to the Germans, but now Berlin became a symbol of Allied contention. Once the Western powers had chosen to go their own way, Berlin as an area of continued four-power management became increasingly an anomaly for the Russians, with the Western presence a constant reminder of a contrasting style of life. Fully aware of this, Americans were beginning to get edgy at the possibilities. On 5 March, Truman wondered in a handwritten note: "Will Russia move first? Who pulls the trigger? Then where do we go?"[34] Clay, in a telegram, expressed his feeling that war "may come with dramatic suddenness."

The Soviets opened their campaign to evict their former allies with a series of harassments, such as stopping trains and demanding the right to search the belongings of the military travellers. When train commanders refused to allow Russian guards to board, the trains were shunted to sidings where they would sit forlornly until they were backed out to the border. Next the Russians prevented all passenger trains from leaving the city. These actions were followed by a series of administrative measures designed to make communications more difficult. In the middle of June, the Russians walked out of the Kommandatura, the microcosmic control council for Berlin.

If the Soviets were gambling that their actions would prevent the Allies from continuing with the London program, they were badly mistaken.

Indeed, they had the reverse effect of fortifying American and European determination to strengthen the West. For it was at this point that the United States decided, in National Security Council memorandum 9, to sign a defensive alliance with other North Atlantic nations in order to confront the USSR "with concrete evidence of determination to resist and with increasing organized force." The Vandenberg Resolution passed that summer in the U.S. Senate left little doubt that such a drastic shift in policy, which would formally renounce the isolationist tradition of nonentanglement laid down in George Washington's Farewell Address, was likely to become a reality.

The Soviets increased their pressure with a blockade of the city, which lay 110 miles within the eastern zone. In justification, they pointed to the embarrassing fact that the wartime agreements had never spelled out the details of transport arrangements or access rights to Berlin. In the early stages of the occupation, Clay had had to make arrangements with his opposite number for the use of three autobahn corridors, plus rail and air access to the city. Nevertheless, the American right to be in Berlin was unquestioned, and the right of access was sanctioned by logic, local agreements between U.S. and Soviet commanders, and the emergence of customary practice.

The Americans had law on their side, the Russians geography. Taking advantage of the strict letter of the agreements, the Soviets shut down all road, railway, and waterborne traffic into the city. To make life even more difficult, they cut off electricity from the power plants in the eastern part of the city and stopped coal shipments. According to Clay, the Soviet zonal commander, Marshall Vasili Sokolovsky, warned his Western counterparts that "the technical difficulties would continue until we had abandoned our plans for West German Government."[35]

As a signal to the Russians not to go too far, Truman ordered the despatch of two squadrons of B-29's, "atomic bombers," to forward bases in England, a step that marked the first use of massive retaliation as part of diplomatic strategy. (Only later was it revealed that this act was a gigantic bluff, since these planes had not been modified to carry nuclear weapons.) Yet from a purely military standpoint, Berlin was indefensible, and some westerners thought that discretion would be the better part of valor. Robert Murphy reported one visiting British general as saying: "We should pull out while we can still do so without too much loss of prestige. In military terms, our exposed salient in Berlin doesn't make sense."[36]

Nevertheless, given the view of European psychology on which American policymakers were then operating, a decision to abandon the city would not only have had devastating consequences for the inhabitants, it would also have cast into doubt American determination to stay on in Europe. Once the floodgates of defeatism were opened, a Europe still gasping for air would surely have been submerged under the red torrent. "If we mean that we are to hold Europe against Communism, we must not budge," Clay argued. "I believe the future of democracy requires us to stay here until forced out."[37]

If the Soviets hoped at a minimum to eject the Western powers from Berlin, the blockade proved spectacularly counterproductive. Reluctant to resort to military measures in such an unfavorable place, gambling that the Russians would not fire the first shot and determined not to be forced out, Truman decided to supply this beleaguered city of 2.5 million from the air, by launching "Operation Vittles," the Berlin airlift. Despite the admission by the National Security Council (NSC) that "without satisfactory resolution, the Western position in Berlin is untenable in the long run,"[38] the external face of U.S. policy was far more confident of the outcome. "We were going to stay, period," recalled Truman in typically terse fashion.

More drastic measures were also considered. Clay and Murphy argued for breaking the blockade forcibly at the Helmstedt border crossing. But Truman felt that "the airlift involved less risks than armed convoys," and the consensus of opinion was that the crisis could be resolved short of taking military risks, especially as the nation was unprepared for war. Nor did American policymakers believe that the Soviets wanted a military showdown. According to Marshall, they did not feel "that the Soviet Government has committed itself so irretrievably to maintain the blockade as to preclude the possibility of some face-saving retreat on their part."[39] Clay and Murphy were overruled at an NSC meeting that opted for continuing the airlift as a means of asserting Western transit rights until the Russians relented.

The airlift strained American transport capacity to the limit. It began with 130 planes making two round trips daily, bringing in 2,500 tons of food and fuel to the isolated city, with a plane taking off or landing every ninety seconds. By the spring of 1949, that figure had more than tripled, with planes transporting as much as had formerly been brought in by land, despite poor flying weather and the constant tension caused by the menacing presence of Soviet fighter planes. Over the life of the airlift, more than 200,000 flights delivered 1.5 million tons of cargo. The Western Allies, in addition, imposed a counterblockade of their own and demonstrated that they, too, could create "technical difficulties." Providing some sorely needed comic relief, Marshall Sokolovsky was caught in a crackdown on speeding by military police and forced to cool his heels for one hour before being released.

The drama in the air was matched by events on the ground as Communist attempts to take over the city government were frustrated by the formation of a separate West Berlin municipal administration under Mayor Ernst Reuter. Similarly, following the dismissal of three students from Humboldt University in the Soviet sector, a secessionist movement resulted in the creation of the Free University of Berlin, an institution with a democratic constitution. As one American observed, the birth of the university was "just one part of a mighty movement, underscored by the constant drone of the planes and the periodic publication of angry international notes."[40]

The airlift was a milestone not only in the cold war, but also in U.S.-German relations. The heroic conduct of the Berliners in the face of hardships and Soviet threats and blandishments changed the perception of Germans in American eyes. The fact that the Berliners were willing to impose a system of self-rationing stricter than that required by the military government was impressive proof of their fortitude and goodwill. The airlift had an important effect on West Germans as well. Buoyed by American determination in the face of Soviet provocation, many now swallowed their doubts about a West German government in return for continued American protection of the former capital.

The actors may have been breathing defiance on the stage, but behind the scenes they were still talking. At the end of July, Ambassador Smith in Moscow, in company with his French and British colleagues, spoke with Molotov and Stalin. The Soviet dictator made plain what was agitating him: the London agreements on a West German government. "If this went ahead," he stated, "the Soviet Government would be faced with a fait accompli and there would be nothing left to discuss." On the other hand, if the London decisions were abrogated, he felt confident that "after much skirmishing they could return to a basis of agreement."[41]

To Smith, it seemed worth the gamble. The Berlin crisis just might provide the necessary jolt to bring the two sides back together. The problems as they had evolved, day in and day out, had created a mare's nest of German issues so snarled that it was difficult at times for the two parties to know what they were arguing about, or why. Another consequence of the Berlin crisis, then, was that it induced the U.S. government to step back and undertake a systematic, high-level reconsideration of the place of Germany in American policy.

Others besides Smith were wondering if the disagreement over Germany had been allowed to go too far, thereby prejudicing any sort of negotiated solution to postwar problems in Europe. One of these people, ironically, was George Kennan, who now feared that if the Allies went ahead with the London Program, "the fight would be on for fair; the division of Germany, and with it the division of Europe itself, would tend to congeal and to become more difficult of removal with the passage of time."

Germany, Kennan sensed, was at a historic "parting of the ways." Reminding his superiors that Germany had "become a problem child in Europe only since it [had] begun to think in national terms," he warned that going ahead with the London Program would crystallize opinion in Germany along nationalist lines and breed discontent for the future. A West German government would "naturally serve as a magnet and channel of expression for nationalist sentiment."[42]

In a series of brilliant essays, Kennan had provided the intellectual rationale for containment, a strategy that sought to build up centers of power in Europe and Asia capable of holding their own against a threatening Soviet

Union. His intent, however, had not been to set this power balance in con-crete. From Kennan's standpoint, containment was designed to end the divi-sion of Europe by providing a foundation for a negotiated withdrawal of Soviet power; it was not intended to perpetuate the Soviet presence in Central Europe.[43] Under his direction, the State Department's Policy Planning Staff prepared an alternative that called for the creation of a neu-tral all-German government through free elections, and for the withdrawal of military forces to garrison areas outside Germany. The time seemed ripe. One of the main benefits of the Marshall Plan, Kennan thought, was that it would enable the United States "to do business over the table with our Russian friends about the future of Germany."[44]

Kennan and Smith, it turned out, were singing an unpopular tune. Another State Department paper sounded notes more pleasing to State Department ears. "A segregated [i.e., neutralized] Germany," it argued, "would be under irresistible temptation to seek, through its central geograph-ic position and potential strength, to achieve dominance in Europe, playing off the East against the West." Furthermore, it would "have a great tendency to revert to extreme authoritarian rule." The argument's clincher: a neutral Germany "would provide a fertile field for the rebirth of aggressive German nationalism and permit a rapprochement with the Soviet bloc. The fear of these developments constitutes the heart of the German problem."[45] Rehearsed here were themes that would become State Department standards in the 1950s. Running through them all like a leitmotif was the cautionary memory of Weimar Germany's shocking 1922 treaty of friendship with the Soviet Union at Rapallo.

There were simply too many negative factors operating against Kennan's neutralization proposal. The momentum generated by two years of policy would have been hard enough to break in any case, but his suggestions also came at an inopportune moment, at a time when the United States had finally set its mind on a European alliance. With military thinking increas-ingly important, the Joint Chiefs of Staff had little difficulty in pointing out the strategically fatal liabilities of Kennan's approach: while Western troops would have their backs nearly against the English Channel, Soviet arms would remain within short striking distance of the German heartland.

The reconsideration of German policy also coincided with the installa-tion of a strong-minded new secretary of state, Dean Acheson, whose approach to the Russians differed greatly from Kennan's. From various high posts within the State Department during the war and the immediate post-war period, this aristocratic son of an Episcopal bishop, a WASP in bearing and waspish in his treatment of those who held contrary views, had conclud-ed that it was futile to deal with the Soviets through traditional diplomatic means. Acheson assumed office without having prejudged the German ques-tion one way or the other, but it did not take long before he ruled against Kennan's proposals.

Acheson started from the same premise as Kennan, that "our concern is with the future of Europe and not with Germany as a problem by itself," but he believed the United States was making progress toward the integration of western Germany into a free and democratic Europe. This, he believed, was a great achievement, and the United States would do well not to "jeopardize this progress by seeking a unified Germany as in itself good." Moreover, Kennan's proposed course of action would only undermine the European morale that the United States had labored so mightily the past two years to prop up. Indeed, when reports of Kennan's proposal were leaked to the Western European governments, they were greatly disturbed.

Thus the die was cast. Only if talks led clearly to the democratic organization of all Germany and the reclamation for the West of the Soviet zone would the postponement of a West German state be considered. Acheson was determined not "to accept anything which would tend to undo what has been accomplished." The clock would not be turned back.[46]

The difference of opinion had nothing to do with the definition of the German problem; both Kennan and his opponents were well-schooled in the lessons of the past, and both worried about a revival of German nationalism. Rather, it stemmed from contrasting definitions of the cold war, which, for all its novelties, Kennan saw as a traditional power struggle capable of being successfully resolved through adroit diplomacy. Now that the period of greatest danger seemed to have passed, he felt that negotiations on Germany, if properly framed, might lead to a withdrawal of Russian power from Europe, whereas Acheson and others in the department believed that the solution to Germany's problem and the key to an eventual Soviet withdrawal lay in a resolute buildup of the West for the long haul.

In each case, the solution to the German problem hinged on different perceptions of the Soviet problem. Kennan believed that the United States could do business with the Russians. Acheson, by contrast, believed that "the most dangerous thing in the world we can do is to again enter into any agreement which depends for its execution upon Russian cooperation and Russian goodwill."[47] The only kind of agreement that one could reach with the Russians was one that registered existing facts. It was the job of diplomacy to create those facts, or the environment conducive to their creation. For Acheson, diplomacy was reserved for one's friends, not for historical antagonists beyond the civilized pale.

Thus, when the Soviets began to waver on the blockade, the American response was well in place. In reply to written questions from a Western reporter, Stalin suddenly hinted at a willingness to do business on Berlin. In February 1949, private discussions between Philip Jessup and Soviet ambassador to the United Nations Jacob Malik confirmed that a deal could be made: an end to the blockade and counterblockade in return for a meeting of the moribund Council of Foreign Ministers.

The new round of CFM meetings began in Paris on 23 May, the Berlin blockade having been lifted ten days earlier. The Soviets had little to offer but the return to four-power control, which was precisely why the United States had gone its separate way in the first place. To Acheson, the proposal was "like asking a victim of paralysis who was three-quarters recovered to return to total paralysis," but it did not come as a disappointment. Finding the Soviet foreign minister, Andrei Vishinsky, to be "long-winded and boring" and the discussions "completely sterile," Acheson spent much of his time in princely ennui, contemplating the frescoed ceiling of the Palais Rose where "satyrs pursued nymphs through clouds without gaining on them even through the double translation of Vishinsky's longest speeches."[48]

Having decided not to reshuffle the diplomatic cards, the American government continued with its plan to create a West German government clothed with "increasing attributes of sovereignty." In the summer of 1948, the minister-presidents of the eleven West German *Länder* were instructed to convene a constituent assembly. Understandably, they feared that such a step would irretrievably prejudice the reunification of their nation and were therefore reluctant to draw up a constitution ratified by a popular referendum. Instead, after some bickering with the military government, a Parliamentary Council of delegates from the eleven *Landtage* was selected to draw up a *Grundgesetz*, or basic law. By implication a full-fledged constitution, or *Verfassung*, would have to wait until reunification.

The Parliamentary Council began meeting in September in Bonn under the chairmanship of Konrad Adenauer, the man who would dominate the first phase of postwar German history. Adenauer, a devout Rhineland Catholic, had been the mayor of Cologne from 1917 until 1933, when he fled from office after he supposedly insulted the *führer*. After the war he was released from a concentration camp by British troops to attend to his shattered city, only to be sacked later by the British for doing his job too enthusiastically. Continuing activity—and fate—revived his political career at a point when most men look forward to retirement. Seventy-three years old when he was made chancellor, Adenauer came to be called "*der Alte*," the "old man," as he became West Germany's father figure. He was, without a doubt, authoritarian and stubborn. One story has it that some member of the Bundestag, the new lower house, once told Adenauer: "Herr Bundeskanzler, we have not come here just to say 'Amen' and 'Ja' to everything you propose," and received the answer, "Gentlemen, 'Amen' is not necessary—'Ja' will do fine."[49] Nevertheless, he would lead the Germans to democracy and civilian rule.

Adenauer was genuinely pro-French—a modern Carolingian—who had always looked more to the West than to the Prussian-dominated East. "A Prussian is a Slav who has forgotten who his grandfather was," he is reported to have said.[50] During the 1920s, he had displayed "separatist tendencies" in his interest in integrating the Rhineland with the French and Belgian economies. Adenauer's view of the cold war reflected his cultural view of Europe. He put his principles into practice by helping found the Christian Democratic Union (CDU), which grounded its policies in "Christian-Western ethics and thinking," in contrast to the materialist doctrine emanating from the East.

Adenauer was far ahead of American statesmen in his conclusions concerning the direction of the postwar world. Unlike many of his countrymen who dreamed of a neutral Germany, from an early date he anticipated the emergence of antagonistic power blocs and warned that West Germany "had to join the one or the other side if we did not want to be ground up between them."[51] In a letter written in October 1945, he had already concluded that the division of Europe into East and West was "a fact," and wrote that in the long run "the situation can only be met by the economic integration of Western Germany, France, Belgium, Luxembourg and Holland." This, to Adenauer's mind, was a solution to the German problem that was "organic and natural," that is, one in harmony with the flow of history, and therefore likely to be durable.[52]

Like Acheson, Adenauer was not seeking a diplomatic solution to the German problem, although he realized that delicate diplomacy would be called for. Nor was he seeking a power political solution, although his Germany would become involved in power politics. Instead, he envisioned a historical triumph of the Western system over that of the Soviets. For the restoration of his country, he was prepared to wait. "Patience is the sharpest weapon of the defeated," he once said, adding, "I have a great deal of patience."[53] His was an outlook perfectly suited to the American cold war posture of the 1950s. As a result, however, his willingness to engage in sincere negotiations with the Soviets on unification was always open to question.

Adenauer's chief political opponent during these years was Kurt Schumacher, the head of the competing Social Democratic Party (the *Sozialdemokratische Partei Deutschlands* or SPD). Schumacher was a native of Prussia and a socialist. He, too, had been imprisoned by the Nazis. Apart from that, about the only thing he had in common with Adenauer was his anticommunism. In this case, "everything seemed to conspire to set the two men in opposition": religion, ideology, native origins, personal history, and temperament.[54] Taking a lesson from the events of 1918, Schumacher adopted an attitude of "preventive nationalism" toward the occupying powers, to guard against a repetition of the events following World War I, when his party had been saddled with the nearly fatal burden of becoming a guarantor of the Versailles settlement. He was most anxious not to be termed a "collaborator," a stance that applied with equal ferocity to the Soviets and the Western powers. ("Chancellor of the Allies," he once called Adenauer, in a breach of civility uncharacteristic even for him.) Dependence on foreigners to achieve unity was useless, Schumacher felt; it was the task of the German people. His dedication to reunification was so total that even the SPD head-quarters building in Bonn had been constructed in sections, on his orders, so that it could be dismantled and reassembled in Berlin on the day it once again became the capital city of a united Germany.

Schumacher's harsh personality did not endear him to Western diplomats. Whereas Adenauer's courtly, humorous, and reasonable diplomatic style soon made him appear indispensable to the Western program, Schumacher was not an engaging man. Indeed, the ravages of chronic illness plus the loss of an arm and a leg had made him an almost grotesque, off-putting figure. What his interlocutors heard only confirmed what their eyes had already told them. One interviewer had no objections to the content of his remarks, "but the way he spoke was simply frightening." He was "dogmatic to the point of fanaticism and authoritarian" and would "not accept criticism or opposition." Acheson found him "a bitter and violent man," one who "combined a harsh and violent nature with nationalistic and aggressive ideas," and his colleagues agreed. Personality aside, Schumacher's Marxism, his belief in a centralized German government, and his neutralism were all anathema to American policymakers. In Acheson's opinion, Schumacher was "hopeless." To the U.S. State Department, he had become "the one man menacing the unity of Western Europe."[55]

Adenauer and Schumacher personified the two foreign policy poles to which West Germans were strongly attracted in the early postwar years. Adenauer would have his people unequivocally cast their lot with the West and wait for history to bring unity. Distrustful of both superpowers, Schumacher would have Germans take their destiny in their own hands. Although Adenauer clung tenaciously to terra firma while Schumacher gazed longingly at the heavens, this is not to suggest that one was more realistic than the other. The future would show that Adenauer had too optimistic a faith in history and that Schumacher overestimated the power of his people to overcome it.

The finely balanced politics of the Parliamentary Council foreshadowed that of the state it would be creating. With each *Landtag* electing one delegate per 750,000 people, the party lineup was 27 each for the SPD and the CDU-CSU coalition (the CSU was the semiautonomous Bavarian branch of the party, something like the old Southern Democrats in the United States), and 5 for the Free Democrats, who proved to be the swing party. Under Adenauer's helmsmanship, the Council made steady progress. After some back-and-forth negotiations between the council and the military governors, centering mainly on the degree of centralization of the new state, the *Grundgesetz* was accepted in May. Elections for the new government were held in August, and the Parliament of the new Federal Republic held its first session in September.

The Basic Law set up a federal government with guarantees of fundamental human liberties, including equality of the sexes. Parties were to abide by internal democratic principles. Parties that sought to do away with a democratic order were defined as unconstitutional, as were actions leading to aggressive war. With an eye to giving the new system a stability that had been absent in the Weimar era, the chancellor could be replaced only by a constructive vote of no confidence, that is, only if the Bundestag could agree on a successor. As a reflection of American influence, the Basic Law incorporated federal principles by creating a second chamber, the Federal Council, or Bundesrat, made up of representatives chosen by the *Länder* governments.

The voting system was a complex compromise between party and individual votes. Each voter cast two ballots, one for an individual candidate and another for a party, with election to the Bundestag possible via either route, through a complicated mathematical formula for vote counting. An additional feature, designed to avoid the revolving door governments produced by the system of proportional representation by which Weimar candidates had been selected, provided that no party list could be considered for membership in the Bundestag unless it totaled at least 5 percent of the national vote.

The new government was not yet a partner of the west nor even a client state, since it possessed no sovereignty. Its creation meant only that the military occupation would be replaced by milder civilian controls. The real center of authority, as planned under the London Program, would be a High Commission whose powers were to be defined by an "Occupation Statute" drafted by the Allied powers. The most urgent task of the new Federal Republic (Bundesrepublik) would be to negotiate itself out from under the limitations imposed by the statute, until it attained sovereignty.

Meanwhile, a parallel process of state creation was taking place in the eastern zone. In March 1949 a People's Congress approved a new constitution. Shortly after the creation of the Federal Republic, a provisional government, based on a single party list of the Socialist Unity Party, took power and the German Democratic Republic (Deutsche Demokratische Republik, or DDR) was formed.

The emergence of two German governments marked the beginning of a third phase of the postwar search for cooperation. There are two basic ways of interpreting these developments. According to the logic of power determinism, the fact that the future Federal Republic and DDR occupied the military boundaries defined at the close of the war meant that the Americans and Soviets, whether they admitted it or not, had agreed to a de facto partition of Germany based on power politics. Their motives were secondary to the fact that the settlement reflected the brute facts of power. All arguments to the contrary were ideological, masking or confusing these underlying realities.

To understand how the German problem developed over the next four decades, however, a different perspective is in order. Despite the fact that no one at the time could come up with a feasible alternative, there was no agreement among the wartime allies that this division of Germany was either acceptable or permanent. That the Americans and Soviets came close to war over German problems in the future suggested that the lines were not as neatly drawn as power theorists would imagine. The Germans, understandably, were not reconciled to their disunity, nor, it seemed, were the Western Allies, who would encourage them in their hopes—if only to keep the Bundesrepublik within the western fold. But talk of reunification was more than mere cynicism. With the Soviet-American confrontation entering a period of great intensity, significant movement toward unity was expected to take place as the cold war moved toward a successful conclusion.

The political reality of the situation was *cuius regio, eius religio*: the ruling powers determined the secular religions of their respective zones. Unlike the Peace of Augsburg, however, which institutionalized the religious status quo in Germany during the Reformation, the Americans and Soviets had not yet arrived at a negotiated peace of exhaustion. To suggest that some sort of tacit agreement was reached on Germany at this point is to ignore the fact that the country's division came at the cost of a dangerous breakdown of cooperation between the United States and Russia. While diplomacy seeks political agreement, the two parties in this case had agreed only to go their separate ways.

This was not a solution at the level of power politics, at least not if one defines realpolitik as accommodation reached on the basis of power. Rather, in its outcome the situation resembled what the German philosopher Hegel called "the cunning of reason." There was indeed an underlying logic to the postwar emergence of two Germanys, but it operated ironically by frustrating diplomatic and national desires, as a series of reluctantly taken decisions led to an unintended solution that pleased no one, but which neither side seemed able to alter. As a result, the German problem drifted beyond the reach of diplomatic settlement and was left for history to resolve.

The immense force of the global superpower confrontation had, like the collision of two tectonic plates, created a new mountain barrier whose most formidable massif was a divided Germany. Reunification would come about not as a result of summit agreements or diplomatic skirmishes in the passes, but only through the long-term erosion of the peaks in the cold war chain. Germans would recognize this historical logic at work and set aside, if only for the foreseeable future, ambitions of their own that were incompatible with it. Only then would it become possible to reach through diplomacy an uneasy accommodation with the spirit of the age. In the meantime, the German problem would remain an explosive issue for years to come.

chapter 4

DOUBLE CONTAINMENT: THE REARMAMENT OF GERMANY

As the Allied armies tightened the noose around Germany in 1945, a desperate Hitler was reduced to fantasizing about a miraculous German-American alliance against the Soviet Union. To Americans this was an unthinkable notion, and it remained so even as the cold war set in and the division of Germany solidified by the end of the decade. Thus, while Allied control may have been liberalized, the Occupation Statute signed by the high commissioners and Adenauer in November 1949 provided for the continued demilitarization of the country and forbade the creation of armed forces of any kind. So strong was the taboo against militarism that even glider planes and fencing were prohibited under the heading of "military exercises."[1]

From today's perspective, the postwar rearmament of Germany seems natural and almost inevitable. To achieve it, however, American policymakers had to clear a long series of hurdles, including self-doubts, widespread European reluctance, and Soviet obstructionism. In George Orwell's *1984*, states could switch sides as easily as people change clothes, but the nations of the West were democracies where human emotion, historical memory, and the passionate beliefs of statesmen themselves often took precedence over cold-blooded raison d'état.

For Americans, the shift in policy was aided by the fact that Germany was an ideological, not a traditional enemy, and by an inability to adhere in the long run to notions of collective guilt. That, however, was not enough. In the political astronomy of the cold war, the planets had to be aligned at precisely the right moment before old fears of Germany could be eclipsed. The Soviet Union may have replaced Germany as the main threat to world peace, but this meant only that the German problem was transformed rather than eliminated. There now existed two interrelated geopolitical problems where formerly there had been only one. As a result, an extraordinary amount of ingenuity and persistence on the part of the Americans and their allies went into the creation of a complicated system of "double containment" to solve simultaneously both the German problem and the Soviet problem.[2] The amazing thing, then, is not that rearmament took place with such enormous difficulty, but that it happened at all.

Old fears died hard. By the beginning of 1950 the West Germans had come a long way toward respectability, but not so far as to encourage any further loosening of controls. George Kennan's views were probably typical in this respect. While he expressed satisfaction at the degree of progress made with West Germany, he warned against excessive relaxation. We must "avoid over-confidence with respect to Germany," he wrote. "We must remember that the German people are still politically immature and lacking in any realistic understanding of themselves and their past mistakes."[3]

High Commissioner John McCloy felt the same way. At a conference of ambassadors held in Rome early in the year, he worried about German fidelity to the West. "Although the German is attracted westward by many things, material, political, psychological," said McCloy, "he cannot help but be aware that the concept of unity comes from the east." Now more than ever, he said, "a reorientation of the German mind [is] essential."[4] Similarly, in March 1950, the director of the State Department's Bureau of German Affairs saw no change of policy in his crystal ball. Believing that the High Commission would continue indefinitely, he suggested that "all other plans for Germany should be made on the assumption that an arrangement of this sort will be maintained for the foreseeable future."[5]

There was some debate over relaxation of the remaining economic controls. In April, McCloy called the lingering vestiges of the punitive approach "unrealistic." Advocating almost total deregulation, he argued that "real security for Western Europe lies not in limiting Germany's production, but in strengthening Western Europe by the addition of Germany as a willing participant and eventually as full partner." The justification, of course, had to do with the Soviets. Citing history, he argued that "as at the Congress of Vienna we must correct false preoccupation with the fallen giant and direct attention to the new threat which again is from East."[6] That did not mean, however, that McCloy was an enthusiast for German rearmament, not even in the form of a German "foreign legion." He believed this was a "defeatist idea," which "would have the effect of making the Germans believe we are dependent on them."[7]

There were other straws in the wind. Already NSC-68, the bureaucratic charter for fighting a global cold war, adopted in the spring of 1950, had suggested that a policy of building strength would require that the West "conclude separate arrangements with Japan, Western Germany, and Austria which would enlist the energies and resources of those countries in support of the free world."[8] On 5 May, the Joint Chiefs of Staff (JCS) finally broke the taboo by arguing forthrightly in NSC-71 that "the appropriate and early arming of Germany is of fundamental importance to the defense of Western Europe against the USSR."[9]

President Truman did not exactly turn handsprings on receiving this recommendation. "This is a most difficult subject about which to talk," he said (one can almost see him swallowing hard). His gut reaction was a feeling that the JCS proposal was "decidedly militaristic."[10] He recalled that the 100,000-man army permitted the Germans in the 1920s "was used for the basis of training the greatest war machine that ever came forth in European history."[11] The idea of a German army also frightened the State Department, which as late as August 1950 declared that it had "opposed, and still strongly opposes, the creation of German national forces."[12] And even if the United States were to change its mind, it could look forward to intense public opposition in Germany, turmoil in the Western alliance, and a heightening of tension with the Soviets.

But then, there was "the logic of the situation." This view was perhaps best expressed by the Parisian daily Le Monde, which predicted that "the rearming of Germany is contained in the Atlantic Pact like the yolk in the egg." Translation: the new balance of power in which the Soviet Union was the opponent made it necessary to bury the past. As a State Department memo argued: "One should certainly not judge the present world or even European situation in terms of the German problem alone but more importantly in light of the overriding Russian menace that in itself makes the German problem acute."[13]

This made it appear as if the change proceeded inevitably from hard geopolitical realities, when actually it was more subjective in nature and far from inevitable. From its aloof global ideological viewpoint, the United States could afford to subordinate the German problem to the Soviet threat. This ideological perspective also facilitated psychological distancing: just as the Soviets were metamorphosed into friends and allies during the war, so could the Germans be afterwards. According to the State Department, the United States could "bring a certain detachment to the treatment of German problems which it is difficult for other peoples to attain."[14]

The changeability of American opinion (born of ideological consistency) contrasted with the long-held and bitter (and ideologically mercurial) attitudes of other European states, particularly France. For the U.S., the newly created North Atlantic Treaty Organization (NATO) was directed against the Soviet Union and its allies. But for the French, it was aimed equally at Germany, as NATO finally provided the security treaty they had been seeking since the end of the First World War. French membership in NATO was conditioned on the assumption that Germany would not become a member; indeed, that was a major reason for France's agreeing to the creation of the

Federal Republic in the first place. Consequently, Allied diplomacy on the rearmament of Germany would always have to reflect compromises between the French and the American points of view: solving the security problem entailed dealing not only with the Russian danger but also, from the French viewpoint, with an equally potent German threat.

So long as NATO remained an expression of political will, without a military force in being, the question of German rearmament could not arise. To be sure, it was talked about. The subject was mentioned in the National Security Council in 1948. In 1949 the American military pointed out the desirability of defending Europe at the Elbe rather than the Rhine. And in November, General Lucius Clay proposed in a newspaper interview the desirability of a "composite military force" that would include German troops. In March 1950, Belgian premier Gaston Eyskens was also reported as advocating the immediate armament of Germany.[15]

At this time, the American government was already seriously contemplating its own rearmament, and its military assistance program looked forward to a large European effort, but Germany did not figure in any of these plans. When asked at 1949 hearings on the Mutual Defense Assistance Program about the continued demilitarization of Germany, Dean Acheson replied: "There is no discussion of anything else. That is our policy and we have not raised it or revalued it."[16] On another occasion, Acheson dismissed any talk at all of a German army as being "quite insane." .

All that changed almost overnight with the Communist invasion of South Korea in June 1950. Until Korea, it was not believed that the Soviets would try to expand militarily. Communism was viewed mainly as a political and psychological problem within the West European nations, one that could be dealt with adequately by economic means. Thus arose the emphasis on psychological fortification of the Europeans through Marshall Plan aid and the NATO commitment.

NATO military planning antedated Korea, but the conflict brought home the possibility of analogous Soviet moves in Europe. Everyone was uncomfortably aware that a divided Germany resembled a divided Korea, the major difference being that a war in Germany probably could not be contained. The use of East German troops on the Korean model, according to Dwight Eisenhower, would "come very close to declaring open, all out, war. This is because of the fact that *her* [Soviet] troops are in actual occupation of Eastern Germany and in actual *control* of that area."[17]

At the same time, the Korean War forced Western statesmen to admit their military vulnerability. Despite America's possession of the atomic bomb, many nervous Europeans felt that a Soviet invasion could occur at any time. Regardless of whether or not the United States chose to detonate nuclear weapons over friendly territory, Western Europe could easily be overrun in a matter of a few days. The Communist invasion of Korea, the menacing aspect of Soviet foreign policy, and NATO's military weakness all combined to make plain the need for augmented conventional forces in Europe as a deterrent.

During the summer of 1950, the American government abruptly changed its views. Acheson bluntly told Truman that "the question was not whether but how Germany should be brought into the general defensive plan without disrupting everything else we were doing."[18] Testifying the next month before the Senate, Acheson asserted that "a program for western Europe which does not include the productive resources of all the countries of western Europe, which includes Germany as well as France, and includes the military power of all, will not be effective in the long-range political sense. Therefore we must include them both."

NATO in 1950 was already planning a "forward strategy" in which defense against the Russians would begin "as far to the East as possible." The Europeans yearned for a unified command and American forces to bail them out, but the decision to introduce American troops to Europe, made in August, was a package deal. Since U.S. forces alone were insufficient for the job, the Joint Chiefs insisted that troop levels in Western Europe be substantially increased, specifically by drawing on German manpower. To the military, and eventually to Truman, it came down to a simple matter of geography and arithmetic.

But to the French, German rearmament was instinctively a repugnant idea. Charles Bohlen did not see how the French attitude, "a natural pathologic Gallic reaction," could be changed.[19] When asked in April 1950 whether Germany might conceivably become a member of NATO, French foreign minister Georges Bidault said this was "impossible," and argued that such a move "would provoke the Russians to war."[20] And while General Marshall (now Secretary of Defense) argued that "the Germans were not much different than the Koreans,"[21] the French disagreed, insisting that the West Germans could not be relied on to fight their eastern brethren.

The problems of German rearmament extended far beyond inbred Franco-German animosities. During 1950, the prominent journalist Walter Lippmann was writing editorials that argued that the rearmament of Germany would be provocative to the Soviets and that a revived German army would be "thinking of a war of revenge and not of the defense of Europe at the Elbe River."[22] Lippmann, however, was getting ahead of himself, for rearmament first required German cooperation, and there happened to be a sizable body of sentiment within Germany fiercely opposed to the idea.

Thus, despite general agreement on the Soviet threat, a German national army appeared out of the question for all concerned. Already, however, there was talk of a way out: the creation of a European army into which German contingents could be merged. Speaking before the Council of Europe in Strasbourg on 11 August, Winston Churchill suggested the creation of such a force. Shortly afterwards, in a conversation with Acheson, Truman agreed that German rearmament was "quite impossible aside from the creation of a European Defense Force."[23] A few days later McCloy announced that any Western European defense arrangements would have to provide for German participation.

Given the military urgency of the situation, there was no time for diplomatic preparation. Acheson would have preferred a less peremptory approach, but he had no choice but bluntly to drop the "bomb in the Waldorf" at a September meeting in New York City with Foreign Ministers Maurice Schuman and Ernest Bevin and the three high commissioners. To drive home the seriousness of his demands, he made clear that the European wish for American participation in a united force under a single command would not come true unless German participation was approved. He also made clear the further implications of European obstructionism: congressional refusal to vote further aid appropriations, and a possible return to a policy of isolationism.

It was a classic good news–bad news dilemma. While the Allies were pleased with the American decision to send troops to Europe, the other half of the package caused great consternation. Bevin was willing to go along with the creation of a West German police force to match the one in the DDR, but Schuman was completely immovable. He told Acheson that even if he were personally in agreement with the American position, "his government would not support him, and even if it did the National Assembly would not support the government." He concluded that the United States had "not thought the problem through, particularly the political setting essential to any German rearmament."[24]

The full NATO council was more receptive. It accepted the idea of a forward defense strategy with an integrated military force under a centralized command, which seemed to imply some German defense contribution, if only because the strategy made no sense without it. But France, although politically isolated, remained obdurately opposed. Apart from some decisions to relax economic controls on Germany and to end formally the state of war, there, for the time being, matters rested.

Shortly afterwards, the French countered with an ingenious initiative of their own, the Pleven Plan. Realizing that his nation's weakness and continued need for American assistance made impossible the persistent exercise of a veto, Premier René Pleven pulled out of his hat the same supranational logic that earlier had been used in the so-called Schuman Plan to form a European Coal and Steel Community, a "government-sanctioned supercartel" designed to ease fears of German economic domination.[25] Pleven's scheme called for the creation of a European Defense Community (EDC) with a single European army composed of mixed contingents that would include German forces. Everything would be under the umbrella of all-European political institutions, including a European minister of defense. According to Schuman, the plan envisaged "a complete merger of . . . armed forces in one uniform, under common discipline, under single command and responsibility—not to individual governments but to all the member governments." Command, supply, and manufacture would operate from a supranational framework.

The Pleven Plan was designed to rearm the Germans without rearming Germany, thereby satisfying the American demand for German rearmament and the French National Assembly's opposition to it. For France, this "French Foreign Legion for Europe"[26] had the attraction of procuring German manpower and resources without creating German military institutions. Since German forces would participate only in small units, perhaps regimental combat teams of 5,000 to 6,000 men independent of a German chain of command, the plan averted what in French eyes was the disaster of creating a German national army.

Acheson publicly welcomed the initiative, but not without serious private misgivings. He did not much like this baroque idea, in which French acceptance of the unthinkable depended on the achievement of the politically utopian. For what the plan amounted to, in effect, was making German rearmament dependent on the creation of a United States of Europe. By sugarcoating the pill, the French were also making it too large to swallow. Understandably, to many critics Pleven's proposal seemed "a politically impossible and militarily unfeasible subterfuge for preventing German rearmament."[27]

Adenauer, for one, welcomed the EDC idea. Early in 1949 he was privately predicting that within four years Germans would once again be in military uniform.[28] Later in the year, he had suggested at a party meeting "that West German manpower be included in a European striking force against Russia."[29] In 1950, he began to press the Allies for a 100,000-man police force to match that being built up in the DDR, although he realized that for the time being rearmament "belonged to the realm of fantasy."[30]

Adenauer was also prepared to turn Western need to his advantage. For while he welcomed the Pleven Plan, he rejected outright its initial formulation, which would have made the Germans little more than mercenaries or cannon fodder in a European army. Late in August Adenauer informed the high commissioners that the price for a German contribution to a European army would be an end to the occupation and equality of status. Some steps in this direction had already been approved, but he was contemplating nothing less than full sovereignty for the Bundesrepublik. For Adenauer the nationalist, the need for German manpower in the EDC seemed more likely than any other state of affairs to lead to sovereignty for the Bundesrepublik. Rearmament, as Franz Josef Strauss later wrote, was "the only escape hatch we had, the only approach that made a comeback possible."[31]

Nevertheless, for Adenauer the convinced Europeanist, the EDC proposal actually represented an improvement over a German national army. He knew that rearmament within a European framework would pacify European apprehensions about a resurgent Reich, but there was more to it than that. Unlike the German leaders of the 1920s, he was not seeking freedom of action for its own sake. "We must free ourselves from thinking in terms of national statehood," he argued, insisting that European civilization could be saved only by adherence to the gospel of multinationalism.[32]

Adenauer's penchant for European solutions was displayed from his first days in office, in the so-called Petersberg Agreement signed with the three high commissioners on 24 November 1949. In return for his acceptance of the International Ruhr Authority, which had been created earlier as part of the London Program's goal of controlling the industrial output of this crucial industrial belt, he was able to secure an end to the tenacious remnants of the dismantling program. For good measure, the Allies also agreed to let the Federal Republic join some international organizations, such as the Council of Europe, the International Monetary Fund, and the World Bank.

Throughout these discussions, Adenauer skillfully asserted his desire for Franco-German reconciliation. He also made a staunch friend of the new American high commissioner, John J. McCloy, Stimson's former under secretary of war, whose influence would later bring him the informal title of "Chairman of the American Establishment." The coincidental fact that McCloy's wife happened to be a distant relative of Adenauer's late wife enhanced McCloy's sympathetic understanding of the German position, an understanding that would prove invaluable to Adenauer in the years to come.

Dean Acheson, however, was an Atlanticist, not a Europeanist. Indeed, from a traditional nationalist viewpoint the EDC was a wildly improbable project. Sticking out in Acheson's memory was Winston Churchill's ludicrous picture of "a bewildered French drill sergeant sweating over a platoon made up of a few Greeks, Italians, Germans, Turks, and Dutchmen, all in utter confusion over the simplest orders."[33] Acheson felt that the original Pleven proposal had been "hastily conceived without serious military advice," and noted that even the French military agreed with their NATO counterparts that the plan was "unrealistic and undesirable."

Although Acheson bridled privately at the "cult" of European federation that slowed progress toward the mundane goal of rearmament, he was constrained by psychological realities. He was acutely aware that the kind of cooperative spirit found in the Marshall Plan was now absent. He realized also that since rearmament had "come to be regarded by Europeans as an American plan imposed upon them by the United States," the push toward a European army and European integration was aimed not only at the Germans; it might also be a reaction against an American-dominated NATO.[34] Given these realities, the idea of European integration, which appealed strongly to many Europeans, just might be an engine with enough political horsepower to pull rearmament along with it.

German rearmament was a drama that the Pleven Plan turned into soap opera. The idea of the European Defense Community would endure so many crises, deaths, and resurrections that the final resolution, when it came, inevitably seemed anticlimactic. But the statesmen knew what they were getting into. The task was undertaken, as McCloy rightly judged, because there was "just no other way open, at least for the measurable future."[35]

After a "sometimes acrimonious debate" at a NATO Defense Committee hearing in October, it was decided that the recruitment of German units would be permitted on a regimental basis under the so-called Spofford Plan.[36] Under its terms, the ratio of German to European units was not to exceed one in five, and the Germans were to operate without benefit of a general staff or heavy armament. The French now agreed "in principle" to German rearmament, on the condition, however, that everyone else accepted the Pleven Plan. On 15 February 1951, the French convened a conference in Paris of all continental NATO members to discuss their European Defense Community proposal. Six months later, a preliminary report announced agreement on the creation of a European Defense Ministry, a committee of ministers to handle important decisions, an interparliamentary assembly, and a court of law to dispose of legal complications and disputes.

Once these agreements were reached, Acheson put his doubts behind him and rolled up his sleeves in full support of the idea. After a series of meetings in July 1951, wholehearted backing of the EDC became official American policy. Nevertheless, Acheson's attitude remained that of an interested outsider, encouraging but not pushing too hard, on the thesis that the EDC was "something of vital concern to Europeans themselves."[37]

American determination was buttressed by the infectious enthusiasm of NATO's new supreme commander, General Eisenhower. At first, he was critical of the Pleven Plan, which seemed to be made up, he said, of "every kind of obstacle, difficulty, and fantastic notion that misguided humans could put together in one package." However, following a tour of European capitals in the spring, he became a convert to the visionary ideas of Jean Monnet and wholeheartedly endorsed the EDC idea to Truman. In one of many private letters written at this time sounding a single theme, he wrote: "In substance, my basic belief is that we must unite Western Europe including Western Germany or there is no logical basis for a long-term, enduring peace for the western world." Now characterizing all other proposals as only half measures, Ike argued: "After all, when a person goes to a hospital for surgery the doctor doesn't operate 10 percent each time." In a speech made in London on 3 July 1951, he came out publicly with a strong plea for the unification of Europe.[38]

Assuming that French doubts could be put to rest, the United States hoped to "proceed with integration and let the rearmament of Germany follow as a normal part of this process."[39] Yet German consent was by no means automatic. As the *New York Times* wryly reported, "the French aversion to arming the Germans appears to be matched only by the German aversion to being armed."[40] The conspicuous absence of any desire for a new national army, an attitude that was more antimilitarist than pacifist as a consequence of Hitler's disastrous adventures, was captured by a slogan then making the rounds among Germans, *"ohne mich,"* which translates loosely as "include me out."

Adenauer's crafty negotiating tactics also caused difficulties. His demands for sovereignty and equality recalled the ill-fated Geneva disarmament talks of the early 1930s, in which the German insistence on equality had proved incompatible with the French demand for security. In one respect, the problem had not changed: an equal Germany automatically made France feel insecure. The difference, in this case, was that the indispensability of a German contribution, as defined by an insistent United States, dealt a strong bargaining hand to Adenauer. Thus, even though the EDC's supranationalism was for Adenauer a splendid idea, he used it to extract maximum gains for his people. "It is a very hard task, making presents to the Germans," said a French high commissioner at one point.

Adenauer also turned his shaky domestic position to negotiating advantage. The Social Democrats strongly opposed rearmament out of the conviction that the EDC would destroy any chance of reunification in the foreseeable future. Their dislike for the Pleven Plan was accentuated because, as originally formulated, it clearly contemplated an inferior status for West Germany. According to Kurt Schumacher, it treated the Germans as "second-class human beings and first-class blood donors."[41]

Traditional nationalism also played a role in the SPD's opposition to the EDC, an attitude plainly evident in Schumacher's caustic comment that "six invalids cannot combine to make one athlete."[42] Nationalist opposition to the scheme surfaced on the right as well, when Adenauer's minister of the interior and later president, Gustav Heinemann, resigned in October 1950 over the issue. McCloy, for one, believed that the EDC would never make it unless the Social Democrats were brought round.

Adenauer masterfully exploited this opposition in his bargaining with Allies who were predisposed to pay his price. At this time George Kennan, like others in the government, argued strongly for a complete end to the occupation on the grounds that existing arrangements were "quite inadequate and in some respects dangerously unsuitable to the task at hand." In particular, he said, decartelization and reform seemed "trivial anachronisms and caprices compared with the issues really at stake." Pointing to some disturbing parallels to the Weimar period, he felt that Germany must be dealt with "on the diplomatic level rather than on the authority of the victor and as with a sovereign power."[43]

The liberalization of Allied controls had in fact been going on for some time. In September of 1950, the Allies agreed to terminate the state of war with Germany, allowed the Federal Republic to establish a ministry of foreign affairs, further relaxed economic controls, and allowed "mobile police formations on a *Land* basis" as a response to the establishment of similar police units in the East. These decisions were put into effect in March 1951 by the high commissioners, following a series of discussions with Adenauer. In October the United States declared a formal end to hostilities.

Talks in Bonn held in parallel with the Pleven discussions in Paris cleared up the technical details of recruiting German forces. In the Petersberg Plan of July 1951 the Germans insisted on and got agreement to a divisional organization with a total force of 250,000 men, far more than contemplated under the Spofford Plan. It was understood, moreover, that Adenauer's political demands would have to be satisfied before recruiting actually began. Negotiations for a German defense contribution then began in earnest in September 1951, following a contentious meeting of the foreign ministers in New York that called for the negotiation of a set of "contractual agreements" or treaties to replace the occupation statute.

Although the communiqué specifically talked about admitting the Federal Republic into the EDC on an equal basis, the French and the British were reluctant to let go of all controls and were insistent on driving a hard financial bargain with Adenauer as the price of admission. Thus when the talks began they offered less in private than they had professed themselves willing to pay in public pronouncements. Adenauer rejected the Allied proposals, especially a provision for a "Council of Ambassadors," calling them "nothing but a reduction of the Occupation Statute, although the Federal Government was striving for an entirely new basis of agreement resting on reciprocity."[44] As much as admitting that the Germans had them over a barrel, McCloy then let Adenauer know that the Allies were prepared to be flexible. By early October, experts were drawing up the details of the contractual agreements in the hope that they could be initialed by the foreign ministers in Paris by the end of the year.

These hopes were overly optimistic. The extent of a German contribution could not be decided until the NATO allies had first agreed among themselves on the degree of their commitment to rearmament. European economic recovery was only in its beginning phases, and European governments were understandably reluctant to sacrifice living standards for the EDC just when they were, at long last, beginning to rise. These economic obstacles, when added to political reluctance, helped explain why the Paris conference was still in session at the close of 1951.

The EDC received a serious setback when the British, traditionally reluctant to become tied down on the Continent, made known their unwillingness to join. Though they were agreeable to garrisoning troops on the Continent and supporting the EDC by all means short of entry, becoming a member was something that, in Anthony Eden's phrase, "we know, in our bones, we cannot do." British aloofness in turn fed French fears of entering an alliance in which they would be left alone to deal with the Germans. Indeed, the National Assembly was having difficulty in summoning the resolve to ratify entry into the European Coal and Steel Community, a dark omen for the far more controversial EDC.

Adenauer took advantage of French ambivalence to step up his demands. The French appointment of an "ambassador" to the Saar territory inflamed German opinion and squeezed Adenauer between the left and right just at the time rearmament was coming up for debate in the Bundestag. Calling the French action "surprising" and "unbearable," Adenauer flatly declared that he would not initial the EDC treaties before he had been satisfied on the Saar and Germany's relationship to NATO. The EDC could not succeed, he said, "unless the causes of friction and the remains of unilateral legislation injurious to Germany are removed."[45] In the background, a wave of strikes and protest demonstrations against militarization (one leaflet asserted that "Stalingrad reminds you to tear down conscription orders") exerted still more pressure on Adenauer.

The Bundestag went Adenauer one better. Adenauer swore that West Germany would not join EDC as an inferior partner: "It is, before God, understandable to everybody that under no circumstances will we place young Germans, just like that, under the authority of a body upon whose functioning and work we have no influence."[46] But the deputies remained unconvinced, and following two days of excited debate they voted a number of provocative resolutions. First and foremost, they insisted on political and economic equality for the Federal Republic in the EDC. Second, they demanded, at a minimum, a voice in NATO councils. The deputies further directed that the Saar problem had to be solved, the occupation ended, and sentences of convicted war criminals reexamined. In this remarkable fit of temper, the Bundestag demonstrated just how complicated German rearmament was: the future of the Saar, NATO, the EDC, and the contractual agreements were all part of a single package.

The Bundestag debate was mirrored by a tumultuous week-long argument in the French National Assembly. "We wanted Europe, but we don't want this abortion of a Europe," said Jules Moch, a co-author of the Pleven Plan. The government of Edgar Faure received a vote of confidence, but with a long string of conditions attached: no German admission to NATO, Anglo-American security guarantees in the event of a German breakaway from the EDC, and financial compensation for French efforts in the Indochina war. France was already spending 10 percent of her gross national product on defense, the highest figure in Europe, and the EDC would only add to the tax burden.

National feelings obviously counted for much, but so too did finances. The United States needed Germany partly because it could not afford to defend Europe unilaterally; France was afraid of Germany because her Indochina commitment had drained resources available for Europe; rearmament would require politically unpalatable increases in European commitments and taxes; and Germany, whose industrial production had trebled in three years, was expected to contribute not only men but also money.

Many of the Franco-German problems were ironed out at an impromptu meeting in London in February 1952, made possible by the death of King George VI. But the big decisions—endorsing the EDC and nailing down solid commitments to a military buildup—were made shortly thereafter at the NATO meetings in Lisbon. "We will succeed because we *must* succeed," Acheson told the delegates. Despite French demands for guarantees in the event of a possible German secession from the EDC, the hard decisions on troop levels were made, following which Adenauer agreed to an acceptable figure for the German financial contribution. "We have something pretty close to a grand slam," an exultant Acheson cabled to the president.

The euphoria was short-lived, however, as the domestic political costs of these decisions became clear. Not long after the NATO meetings, the Faure cabinet was forced to resign because of its request for a 15 percent tax increase needed to meet France's obligations under the Lisbon program. At the same time, the British government announced that its three-year program of military expansion would be stretched out considerably past that period of time because of economic problems. And in the Federal Republic, Gustav Heinemann announced that the Lisbon decisions "destroy all hopes for a united Germany in the foreseeable future."[47]

At this point, the Soviets decided to further complicate the situation. Realizing after Lisbon that the specter of West German rearmament was no longer an abstract possibility, their diplomacy threw sand into the delicate Allied machinery by playing on German nationalist sentiment. For years the Soviets had refused to consider any plausible steps leading to unification. Now with rearmament in prospect, they played their strongest card in the hope of influencing not only the Germans, but also the lukewarm French and the Pollyannaish left-wing elements throughout Europe who longed for some sort of negotiated settlement between East and West.

Reunification was the supreme goal of German foreign policy. Indeed, it was constitutionally mandated in the preamble to the Basic Law, which called for "the unity and freedom of Germany." No doubt Adenauer was sincere in his belief that collaboration with the West was the surest route to reunification, but it was widely held that the two were mutually exclusive—at least until the end of the cold war. According to a *New York Times* correspondent, "the unity of Western Europe, as now planned, including as it does Western Germany, implies the more or less permanent disunity of Germany."[48] As early as 1950, Acheson had told a Senate Committee behind closed doors that "at the present time there is a line drawn across Europe which, so far as we can see, looks as though it were permanent." Many Germans were unwilling to wait that long.

The tension between the ideal of *ein Volk, ein Reich,* the need for security, and the desire for a European identity created an almost schizophrenic public opinion within the Federal Republic. By the middle of 1953, nearly 40 percent of the public felt that reunification was the single most important question facing German foreign policy. According to public opinion polls taken during this period, more than nine out of every ten West Germans viewed reunification as a desirable goal, but their enthusiasm cooled considerably when asked if they were willing to risk their economic or military security to achieve it. Most felt threatened by the Soviet Union. At the same time, most favored some sort of close association with Western Europe, while a 1951 poll had only 16 percent declaring themselves in favor of neutralism.

Although favorable to reunion and to close ties with Western Europe, West German opinion on rearmament ranged from overt hostility to indecision. During 1950 and 1951, at least, there is little doubt that the overwhelming majority of West Germans were opposed. The popularity of rearmament increased as time elapsed and the EDC came nearer to realization, but at no time did the EDC gain the unqualified support of more than one-third of the West German public.

The confusion of public opinion paralleled the dilemmas facing German politicians. While most favored the EDC, the majority also opposed the sine qua non for membership: rearmament, and of course its consequences for German unity. Public opinion, however, did not make policy in the Federal Republic, where the tradition of cabinet diplomacy was still strong. Assuming that Adenauer could weather challenges in the Bundestag, where foreign policy issues were drawn on a strict party-line basis, victory for his approach seemed likely.

Kurt Schumacher and the Social Democrats focused on the restoration of unity and self-respect. They quite unabashedly advocated trading off the Federal Republic's membership in the Western alliance system in return for Soviet concessions that would hasten the return of the eastern zone, precisely what Adenauer most feared. He and the Christian Democrats favored reunification, too, but only in "peace and freedom." This precluded neutralism, which he felt would force Germany to deal with both Soviets and Americans from a position of permanent weakness.[49]

There were also narrower party motives at work. The eastern areas of the Reich had historically been the source of the SPD's greatest support, whereas the Catholic-dominated west was the bedrock of CDU strength. From the standpoint of electoral politics, recapturing their silent constituents in the east would automatically catapult the SPD into the position of majority party. The EDC would make problematic the party's political future in Germany, and the dilution of Socialist ideals in a conservative, clerical, and non-Socialist Western Europe threatened its ideological future as well. These fears proved to be well founded.

The Russians had growled as soon as they sniffed trouble. In the fall of 1950 they served notice that they would "not tolerate" measures "aimed at reviving the German regular army in West Germany." Later they sent another note urgently requesting a Council of Foreign Ministers meeting to fulfill the Potsdam pledges regarding demilitarization. Unity was hinted at, but only under four-power demilitarized status.

To Acheson such invitations to talk were just so much stale beer and came much too late. Because Soviet-American disagreements had spilled onto a global flood plain, it was silly to suppose that they could be diverted successfully into the narrow channels of the German problem. Nevertheless, European public opinion demanded to be satisfied that an accommodation with the Soviets could not be reached. Not wishing to get bogged down in endless parleys, yet unwilling to appear intransigent, the Allies agreed to a meeting of deputies in Paris in the spring of 1951 to prepare an agenda for a CFM meeting. The Allies wished to start with the general causes of tension and only lastly to discuss Germany; the Soviets insisted, but to no avail, on the reverse agenda.

To this point, Moscow had had little to offer except a tired emphasis on Potsdam. But Soviet policy began to shift in the fall of 1951 when Vladimir Semenov, the political advisor to the Soviet high commissioner in Berlin, announced that the USSR was now prepared to see Germany reunited, on condition that she remain an unarmed neutral. Shortly thereafter, the East German Volkskammer proposed the holding of all-German elections to set up a provisional all-German government. Replying tartly to the accusation that these moves were designed to wreck Allied policy, East German propagandist Gerhard Eisler said, "You don't have to be a Columbus to make that discovery."[50]

The Allies had learned their lesson at Yalta, which had called for free elections throughout Eastern Europe but without any built-in safeguards that they would in fact express the will of the peoples involved. Now they set out to use the elections ploy to their advantage. On 4 October, Adenauer suggested that a "neutral international commission" under UN auspices be set up to determine, through investigation in the Federal Republic and the DDR, whether the conditions for free elections existed. The high commissioners approved, citing the desirability of "free, general, equal, secret and direct elections in the whole of Germany," which would accomplish the reunification of Germany "along democratic lines insuring the creation of a free Germany able to play its part in a peaceful association of European nations." The proposal was put to the United Nations and adopted by the General Assembly on 20 December.

As anticipated and desired, this sort of proposal was bound to founder on the rock of Soviet and East German insistence that elections were an internal matter. No self-respecting Communist government was willing to allow capitalist outsiders to investigate "the various aspects of personal freedom" necessary for uncoerced elections. The Soviets were being asked, in effect, to assist the commission in certifying that basic democratic freedoms in the eastern zone had been abrogated. Predictably, the commission received no response from the East and, thus, never got to begin the work it had never been expected to do.

These were but the warm-ups prior to the main event. On 10 March 1952, Soviet foreign minister Andrei Vishinsky finally issued a startling set of new proposals. According to the new Soviet scheme, Germany should be unified forthwith within the frontiers established at Potsdam. All foreign forces should be withdrawn no later than one year following entry into force of the treaty. Reassuringly, democratic "rights of man and basic freedoms including freedom of speech, press, religious persuasion, political conviction, and assembly" were to be guaranteed to all Germans, as was the free activity of democratic political parties. To drive home the point that bygones were bygones, full civil and political rights would be granted to all former Nazis, excluding those serving sentences for war crimes.

In its external relations, Germany would be neutral in the cold war, but there would be no limitations on her economic development. Foreign trade would be unrestricted, with full freedom of access to world markets. These kinds of proposals were novel enough coming from the Russians, but then came the truly startling departure: as a counterweight to Western promises of rearmament, the proposed draft treaty provided for German armed forces and the right to manufacture military equipment within limits to be set by the treaty. This was an embarrassing point for foreign Communist parties, which had been trumpeting the line that the USSR was the sole guarantor against a revival of German militarism.

To many in the West, this was an extremely attractive proposal, especially as it appeared that Stalin was now willing to accept a Western-style democracy and to dump the East German regime in exchange for an end to West German entry into the EDC. Acheson, however, smelled a rat. He interpreted this "familiar Russian gambit" as a "spoiling operation" and a "last ditch effort to prevent German integration." Recalling the Greek myth of the judgment of Paris, he argued that "several golden apples had been tossed over the Iron Curtain in the hopes of creating discord."

With the full backing of Truman, who as usual on the German question was content to allow policy to be set by subordinates, Acheson resisted the idea of talks with the Soviets unless they produced some hard evidence of good faith beforehand, such as cooperation in producing an Austrian peace treaty, or perhaps help in expediting an armistice in Korea. John McCloy reaffirmed this skeptical approach: "We are not prepared to play the role of Alice in Wonderland. We want firm evidence, firm facts. We have all suffered too much—Germans included—to jeopardize the progress we have made."[51]

Nevertheless, Acheson was painfully aware that the Soviet offer was well aimed, not only at Germans who yearned for unity and might appreciate a national army free of the EDC's apron strings, but also at European and American critics of the cold war who desired a negotiated end to great power squabbling in Europe. For that reason, he said the Allies would be "ill-advised . . . to turn it down out of hand," but needed to "tread warily," guarding against a replay of the divisive discussions of the early postwar years which would only deflect them from the common policies so painfully arrived at.[52]

Whether or not Stalin was sincere is still unclear—as one might expect, the 10 March note was ambiguous on crucial points. But Stalin was definitely worried about the effects of rearmament and may well have been willing to work out a deal along the lines of the security treaty proposed by the Americans in 1946. In his 1952 work, *Economic Problems of Socialism in the USSR*, Stalin predicted a revival of German power. Once rearmed, Germany would "break out of American bondage" and start yet another war. If his fears were as genuinely deep-seated as this text indicates, then the proposal might have been seriously intended. Realizing that the Federal Republic was firmly betrothed but not yet wed, this proposal was designed to prevent Adenauer from saying "I do."

For all the talk of the German problem's being at the heart of the cold war, the American response to this initiative demonstrated the contrary. Only if the Russians retreated from Europe, and not merely Germany, could there be a satisfactory resolution of the German question. To be sure, the United States favored reunification, but only in an ideal world where there was no cold war. And even if the Soviet proposal were totally genuine, so what? The idea of a neutral Germany horrified the Americans, bringing immediately to mind the possibility of a "new Rapallo," in which Germany would maneuver to best advantage between East and West.

Adenauer's route to German unification paralleled Acheson's path to cold war victory; both depended on building positions of strength with the hope of winning concessions from a Soviet Union that faced the facts. Adenauer was unwilling to sacrifice the sure thing of sovereignty and equality in association with the West for a leap into the political unknown of reunification and neutralism. Whatever the effect on unity, Adenauer's position was in keeping with the supranational political realities of the cold war, whereas the Social Democrats were still mesmerized by the nationalist myths of a bygone world.

Western unwillingness to find out whether the Soviets were indeed serious led some years later to accusations of a "stab in the back" from disappointed advocates of unification. But for Acheson, whether or not the proposal was made in good faith was beside the point. It was years too late in coming, the Soviets having missed the boat at the time of Byrnes's treaty proposal in 1946. Negotiations had been possible in a pre–cold war framework, but it would have required a total reversal of historical perspective for most Americans to believe that an end to the cold war could be negotiated. Still, one could not answer with a flat "no." Popular delusions had somehow to be defused, especially in Germany and France. If bad faith was involved, it lay in the unwillingness to lay the issues candidly before public opinion.

Thus began the "Battle of the Notes," as Eden called it. In an identical message dated 25 March, the Allies stuck close to shore by resorting to a time-tested method of bringing negotiations to a halt. Talks, if held, were to be limited to discussion of free, UN-supervised elections for an all German government and were not to range into deeper political waters. As before, these electoral proposals were made "in the firm belief that the Russians will reject them." The Allies also rejected the unilaterally imposed Oder-Neisse line, which had been the de facto German-Polish border since the war's end.[53]

The Soviet reply on 9 April brushed aside the Western counterproposal and suggested instead a four-power electoral commission. This proposal, they argued, was better than the alternative of "hireling troops of revanchistes headed by Fascist-Hitlerite generals ready to engulf Europe in a third world war." The exchanges ground on into September 1952, with neither side making substantial alterations of position.

Acheson was relieved that the Russians did not agree to talks, for that undoubtedly would have stalled the EDC. But the Soviet notes did have their intended effect in stirring dormant political passions and in rousing neutralist sentiments throughout Europe. Adenauer now faced such enormous pressure from nationalist opinion of all stripes in the Bundestag that he was forced to call for four-power talks on unification, much against his personal inclinations, although he was careful to include the electoral conditions as a poison pill. The sense of historic opportunity was quickened by *Pravda's* blunt assertion that German reunification was a "now or never" proposition. Trying to calm the excitement, Adenauer told the Bundestag that the Soviet offer had been prompted by the Western policy of building strength and suggested that better offers would be forthcoming if the process of rearmament and integration went ahead full steam. But Western expectations made it questionable whether such a policy could ever lead to negotiated unity. As a National Security Council memo drafted a few months later put it: "If the free world acquires such strength, the internal contradictions of the Soviet totalitarian system will, with some positive assistance from us, cause that system gradually to weaken and decay."[54] The emphasis was clearly on historical capitulation, not negotiation.

The French, too, by now were beginning to waver on the EDC, as public opinion put great pressure on the cabinet to attempt exploratory quadripartite negotiations. At the same time, worried about a possible German breakaway, they sought security guarantees from the British and the Americans above and beyond those provided in the EDC text. Meanwhile in Great Britain, the Labor Party, having shifted to a neutralist course following its loss of control of Parliament in the October 1951 elections, also came out in favor of talks.

But if the Soviet démarche was calculated to disrupt Allied progress, it had exactly the opposite effect—by now a familiar pattern. For all the commotion it stirred up, the Soviet gambit had the unintended result of convincing Americans of the need to promptly squelch the debate over the precise nature of Germany's future. The months following the release of the Soviet note thus witnessed an all-out American push to speed the interminable EDC and contractual negotiations to a conclusion.

There was some hard bargaining, including some grueling all-night sessions toward the end, with the tireless Adenauer getting the better of it. At one meeting, Adenauer was told that "the United States would not budge from the principles for which she had fought the war . . . for all the German divisions in the world."[55] But "der Alte" realized that the military necessities of the cold war were working to his advantage. "Time is on our side," he told his political intimates. "American insistence on a German army will eventually force the Western powers to accede to our demands." Acknowledging this reality, at one point McCloy said, not entirely in jest: "All right, then. This is now the one hundred and twenty-second concession the Allies have made to the Germans."[56]

In this frantic atmosphere of haste, modifications continued to be made until the last minute. But finally the contractual agreements and the EDC treaties were ready for signing at the end of May 1952 in Bonn and Paris, respectively. The sheer volume of the intricate agreements was mind-boggling. In Bonn alone, Maurice Schuman signed at least twenty-one separate treaties, conventions, protocols, and letters, with Adenauer's busy hand not far behind.

By replacing the Occupation Statute of 1949, the contractual agreements provided for the restoration of German sovereignty. The occupation would be terminated and Allied controls ended. However, the Allies retained certain residual rights relating to Berlin, which was not part of the Federal Republic, and to all-German questions left unsettled by the war. Allied troops would remain in Germany, not as an army of occupation but to provide essential mutual security. At the last minute, Adenauer extracted an important concession: even if the EDC failed to be ratified, the contractual agreements would go into effect. The metaphysical issue of whether a reunified Germany would continue to be bound by all these agreements, which preyed on French and German minds alike, was not so much settled as obscured to everyone's satisfaction.

The following day the statesmen flew to Paris for signature of the EDC accords. There, too, negotiations continued to the last minute. French fears of a German pullout were temporarily stilled by a British agreement to extend the guarantees of the 1948 Brussels Treaty (a fifty-year mutual defense treaty between Britain, France, and the Benelux countries) to the EDC as a whole in the event of an armed attack. As an official of a lame duck administration in an election year, all Acheson could do was agree to a declaration that a serious threat to the integrity or unity of the EDC would be examined in accordance with the terms of the North Atlantic pact. The EDC treaty as finally signed provided for the creation of twelve German divisions, as well as an air force and a navy, as part of the European military establishment.

The treaties still needed to be ratified, however. In the Federal Republic, Schumacher vowed to continue his party's opposition, arguing that they had been "signed on the backs of some twenty million helpless Germans who suffer under Communist dictatorship."[57] In France, Acheson quickly discovered that having the French signature on the dotted line was no guarantee of ultimate approval by the National Assembly. In an interview with French president Vincent Auriol he was subjected to an anti-German tirade and accused of committing a tragic error of judgment.

While France and Germany continued to be preoccupied with their attempts to come to terms with the treaties, the changing international situation cast even darker shadows of uncertainty over the outcome. The death of Stalin in March 1953 seemed to provide a heaven-sent opportunity for a break in the East-West deadlock. Even a staunch cold warrior like Winston Churchill called for four-power talks. An uprising in East Berlin in June 1953 that was brutally put down by Russian tanks pointed to explosive dissatisfactions in the eastern zone. Meanwhile, American policy was paralyzed by the presidential elections, which resulted in the victory of the war hero Eisenhower, and by the overriding importance of the Korean War as an issue in American politics.

Early in the new administration, a sweeping reexamination of America's international position, code-named "Project Solarium," called for remarkably little change in policy. In one of the task forces, George Kennan as usual argued in lonely fashion for "a better United States stance on the unification of Germany, which may mean letting EDC die a quiet death."[58] He urged "the preparation, as a matter of urgency, of a strong and plausible United States negotiating position on the reunification of Germany," in order to "exploit and intensify Soviet internal stresses and achieve, in due course, the first major roll back of Soviet hegemony over Eastern Europe."[59] Kennan feared that United States policy, as in 1949, was so committed to its military solution that it would only intensify the German problem and the division of Europe rather than alleviate it.

If anything, the change of administrations resulted in a stronger American commitment to the EDC. Eisenhower came to power partly as a result of popular dissatisfaction with the cold war, a feeling captured by his secretary of state, John Foster Dulles, in his call during the 1952 presidential campaign for the "liberation and rollback" of Communist power in Europe. The dramatic objective of freeing Eastern Europe had generated some controversy, but it relied basically on building strength in the West, an approach that had bipartisan acceptance. Viewing the EDC in that hopeful light,

Dulles had argued that "the present series of complicated treaties and con-tracts will produce only barren and bitter fruits if they are looked upon as establishing some new balance of power by a new and rigid political struc-ture."[60] Eisenhower, too, looked for results on the German question. In a let-ter to William S. Paley, he remarked that "we are going to solve this German problem or the Soviets are going to solve it in their favor."[61]

In response to criticisms that the United States was digging a hole for itself in its German policy, the Eisenhower administration chose to dig deep-er. The discussion of options resulted only in a greater determination to push for the EDC and, failing that, to consider rearming Germany bilaterally if need be. In his defense, Eisenhower insisted that "he was certainly the last person in the world to decry thinking, but that to him there simply was no satisfactory alternative to EDC."[62] So long as there was a shred of hope, he would not be convinced otherwise.

Eisenhower refused to believe that there was "anything incompatible between German unification and German participation in the EDC." According to the "magnet theory" then dominating administration thinking, a successful conclusion of the EDC project would "greatly increase the pres-sures inside Eastern Germany for joining up with the other part." Indeed, events might develop to the point that it might even "become impossible for the Communists to hold the place by force."[63] In an NSC discussion, Ike stated that "what we must do is to throw all our weight behind the EDC objective."[64]

Eisenhower, who knew his European politics, felt Adenauer was so vital to American policy that privately he expressed a willingness to "do almost anything to help the German chancellor."[65] Feeling that Adenauer was "our ace-in-the hole," Eisenhower and others shuddered to think what direction the Federal Republic might take if the old statesman's policies were discredit-ed and he were forced from power. Amazingly, Adenauer and Dulles hit it off on a personal basis, to the point that it was said they used to pray together. Adenauer's visit to the United States in April 1953 not only publicized Germany's new status but also let the Germans know that American policy-makers "were putting their money, were so to speak betting, on Konrad Adenauer."[66] A plea from Adenauer for help in the September 1953 elec-tions produced an unusual public endorsement from Dulles, who asserted that Adenauer's defeat would be disastrous for Germany and freedom. Adenauer's impressive victory in the fall balloting, which gave his party a strong working majority, assured that West Germany would remain commit-ted to American goals.

The Eisenhower administration also held strong views on the undesirabil-ity of a unified but neutral Germany. According to Dulles, neutrality was all well and good when applied to a tiny nation like Austria, but it had absolute-ly "no application to a country of the character of Germany."[67] To imagine such a powerful nation not taking sides in the cold war was to be carried away by fantasy or wishful thinking. The administration, like its predecessor, believed that a neutralist solution, besides denying German strength to the West, would "open up the whole of Germany to Soviet manipulation and intrigue."[68] The idea of a neutral Germany that was free to tack back and forth was simply unthinkable.

An NSC staff summary of the Project Solarium reports concluded that "the EDC nations should be informed that if they do not constitute their defense community by the end of this year, the United States will rearm West Germany on a bilateral basis."[69] This was, however, a last resort the administration was not yet willing to contemplate. As Ike made clear in December at the Bermuda summit meeting with Churchill and Joseph Laniel of France: "To resort to a national army was a second choice so far behind EDC that there could be no comparison." If the EDC failed, he said, it would be a "cataclysmic" eventuality.[70]

From the global standpoint, if a German national army were substituted for the EDC solution, Ike feared that "France would become so frightened in Europe that she would not be able to spare a single man for overseas duty."[71] For the moment, raising the specter of a national Germany army was useful mainly as a negotiating counter. As Dulles said, "We are not thinking of how to give up the EDC; the question is how to get the EDC. An alternative is necessary if we are going to get it."[72]

While the substance of American policy did not change, there was a marked shift in style, especially in the modus operandi of the new secretary of state, John Foster Dulles. Dulles had long experience in European and German affairs, beginning with his service as a reparations expert at the Paris Peace Conference in 1919; he believed that the outcome had been unjust to the Germans and productive of yet another global war. He was a serious— some said dour—man of deep religious faith, whose long historical view of the cold war gave an apocalyptic edge to Soviet-American disagreements. This spiritual evaluation of history was extremely close to Adenauer's views and helped cement their relationship, even though neither could speak the other's language.

Dulles's concern for European unity antedated the cold war. On numerous occasions during World War II he had called the Continent a "firetrap" and concluded that the only way to solve its difficulties and the German problem was through some sort of European unification. In 1946, for example, he had argued that the United States ought "to envisage the German problem in the setting of an increasing economic and political unity for western Europe."[73] Even if the Soviet Union were suddenly to disappear, Dulles believed that there was "an urgent, positive duty on all of us to seek to end that danger which comes from within. It has been the underlying cause of two world wars and will be disastrous if it persists."[74]

His logic with regard to the EDC was somewhat more complex, especially when one considers that its near-term effect would work against European unity. But the cold war was a long-range historical undertaking. To Dulles, the EDC was a means not only to rearmament and stability, but also to the rollback of communism. Long convinced that diplomacy failed when it aimed at preserving the status quo (the cardinal sin of the 1920s and 1930s), Dulles was determined to make movement possible in the cold war. Employing the same logic, National Security Council memorandum NSC-160/1 argued that a united Western Europe would "exert a strong and increasing attraction on Eastern Europe, thus weakening the Soviet position there and accelerating Soviet withdrawal from that area."[75] A united Western Europe would then achieve the unification of the entire Continent. According to Eisenhower, it would "ultimately attract to it all the Soviet satellites, and the threat to peace would disappear."[76]

Unlike Acheson, Dulles believed that the Europeans could not be relied on to achieve this by themselves. Needed was some "friendly but firm outside pressure."[77] Thus, immediately on assuming office in January 1953, he took a trip to seven European capitals to provide mouth-to-mouth resuscitation to the limp body of the EDC. On his return, he told Eisenhower that his trip had "at least taken this project out of mothballs" and estimated the odds in favor of passage as being about 60 to 40.[78] He hinted not so subtly that if the EDC failed of prompt enactment, U.S. policy would require "a little rethinking." At a NATO council meeting in December, Dulles would at last say it directly: the failure to adopt the EDC "would compel an agonizing reappraisal of basic United States policy."

That was the stick, used time and again (although the prospect of America's retreating to isolationism must have come as welcome news to the Soviets). Dulles made the point as often as he could to French policymakers that "if France were to choose to stand alone, the weight of public opinion in America would move towards isolationism."[79] Later the Eisenhower administration dangled the carrot by promising to have American troops remain in Europe as long as the need existed.

Neither inducements nor punishments managed to budge the increasingly stubborn French. First France, under Premier Pierre Mendès-France, proposed a series of radical amendments that would have shattered the supranational features of the EDC. Then, with the French government putting the issue without any sign whatever of enthusiasm or conviction, on 30 August 1954 the National Assembly refused overwhelmingly to have anything further to do with the plan first put forward by its own statesmen. The EDC was effectively dead.

Even in the Federal Republic, where conditions were more favorable, Adenauer had his hands full. With Kurt Schumacher's death in August 1953, the more moderate and amiable Erich Ollenhauer took over the SPD leadership. Despite Ollenhauer's claim to oppose not the principle but the form of the agreements, his party's opposition remained unchanged. The SPD continued to insist that only if unification were conclusively proved to be impossible would the German people be prepared for full integration with the West.[80] The SPD also played on French opposition to the treaty by making provocative statements certain to arouse emotional counterstatements in France. A final headache was caused by questions concerning the constitutional legality of ratification.

Dulles's initial histrionic reaction to French rejection was to call it "a crisis of almost terrifying proportions." But since the administration had earlier taken this possibility into consideration and had already decided against pulling out of Europe, Dulles was quick to add that the "tragedy would be compounded if the United States was thereby led to conclude that it must turn to a course of narrow nationalism."[81] Thus, all his threats notwithstanding, it was clear that the United States was not about to pick up its marbles and go home.

Adenauer was understandably bitter at having wasted three years in promoting a plan with nothing to show for it. Having bargained in good faith, he now demanded sovereignty anyway, a demand that the United States had decided to grant before it was made. Nevertheless, he was sorely disappointed that the French had wrecked the "European idea." With German rearmament likely in any event on a national basis, he feared a revival of nationalist sentiment in his country and a reversion to Rapallo-like overtures to the Russians. "I am firmly convinced," he reportedly said, "one hundred percent convinced, that the national army to which M. Mendès-France is forcing us will be a great danger for Germany and Europe."

It was at this point that Anthony Eden devised a suitable way out. While lazing in the bathtub one Sunday morning, the idea came to him of expanding the Brussels Pact of 1948 to include both West Germany and Italy. Under that treaty's provisions, West German forces could be suitably regulated by a supranational council, though with nowhere near the authority contemplated under the EDC. As General Alfred Gruenther of NATO made plain, there would be no superstate to "constantly check up on baby carriage factories to make certain [Germans] were not manufacturing guided missiles in secret."[82] As a sweetener for France, Eden promised to maintain British military forces on the Continent for fifty years, a guarantee the French had long been seeking.

Given the French veto in the occupation, Germany could not be rearmed without French assent, but this was hardly cause for elation in Paris inasmuch as the consequences of continued Gallic intransigence promised, in their own way, to be equally disastrous. Clearly, the Eisenhower administration was determined to take the German side of things, for the simple reason that Germany counted for more. "We could get along without France but not without Germany," Ike told Dulles on one occasion. Seeing the handwriting on the wall, the French realized at this point that a completely obstructionist attitude would leave them totally isolated in Europe. Across the Atlantic, American policymakers were already beginning to think of writing off

France, and were likening her hysteria to the nervous collapse she had suffered in 1940.

Despite some last-minute tantrums, the end result of French policy was acceptance of what Paris had originally set out to avoid. In October 1954, the foreign ministers agreed to admit the Federal Republic to the reconstituted Western European Union. In May 1955, West Germany attained sovereignty, the occupation ended, and a few days later it was admitted to full NATO membership. Thus the melodrama sputtered to an end, with America and the Federal Republic appearing to achieve their objectives.

And yet, as is often the case in such complex affairs, the episode created new problems at the same time that it left others unsolved. The entire EDC scheme had been premised on the idea that NATO and the EDC would coexist. A united western Europe would be a third force in world politics and could take care of itself, thus making possible an American withdrawal. But now the German problem had branched out to the point where it required a permanent American military commitment to NATO. By default, NATO would have to become the core of the "magnet theory."

When he assumed the NATO supreme command, Eisenhower had said, "In the long run, it is not possible—and most certainly not desirable—that Europe should be an occupied territory defended by legions brought in from abroad, somewhat in the fashion that Rome's territories vainly sought security many years ago."[83] Though tired of loose talk about the United States withdrawing her troops from Europe, at the same time he had felt that "we cannot allow anyone to get up and protest that we are going to keep troops in Europe forever."[84] In 1951 he had expressed the hope that American ground forces could begin their withdrawal from Europe within four to eight years and that NATO itself might be needed for only ten to twenty years.[85] With the failure of the EDC, however, the idea of temporal limits disappeared entirely.

The NATO solution caused other problems. Though NATO, like the EDC, was supranational, it was a hierarchical organization inevitably dominated by the United States. With the French ultimately taking the line of least resistance with only a minimal sacrifice of sovereignty in return for an indefinite American presence in Europe, the corresponding acceptance of German equality with France came at the price of everyone's inferiority to the United States. The NATO solution also affected Adenauer's quest for sovereignty and equality. While these goals were achieved in theory, in a hierarchical NATO whose European members were less equal than the United States, the Federal Republic would in practice rank lower even than the "lesser equals."

As for the Americans, the open-ended commitment to NATO would be in large measure responsible for perpetuating among Europeans the very sense of weakness it was designed to remedy. Eisenhower still hoped to see emerge in Western Europe "a third great power bloc, after which development the United States would be permitted to sit back and relax somewhat."[86] The NATO throne, however, was destined never to become an easy chair for the Americans.

The NATO solution did not abandon the system of "double containment" of the USSR and Germany. Instead, it required the United States to do the containing in each case. The German problem, which would have become a European problem with the success of the EDC, was shifted for an indefinite duration to American shoulders. As a result the Americans became self-made victims of an almost Newtonian dynamic in which every action toward the USSR in the cold war would have an equal and opposite reaction on the German question, and vice versa. If one wanted to be perverse, one could even call this a system of triple containment, as the United States spun a German web around its diplomacy from which it could free itself only with great difficulty.

Still, these were minor concerns when compared with the larger questions. Would the rearmament of Germany achieve its objectives in the cold war? Would the militarization of cold war alliances produce the reunification of all Europe, or would the laboriously achieved rearmament prejudice a diplomatic solution to the German problem and the cold war? Adenauer's policy of reunification through freedom and the American strategy of building strength would now be put to the test.

chapter 5

TWO GERMANYS: THE FAILURE OF REUNIFICATION

In contrast to the perception of the cold war in the 1980s as a standoff in which change occurred glacially if at all, statesmen of the 1950s saw a very fluid international situation. In that fast-paced environment, the rearmament of the Federal Republic and its integration into the Western alliance, though a tortuous and seemingly endless diplomatic process, was not supposed to be an end in itself but a start toward the settlement of several connected problems. Rearmament, of course, was designed to bring security, but it was also intended as a giant step toward ending the cold war. Once rearmament was agreed on, therefore, the focus of diplomacy shifted to the problems of German reunification and larger issues of European security.

The German problem was analogous to the dual key system that Americans use to control the launch of nuclear-tipped missiles—nothing happens unless both operators agree to turn their keys simultaneously. Until 1955, rearmament had been primarily a matter of intra-Western diplomacy, but no solution of the German problem could get off the ground without the approval of the other key holder, the Soviet Union. Following the Berlin airlift, the Russians had been reduced to playing a background role—a noisy one, to be sure—as American and German statesmen treated Soviet proposals as just so many nuisances. With the death of Stalin in March 1953 and the emergence of a new Soviet leadership that protested its desire for peaceful coexistence, the heavens seemed properly aligned for a negotiated settlement.

And yet, even though the immediate post-Stalin era was filled with summitry and high-level East-West negotiations on Germany and other issues, the more the superpowers talked, the less they solved. The West's single-minded determination to make rearmament a fact had meant that doubts had been suppressed and questions put off until the future. Now, however, as larger issues were taken out of storage, the drawbacks of a Germanized NATO became evident to the Bundesrepublik and the United States. Contrary to expectations, the Soviet response to the Western policy of double containment not only frustrated German and American hopes, by the early 1960s it also led to tensions that threatened to break out in nuclear war. Instead of ending the division of Germany and Europe, this new phase witnessed its solidification.

By the mid 1950s, the success of one aspect of American policy was plainly evident in Germany's amazing economic recovery. Beginning in 1949–50, when the Federal Republic's foreign trade doubled in a single year and continued to advance with giant strides thereafter, the German phoenix began its spectacular rise from the postwar ashes. By June 1951, the country was self-supporting. In 1953, the industrial index reached 158 percent of the 1936 index, 1936 generally being accepted as the last normal prewar year. Industrial productivity trebled between 1954 and 1964, while unemployment dropped from 9 percent in 1949 to less than 1 percent in 1961, with further reductions still to come. Inflation remained low and real wages doubled between 1950 and 1962. By the end of the decade, the Bundesrepublik was the world's third-ranking industrial power.

Favorably comparing the new Germany with what he had seen in the 1920s, Eisenhower's new ambassador, Dr. James Bryan Conant, reported "a brisk and prosperous Germany" in which the people were "healthy-looking, alert and well dressed." Everywhere one turned in the cities, construction cranes were transforming war-inflicted wounds into memories whose basic content, like the pain of a past toothache, could no longer be recalled. Not only the cities but also the towns and the landscape regained their customary manicured appearance. In the villages, too, modern technology had penetrated to transform the peasants into consumers of the latest commodities. All this was accompanied by a massive program of social reconstruction. By the end of the decade, more than 10 million refugees from the East had been successfully integrated into West German society.

Although the emphasis was on market forces, Ludwig Erhard's "social market economy" (Soziale Marktwirtschaft) created one of the world's most advanced welfare states. Taxes were among the highest in the free world, but in return employees received free health insurance and medical care, generous unemployment benefits, and old age pensions. In addition, the prevailing ideology accepted a necessary role for state intervention in the economy when called for by extraordinary circumstances. The antagonism between capital and labor was muffled in major industries by the practice of co-determination (Mitbestimmung), in which labor was given some voice as a partner in management decisions. More important, the powerful labor unions were kept happy by the wage increases made possible by unbroken prosperity.

The causes of this economic miracle were, as always, varied and complex. It was a product in varying degrees of German industriousness and know-how, long pent-up consumer demand that provided stimulus, an export boom caused by high international demand for capital goods in the 1950s that provided a substitute for Germany's traditional markets in Eastern Europe and the Balkans, stable prices, the ability to concentrate efforts in the most promising branches of industry, and cost efficiencies resulting from the need to modernize industries and plants destroyed by the war. As a result, the *Wirtschaftswunder* transformed West Germany in the 1950s into an advanced industrial economy.

As American policymakers had hoped, German success was tightly knotted to Western European prosperity. The unhappy derailment of the European Defense Community was a setback for European integration, but dedicated Europeanists quickly switched tracks by taking the economic route to unity pioneered by the European Coal and Steel Community. Following the EDC's demise, the Treaty of Rome, which created the Common Market, was signed in March 1957, with the Federal Republic as a charter member. Bonn's partnership with Europe was significantly helped along by the settlement of the Saar issue with France, which had been an irritant since the end of the First World War. Following a feeble attempt at Europeanization, the French government finally threw in its hand and agreed to let the Saar rejoin the Federal Republic in 1957.

Politically, too, the Bundesrepublik exceeded all expectations in the ease with which it took to democracy. The fear of creating another Weimar, with its revolving-door governments, proliferation of parties, and lack of legitimacy, was rendered groundless by the new government's surprising stability. Beginning with the convincing electoral victory of 1955, Konrad Adenauer's Christian Democrats enjoyed solid majorities in the Bundestag for the next decade. Though there were extremist parties, like the neo-Nazis, and those who pushed for a more aggressive policy aimed at recovering the eastern territories, these were clearly fringe groups. Perhaps the most outstanding achievement of the Adenauer era was that he accustomed his countrymen to the idea of civilian rule in a nation that was prone to believe, as one historian put it, "that leaders could only be taken seriously when they wore uniforms."[1]

True, there were some worrisome reminders of past behavior. Having agreed to take over from the Allies the responsibility of prosecuting war criminals, the Federal Republic tended to drag its feet in bringing ex-Nazis to justice. However, according to Thomas Schwartz, by this time the Americans, more interested in securing German allegiance to the Western alliance, also "had abandoned their search for justice against the Nazis" by commuting the sentences of many convicted war criminals.[2] In industry, the ambitious attempt at decartelization proved to be a flop, as the Germans reverted to their time-tested practices of industrial coordination. A sign, too, of lingering insecurity with the idea of full democracy was the Federal Republic's outlawing of the Nazi and Communist parties. This fear that extremist elements might somehow be able to poison the entire system would later find expression in the so-called *Verbot,* which banned opponents of the state from any government service. The implication was that the democracy was so new and weakly rooted that it was not strong enough to stand on its own.

To critics, the Federal Republic's democracy seemed wholly negative and devoid of any positive spiritual appeal, offering in place of ideals a shallow commitment to naked material values. The reluctance to bring up the past, the idea that 1945 was the "zero hour" from which the nation had made a fresh start without looking back, gave the society a historically rootless feeling. The Germans were certainly disillusioned with Hitler, or, more precisely, with the consequences of Hitlerism, but there seemed to be no new inspiring political credos to fill the void. In particular there were grave concerns about the lack of idealism found in the generation born after the war. A fetishism of commodities was understandable for a generation that had suffered through postwar deprivation, but what sort of legacy besides hard work and material enjoyment could the older generation bequeath? Representative of this feeling of spiritual malaise was a German girl who is reported to have said that the two most important influences on her life were her father's checkbook and her mother's cookbook.[3]

As the decade drew to a close, the trend to political moderation received a welcome boost from the new program adopted by the Social Democrats at their 1959 Bad Godesberg party congress. Repeated defeats at the polls and the realities of the cold war led a frustrated SPD to renounce Marxism as an ideology and socialism as a final goal. Realizing that Marxist principles had aged badly in the modern world, the Social Democrats agreed to work within the framework of free market principles, adopting the slogan: "As much competition as possible—as much planning as necessary." With this peaceful but drastic ideological metamorphosis, the SPD, once exclusively a worker's party, now became a party of the people.

Despite these changes, the party remained more dovish on the cold war and more interventionist in the economy than the Christian Democratic Union, but henceforth its policies were clearly within the bounds of the kind of consensus politics preached by the Americans. The SPD's turnabout reflected the lessening appeal of Marxism in the West at the same time that it made less terrifying to the Western powers the coming of the true test of democracy: the alternation of power. As one analyst put it, the SPD now "became a Party like the others and ceased to consider itself as a community of political saints."[4]

In foreign affairs, change was harder to come by. Whatever the rhetoric of the Allies with the conclusion of the October 1954 agreements, the Federal Republic's status was not transformed overnight by signatures on pieces of paper. Bonn acquired sovereignty, but it was a curious sort of sovereignty hedged about with all kinds of fundamental restrictions created by the system of double containment. Her ability to deal independently with the East was curtailed by Allied retention of ultimate authority over Germany's future. The Allies retained their rights in Berlin, the right to continue to station troops in Germany—albeit on terms negotiated with the Bundesrepublik—and, most significant, they reserved their powers with respect to all-German questions such as the peace treaty, which of course involved the vital matters of frontiers and reunification.

In addition, Bonn's relationship to the West was tightly sealed in its NATO wrapper and in a variety of other West European supranational institutions that limited her capacity for a seesaw policy between East and West. Acting the role of Caesar's wife in the alliance, Bonn tried to rise above suspicion by agreeing to renounce the manufacture and use of atomic, biological, and chemical weapons. But try as she might to behave in a manner beyond reproach, the fact that she was clearly on her best behavior inevitably suggested to some that she was presenting a false face to the world. In the event, the Federal Republic was granted sovereignty in all matters except those most essential to sovereignty: those pertaining to self-definition.

Trying to determine whether the times were in fact auspicious for diplomatic change was much like trying to predict the weather. Superficially, the auspices seemed good. In many small ways, following Stalin's death, the winds from Moscow began to blow more warmly and would continue to do so for a number of years. Illustrative of this was the Soviet contention in August 1953 that the recently concluded Korean armistice was a sign that "favorable conditions have been created for a lessening of tension in the international situation."[5] A small degree of liberalization in East Germany prior to the June 1953 rebellion appeared to some Kremlinologists to be a straw in the wind, an indication that the Soviets might be prepared to change course in their overall German policy. In 1955, the Soviets finally agreed to an Austrian State treaty, which John Foster Dulles hoped would be "contagious."

With the exception of a sharp rise owing to the Soviet suppression of the Hungarian rebellion in 1956, the temperatures on the diplomatic chart in Europe during this period remained for the most part moderate until the closing stages of the Eisenhower administration. Following Stalin's death, in particular, there was considerable debate among Western leaders as to the prospects of a détente with the Soviets. Winston Churchill thought a summit would be desirable in order to discover what manner of men the West would now be dealing with. Eisenhower, while not eager for a summit, was nevertheless anxious to take advantage of any trend toward liberalization. As he put it, he did not wish "to freeze the tender buds of sprouting decency, if indeed they are really coming out."

Dulles and Adenauer, however, were unhappy with the idea of a summit. During his visit to Washington, Adenauer argued that the mating calls emanating from Moscow following Stalin's death "were nothing but a sign that the new Soviet leaders needed a lull to settle their internal affairs and therefore wanted to ward off any disturbance that might impinge from outside." Dulles, like Dean Acheson before him, worried that a disposition to talk might deflect Western resolve and endanger the ongoing struggle for ratification of EDC. Nevertheless, the ardent public hopes for a relaxation of tension, which later came to be known as "the spirit of Geneva," made a meeting inevitable.[6]

American leaders were aware that ever since the Korean War, the fear of war had been declining in Europe and that expectations of a negotiated East-West settlement were on the rise. Although many American policymakers viewed this as "wishful thinking," nevertheless they recognized that it removed "the sense of urgency and willingness to sacrifice which marked the early NATO buildup."[7] Predictably, following the drawing up of plans for West Germany's admission into NATO, Pierre Mendès-France insisted on talks with the Russians, if only to demonstrate to his people that rapprochement was impossible. Eisenhower may have been irked by what he called the old French game of "diplomatic doodling,"[8] but the United States had little choice but to put on its Sunday suit and go through the pious motions of diplomatic ritual.

In response to French pressure and Adenauer's request that a four-power meeting be scheduled to help him with upcoming general elections, a meeting of foreign ministers was held in Berlin early in 1954. The conference appeared to be just another performance of a stale play in which the bored actors ran through their lines, but the positions adopted by the two sides were nevertheless interesting, because they suggested that the show was about to close.

The three Western powers put forward the so-called Eden Plan, which called for free elections for a constituent assembly, a four-power commission to draw up the electoral law, and a system of security guarantees to allay Soviet fears of a united Germany tied to the West. Here they were publicly broaching what they had long privately desired as an ideal objective: a united Germany in NATO. The Soviets, too, went beyond earlier demands by broadening the terms of discussion. Germany could be reunited, Vyacheslav Molotov said, if a general European security pact were signed that would involve not only the dissolution of the EDC and NATO, but also the withdrawal of American troops from the Continent. To this proposal the Americans responded with amazed laughter.

In the course of the next year, the two sides drifted further apart. The Soviets did agree to free elections, but they insisted as always that the elections must be arranged between the two Germanys and that the end result must be a guaranteed neutralized Germany. More impossibly yet, however, the Soviets frankly stated that before such an agreement could be made, important social and political changes would have to take place inside West Germany. Not only would this mean neutrality, something the West was not willing to accept in any case, but also a Germany tilted ideologically toward the East.

Despite Adenauer's fear that the Soviets might actually accept the Eden Plan and take advantage of it to cause turmoil in the Federal Republic, the cold war differences on Germany during this period were widening, not narrowing. The Americans now maintained that a united Germany, even if united through free elections, should be free to join NATO. The Russians, for their part, began to insist that the German problem could be solved, on their terms, only when prior solutions to East-West problems had been arrived at.

At the Geneva summit of July 1955, the atmospherics were encouraging, but the substantive outcome was not. For all the hoopla and media attention of the time, Geneva became just another obscure footnote in the cold war. The Americans tried repeatedly to convince the Soviets that a united Germany in NATO would be in their best interests, since it would safely restrain German power while taking the steam out of dangerous nationalist sentiment in Germany. For example, Assistant Secretary of State Livingston Merchant insisted that "the character of existing western collective defense arrangements is not only defensive in purpose and intent but as a practical matter incapable of aggressive use or domination by a single power." But the Soviets simply shrugged off the Western proposals. Asked why they rejected the free elections formula for Germany, the emerging strongman Nikita Khrushchev replied frankly, "The German people have not yet had time to be educated in the great advantage of Communism!"[9] With equal candor, Soviet Premier Nikolai Bulganin informed Eisenhower that Western diplomacy had made reunification impossible. With West Germany now in NATO, any realistic chances of reunification were receding in the rearview mirror of history.

The hardening of the Soviet position clearly indicated that Moscow now sought to stabilize the status quo by holding on to what it had. Shunning proposals related specifically to Germany, the Russians suggested that the problem be set aside in favor of talks on an overall European security pact, which would lead to the easing of tensions (and the dismantling of NATO). Only with the establishment of a favorable new climate could serious discussions leading to German unity take place.

Reunification was thus turning into a chicken-and-egg problem. Though Eisenhower personally was less interested in the German question than in disarmament, the Americans believed as a matter of policy that starting with the European chicken instead of the German egg would confirm rather than ease the division of Germany. Rather than draw the line on this crucial issue, at the last moment the Russians consented to discuss the idea of reunification through free elections, along with general security matters, at a follow-up meeting of the foreign ministers to be held later in the year.

Adenauer realized that coupling broader European security issues to discussions of the German problem was an ominous development. Any tendency to superpower agreement, on force levels for example, that was not based on prior agreement on German unity would tend to make the status quo more acceptable. Once agreed on larger issues, the superpowers would no longer be inclined to rock the boat over Germany. German reunification would then automatically become a peripheral concern, and the drift toward two Germanys might harden into a mutually acceptable division of his country. The nagging fear of a deal being made behind his back led Adenauer repeatedly to seek reassurance from his friend Dulles that the Federal Republic was not being abandoned in its cradle.

In the foreign ministers' meetings in Geneva in October, the Soviet position was illuminating, because it unambiguously preferred to maintain the status quo in Germany. The Eden Plan was unacceptable, Molotov said, because it "ignore[d] the conditions actually existing in Germany" and might lead to "the violation of the vital interests of the working masses of the German Democratic Republic, to which one cannot agree."[10] To the creation of Western facts, the Soviets were opposing hard facts of their own, in the form of a two-Germanys policy.

In fact, they had begun as soon as the war was over to install their system in the East. Shortly before Hitler committed suicide, the Soviets flew in a number of Communist exiles from the Nazi era, including Walter Ulbricht, who with his long dominance of party leadership in the postwar era would be East Germany's answer to Adenauer. Realizing that the small German Communist Party (Kommunistiche Partei Deutschlands, or KPD) could not become the vehicle of mass control, in 1946 they forced a merger with the SPD that created the Socialist Unity Party (Sozialistische Einheitspartei Deutschlands, or SED), a merger with which Kurt Schumacher's western SPD refused to go along. Predictably, Moscow's men dominated this new organization. Using strong-arm tactics to intimidate opposing parties, the SED quickly took control of the eastern zone's political apparatus.

Unlike the Americans, the Soviets wasted no time in rearranging things to suit themselves. One of their first moves was a drastic land reform in which East Germany's large estates were broken up into small holdings that allowed 400,000 peasants to become landowners. The policy of reparations in kind was abandoned in 1946 as Moscow came to realize that most of the purloined equipment lay rusting on railroad sidings. Instead, the Russians acquired majority ownership of stock in more than two hundred firms—SAGs they were called (Sowjetische Aktiengesellschaften)—whose production was requisitioned for Soviet use as reparations. Through this device the Russians acquired perhaps as much as twice the 10 billion dollars that they had demanded at Yalta and Potsdam. The actual exaction of reparations turned out to be much less of a problem than the diplomatic wrangling over dollar amounts had suggested.

The degree to which Stalin had been committed to the East German regime is a matter of conjecture. He was clearly concerned about conditions

in West Germany, enough so at least to make frequent overtures toward unification on a neutralist basis that would have spelled finis for the Ulbricht
regime. And while Western statesmen suspected that Stalin's unification
proposals were designed with an eye to communization of the entire country,
there are those who argue to the contrary, that a German Communist behemoth would have constituted so great a challenge to Soviet leadership that
its creation was to be avoided at all costs. In any case, once the Soviets lost
their ability to influence developments in the West, Stalin's successors
decided to strive for the stability of Ulbricht's government in the East. The
uprising in Berlin in June 1953, fueled by frustration at harsh living conditions, was a landmark, for it marked the end of the USSR's exploitative
treatment of the eastern zone.

In the early 1950s the Soviets had been willing to grant concessions in
response to Western initiatives, but now they sought to make clear that the
time for making deals was over. In 1954, the Russians announced that they
were granting sovereignty to the DDR. This was a move the West refused to
acknowledge, especially as it might prejudice their position in Berlin. The
Americans let it be known that no decision regarding the future of Berlin
and no actions prejudicial to Allied rights could be taken without their consent. One week following the Federal Republic's formal entry into NATO,
the Warsaw Pact was signed and East Germany was integrated into the
Soviet military alliance.

In response, the Federal Republic became adamant in its opposition to the
trend toward two Germanys. It refused to recognize the DDR, those countries that did recognize this hated regime, and the permanency of the postwar
borders. For Adenauer and his countrymen, East Germany was always
referred to as "*die Zone*," the Soviet occupation zone, while the government
next door was always the "so-called Deutsche Demokratische Republik."
More unyieldingly yet, many West Germans insisted on referring to it as
Mitteldeutschland, the clear implication being that even the lost territories
further to the east would one day be recovered.

Increasingly the foreign policy of the Bundesrepublik came to rely on
diplomatic incantations by which it sought to dispel unpleasant realities.
The Western powers did provide a small measure of comfort to the West
Germans by refusing to recognize the sovereign status of East Germany's
Pankow regime (Pankow being the suburb of Berlin where it made its home),
but this did so little to stem the tide toward permanent separation that Bonn
felt compelled to take further action. In December 1955, it enunciated the
"Hallstein Doctrine," a policy of refusing to have diplomatic relations with
any nation that recognized the government of the eastern zone. The doctrine
was most effective with Asian and third world nations that counted on the
Federal Republic's generous aid programs.

Ironically, the trend toward lasting estrangement received an unexpected
boost when Adenauer decided to fly to Moscow in September 1955.

Adenauer had been invited by the Soviets after the Geneva summit to discuss the establishment of diplomatic relations. No doubt as the result of the failure of four-power discussions, they viewed this as a fitting way of promoting the two-Germany concept. Perhaps aware that the opportunity for unification was rapidly being passed on for settlement from diplomacy to history, Adenauer revived Western apprehensions of a second Rapallo by entering the bear's cave. After consulting with his allies, he reassured the public that he was going to discuss unification and claimed brazenly that the Soviet offer constituted, in point of fact, "a success for the consistent and determined policy of the West."[11]

Whatever hopes Adenauer had of serious discussions on reunification were quickly deflated as the Russians pushed hard for the recognition of two Germanys in the interest of a general relaxation of East-West tensions. As Adenauer's diplomatic advisor, Herbert Blankenhorn, noted in his diary: "We had the impression that the Soviet point of view has significantly hardened, and that the Russians will not—certainly for a long time—let the East zone out of their sphere of influence." The visit featured some rough-and-tumble sessions, punctuated by shouting, cursing, and fist-waving, in which Adenauer and Khrushchev exchanged recriminations about the past.

The meeting ended with an agreement to establish diplomatic relations in exchange for the release of some 10,000 German prisoners of war still interned by the Soviets as "war criminals," these being the only survivors of some 750,000 deported to the USSR following the war to provide reconstruction labor. Adenauer insisted that this deal in no way prejudiced the Hallstein Doctrine or the drive toward unification, but U.S. ambassador to Moscow Charles Bohlen angrily disagreed. Bohlen was "astonished when [Adenauer] buckled" to a Soviet tactic that was transparently intended to "formalize the division of Germany."[12] As if to underline the point, immediately following Adenauer's departure the Soviets formally recognized the sovereignty of the DDR.

The nuclearization of NATO's military strategy led to further setbacks in Adenauer's policy of reunification through strength, and in addition highlighted the Bundesrepublik's inferior status in the alliance. One of Eisenhower's abiding principles was a determination to hold down military budgets so as not to be bankrupted by the expense of waging the cold war. Seeking "more bang for the buck," his administration began increasingly to rely on nuclear weapons rather than on (presumably) more-expensive foot soldiers as a deterrent against Soviet expansion in Europe. As early as 1954, Supreme Commander General Alfred Gruenther of NATO had concluded that any major war in Europe would "inevitably be atomic," and U.S. forces in Europe were rapidly being equipped with nuclear arms.

In June 1955, the press leaked a proposal by Admiral Arthur Radford, chairman of the Joint Chiefs, that advocated reducing U.S. conventional forces by some 800,000 men in order to concentrate on nuclear deterrence.

The Radford proposals were never translated into policy, thanks in large measure to Adenauer's determined lobbying with Dulles and even with members of the Democratic Party. Adenauer argued that the creation of the Bundeswehr, the new German army, had been a vote of confidence in America's continued commitment to station troops in Europe; a reduced force commitment could not help but weaken German and alliance morale. In a conversation with CIA director Allen Dulles, he contended that NATO was being threatened with "senility" at the very moment it was supposed to be coming of age.

Nevertheless, the nuclearization of NATO went forward, trailing controversy with every step. The NATO decision of December 1957 to authorize the use of tactical nuclear weapons was especially divisive, since many Europeans feared that a minor incident in Germany would escalate to the point that all Europe would become an atomic battlefield. It was no secret—indeed, the effectiveness of policy depended on its being public knowledge—that the Eisenhower administration was fully prepared to use these weapons first, if need be, to compensate for NATO's conventional inferiority. The issue was made more urgent by the seductive argument, advanced at the time by Henry Kissinger and others, that a war fought with tactical nuclear arms could be successfully controlled without further escalation to the strategic level of all-out "spasm" war.

For nervous Europeans, this raised the horrifying prospect that Europe's defense might actually be "decoupled" from that of the continental United States. That is, a nuclear war could be fought solely on European territory, leaving the superpowers untouched. The Soviet launch of the first earth satellite, Sputnik, in August 1957 added to these fears, for the U.S. policy of massive retaliation lost what credibility it had possessed when the Russians acquired an intercontinental retaliatory capacity. As the calamitous consequences of starting a nuclear war became clear, the willingness to start an all-out conflict over some local confrontation became less and less credible.

Understandably, many Europeans were not enthralled at the prospect of the two giants fighting to the death of the last European. Though the term "tactical" suggested otherwise, the explosive force of these weapons was roughly equivalent to that of the devices dropped on Hiroshima and Nagasaki at the end of World War II. Their devastating power was amply driven home by the results of a NATO exercise named Carte Blanche, held in June 1955, which showed that an attack on military targets by 355 bombs would leave a total of 1,700,000 dead and 3,500,000 wounded, without including the indirect effects of lethal radiation released by the bombs. The conclusions derived from the exercise directly contradicted Adenauer's assertion that membership in NATO would no longer make the Federal Republic of Germany the battlefield of Europe. As his critics saw it, the Bundeswehr was contributing not to defense, but to a nuclear catastrophe that would obliterate the nation.

There was, however, a flip side to these criticisms of nuclear policy, for the absence of a nuclear deterrent seemed an open invitation for Soviet arms to overrun a supine and defenseless Europe. Given these contradictory fears, and Western Europe's reluctance to build up its armies to a level where conventional deterrence alone would suffice, the concern for economy overrode all else. By default, the Europeans settled for a "trip wire" or "plate glass" defense, in which sacrificial ground troops would sound the alarm and slow the Soviets until American nuclear arms took over.

Although Adenauer originally had his doubts about the nuclear strategy, it was not long before he and his defense minister, Franz Josef Strauss, became stalwart supporters of the American position, but not before the policy of nuclear deterrence had cast doubt upon the dogma of reunification through strength. After all, why should the Soviets negotiate when they, too, possessed the deterrent? Predictably, the Social Democrats deplored nuclear deterrence, not only for its inhumanity but also because it seemed to prove that the policy of rearmament relentlessly pursued by Adenauer was a self-defeating charade.

The growing reliance on nuclear weaponry was prompted also by the chronic failure of NATO to build up to agreed troop levels. Like its fellow NATO members, the Bundesrepublik took advantage of America's nuclear pennypinching to lower the projected size of the Bundeswehr. At the time of its admission to NATO, it was expected that West Germany would contribute a force of some 500,000 men. By the end of 1956, only 67,000 men had been raised for the new army, and there were only 230,000 by the end of 1959, despite Dulles's active prodding. When Strauss became defense minister in 1956, he cut the force goals for the Bundeswehr for 1957 and reset the final total force goal to 325,000, while reducing the period of conscription from eighteen to twelve months. These reductions were a response to the cutbacks envisioned in the Radford Plan, despite the fact that the admiral's proposals were never adopted and even though Dulles consistently promised not to reduce the American troop commitment. If the intention was to keep American troops in Germany, this proved to be an excellent means of assuring their continuing presence.

For many, the real specter haunting the nuclear issue was the prospect that the Federal Republic would in due time seek nuclear arms for itself. Despite repeated past disavowals of any such ambition, by September 1956 the chancellor was requesting nuclear weapons for his new army, with the warheads to be kept under American control, arguing that the general European failure to meet troop commitments made a conventional defense uncredible. The more likely reason was the desire for equality. With the almost certain prospect that Bonn's NATO allies were about to begin national nuclear development programs, the resulting inferiority of the Federal Republic to her partners would undercut Adenauer's position in the Bundestag and make less believable the argument of unification through strength. Thus he put in his bid for nuclear parity by insisting that "Germans must adapt themselves to new circumstances."[13]

Seeking to lessen the shock of this change of position, Adenauer claimed in 1957 that tactical nuclear weapons represented "nothing more than a development of artillery." The following year, Strauss argued that "those who ask us—quite rightly—to accept Soviet power as a reality should after all not deny their own people the right and opportunity to become likewise a reality."[14] In the spring of 1958, Adenauer pushed through the Bundestag a vote favoring the acquisition of nuclear arms, but not without an extraordinarily acrimonious debate and massive demonstrations throughout the country organized under the name *Kampf dem Atomtod* (Struggle against Atomic Death).

Over the next few years, the Bonn government would be given access to some nuclear-capable delivery systems (not to nuclear warheads, which remained under American ownership and control), but the issue refused to die and continued to generate dissension in NATO. With France and Great Britain going ahead with the development of their own nuclear deterrents, some relatively noncontroversial method would have to be found to prevent the Federal Republic from becoming a second-class citizen of the alliance.

Although George Kennan desired the contrary, a clear sign that the sands of the hourglass had run out for negotiation was provided by his 1957 series of Oxford lectures, which briefly shook the alliance. Kennan had never liked a militarized NATO, since he did not define the Soviet danger in military terms. A more catty view had it that "he probably disliked NATO because he had neglected to invent it."[15] Originally conceived as a means, NATO appeared to have become an end in itself, blocking rather than furthering negotiations. Concerned that the installation of tactical nuclear weapons in Germany would hopelessly complicate the task of ending the division of Europe and Germany, Kennan went public with the themes of neutralization and disengagement he had been privately advocating since 1949.

Kennan argued that the American and West German position was unrealistic, since it expected the Russians to acquiesce to a unified Germany, married to NATO, without receiving anything in return. It was possible the Kremlin would not want a unified Germany under any conditions, but Kennan felt the only way to find out was through serious talks. Failing those, he glimpsed a dark future: the eventual weakening of Western resolve to hang on to the exposed position in Berlin, a tense situation in the heart of Europe, where two nuclear-equipped armies stood face to face, and the consignment, by implication, of Eastern Europe to Soviet control. Not least, the German problem would remain a time bomb waiting to explode the peace in Europe. Might not a West Germany eventually armed with nuclear weapons feel tempted to strike a separate deal with the Russians? Finally, Kennan wondered whether the American nuclear presence, by encouraging among otherwise vigorous European states an undesirable syndrome of dependency, was not unnatural, for both parties. He doubted whether the United States could be counted on indefinitely to garrison troops on the Continent. Should the United States one day, for reasons of its own, wish to reduce its troop commitments, what then?

Kennan's critique evoked much sympathy among those in European circles who were searching with increasing desperation for a solution to the division of Europe before the point of no return had been reached. The Polish foreign minister, Adam Rapacki, moved by the prospect of a Bundesrepublik gone nuclear, suggested a nuclear-free zone in the heart of Europe. Britain's Labour Party leader, Hugh Gaitskell, was thinking along similar lines, as were Conservative leaders Macmillan and Eden. Predictably, the idea appealed most strongly to the Social Democrats in Germany, for whom Adenauer's policy of unquestioned allegiance to the West had always seemed a grave mistake.

On balance, however, the reaction to Kennan's eloquent plea for reconsideration was intensely, even vehemently, critical. As one might expect, the architects of the current policy of double containment—Acheson, Dulles, Adenauer—unanimously rejected his views. "Poor George," said Acheson pityingly to his friends, as if Kennan had taken leave of his senses. In a rebuttal in the journal *Foreign Affairs*, Acheson argued that abandoning the American presence in Germany, regardless of Soviet good faith, was unthinkable. "Disengagement—it is called now; but it is the same futile and lethal attempt to crawl back into the cocoon of history."[16] If it came to pass, the West would live in constant dread of "a sort of new Ribbentrop-Molotov agreement." Dulles fully agreed, arguing that a neutral, united Germany "would be under an almost irresistible temptation to play one side or the other, and that this would be a very dangerous situation, dangerous for the West, dangerous for the Soviet Union and dangerous for the Germans themselves."[17]

Most telling of all was the criticism offered by the French intellectual Raymond Aron, who saw the division of Germany as a solution preferable to all others. Arguing along the same lines, Walter Lippmann, who for the past decade had agreed with Kennan, now reversed himself in a series of influential newspaper columns. According to Lippmann, the partition of Germany was no tragedy but instead was "regarded on both sides as not intolerable, and on the whole, preferable to reunification."[18] Lippmann predicted that "what we are going to see, it seems to me, is—as unfortunately only the Russians have had the wit to suggest—negotiations between the two German governments." These talks would result in "some sort of political arrangement which might one day take the form of a dual state."[19] Arguments like these led Kennan to believe that he had smoked out the West's dirty little secret. As he put it, "The pious lip service to the cause of German unification on the part of all the Western statesmen from Adenauer down was the sheerest hypocrisy."[20] Ordinarily an analyst of great refinement, Kennan here resorted to the crudest of explanations, one that would unfortunately have great appeal. Kennan had won acclaim as an acute critic of his country's childish idealism, but he now imagined a cynicism on its part that would have made Machiavelli blush. Indeed, he came perilously close to assuming the kind of tacit East-West complicity that right-wing critics of FDR claimed lay at the heart of the Yalta settlement.

It is true that the American proposals since 1947 were artful. They had been designed for their influence on public opinion at home and abroad, in the certainty that they could not be accepted by the Soviets. Undoubtedly, too, there were many Europeans for whom the situation was a happy one, like the Frenchman who is supposed to have said: "I like Germany so much that I am happy that there are two of them." Nevertheless, when Dulles characterized the continued partition of Germany as "a scandal" and "a crime,"[21] this was not artifice, nor did it mean that German reunification was not an authentic American goal. True, American policymakers had always subordinated German unification to the more urgent need to strengthen western Europe's defenses. But keeping the Federal Republic tied to NATO meant that the German dream of unity could not be casually dismissed. "We have got to keep our allies," said Eisenhower. In contemplating this issue, a breakaway West Germany, disillusioned with half-hearted western support for unity, was not difficult to imagine.[22]

Kennan failed to realize that the position held by Aron and Lippmann required just as great a change in the American mentality toward the cold war in Europe as it did in the German. To deliberately seek a balance of power and to have one forced on you are not the same thing. Otherwise the two parties could quite easily have reached an agreement on the partition of Europe based on the military balance obtaining at the end of World War II. But instead of realpolitik, the American position was based on a frustrating search for victory in a cold war whose first rule was survival. That victory, it was believed, would also solve the German problem. It was only as the need for cooperation with the USSR, however unpalatable, became undeniable that the search for a path to German unification would be called off.

That need was not yet apparent in the 1950s. Kennan's faith in change through diplomacy, and his belief that it had been cynically rejected, failed to take account of the seriousness with which American policymakers viewed the cold war as a historical struggle not resolvable by diplomacy. To acquiesce openly to the permanent division of Germany would have seemed an act of appeasement. The absence of cynical collaboration with the Russians, of under-the-table kicks and sly winks, was made plain by the ambiguities of the American response to the second Berlin crisis, which lasted, on and off, from 1958 to 1961.

Berlin possessed no strategic value—on the contrary, its enclave status made it a distinct liability, with the exception perhaps of its espionage value—but it was a potent symbol. For the West Germans, Berlin was and would remain the capital of a united Germany. Should it come under East German control, as the Soviets desired, the division of Germany would take on a symbolic finality most Germans were not willing to accept. For this reason, and because all great capitals require costly cultural institutions—museums, symphonies, educational institutions, buildings of all kinds—the West Germans were willing to sacrifice financially for Berlin.

Berlin was also a symbol of an occupation that had never ended and a peace that had never been concluded. West Berlin remained under four-power control, despite Bonn's desire to extend its authority there, because the Allies, anticipating an eventual end to the cold war, insisted on maintaining their right to decide the final terms of Germany's destiny. Nevertheless, the Federal Republic took great pains to make the city a de facto part of West Germany. Laws and treaties were crafted so as to apply as much as possible to West Berlin, generous subsidies allowed West Berlin to balance its budget, and from time to time symbolic meetings of the Bundestag were held in the city.

The city was also a sensitive symbol of cold war determination in the struggle for world opinion, for once the pebble of doubt was allowed to slide down the mountainside, the avalanche of defeatism seemed sure to follow. It was a particularly vulnerable symbol, too. "Berlin is the testicles of the West," said Khrushchev. "Every time I give them a yank they holler."[23] Though West Berlin contained no NATO forces, its defense was assured by numerous alliance guarantees. Precisely because of its militarily naked position, the Soviets could take no action without seeming to be indecent bullies and suffering a massive propaganda defeat.

Berlin in the 1950s was unique because, as an open city, it was the only meeting point between East and West in which the Iron Curtain did not get in the way. Until 1961, nearly 100,000 workers traveled back and forth across city borders to their jobs. The glittering Western showcase, with its bonanza of consumer goods, stood in reproachful contrast to the shabby and meagerly provisioned East, where crowds formed in the department stores merely to get limited allocations of detergent. The East German population found it easy to judge for itself the relative benefits of two contrasting ways of life.

The open borders also made it possible for East Germans fed up with life in the Soviet zone to flee to the West. All that was required was a five-cent subway ride, or a simple street crossing, into one of the Western sectors, where one could declare one's intentions and be spirited away by airplane to the Federal Republic. All-German elections had never been held, but those in the East could vote with their feet. Of course, the traffic went two ways, but the overall flow of population was overwhelmingly to the West, thus highlighting the unpopularity and artificiality of the entire Communist system. Said one refugee in 1960: "I was in West Berlin once before, eight years ago, and the lights and displays in the shop windows were something I just couldn't forget."[24] Berlin was thus more than symbolic. It was a fluid stream in an otherwise frozen cold war landscape.

Following the airlift, the city underwent a severe economic crisis, with heavy unemployment, but the boom of the 1950s and subsidies from Bonn restored it to a pulsing cosmopolitan prosperity. Berlin became an active center of commerce, an intellectual and artistic mecca, an international conference center, a tourist attraction—all in addition to its role as a sanctuary for escapees from the East.

Since the end of the blockade in 1949, the Berlin problem had been on the back burner. Throughout the middle of the decade, in addition to everpresent fears that, present prosperity notwithstanding, West Berlin might be a dying city, there had been occasional causes for concern. The failure of the Western powers to respond with more than words to the June 1953 East Berlin uprising was interpreted by some to mean that their resolve to hold on to West Berlin was not of the highest order. The patent unwillingness of the Western powers to stand up vigorously to a series of administrative harassments also bespoke a disposition to appeasement. For instance, they accepted a 10,000-foot ceiling in the air corridors, compromised over Soviet paperwork requirements for access and egress from the city, and put up with occasional delays on the autobahns.

So long as affairs remained at this level of petty annoyances, the status quo was clearly acceptable to the West. However, it was becoming increasingly intolerable to the Soviets. If Berlin for the West was a militarily exposed nerve, for the Russians it was, as Khrushchev said, "a bone in my throat." The population of the German Democratic Republic, which stood at 18 million in 1949, was reduced by emigration to about 16 million twelve years later. Moreover, an alarmingly high proportion of the refugees were young professionals and technically skilled people who despaired of being rewarded for their talents. These were precisely the kind of people indispensable to the functioning of a modern industrial economy.

For the USSR to make a success of a two-Germanys policy, it would have to stanch this debilitating flow of talent; either that, or leave its client state a bloodless corpse. From Khrushchev's perspective, the DDR was submitting to a blood-letting at the hands of the West. In his words, the "drain of workers was creating a simply disastrous situation in the DDR, which was already suffering from a shortage of manual labor, not to mention specialized labor."[25] Having failed to reach a negotiated solution to the German problem, he determined to achieve one unilaterally if need be.

The second Berlin crisis began in November 1958, when Khrushchev announced that the time had come to "renounce the remnants of the occupation regime in Berlin." A note delivered to the Western powers shortly thereafter expanded the argument. Berlin, intended to be the seat of the Control Council and to symbolize Allied unity, had instead become "a dangerous center of contradiction between the Great Powers . . . a smoldering fuse that has been connected to a powder keg." Citing the inability to agree on the basis of the Potsdam accords, it argued that "an obviously absurd situation" had arisen in which the Soviets were supporting a virtual NATO outpost at the expense of its Warsaw Pact allies. Of all the Allied agreements on Germany, the only one still being carried out was the one on the quadripartite status of Berlin. Inasmuch as earlier agreements had been overtaken by events of the past thirteen years, the Soviets declared that henceforth they also considered both Potsdam and the presurrender Berlin agreements to be null and void.

Then the note resorted to the carrot-and-stick approach. The USSR threatened that if a suitable accord was not reached on Berlin within six months, it would sign a separate peace treaty with the DDR and hand over control of traffic to the East Germans. This would force the West to deal with Pankow, a regime it did not recognize, in which case four-power control would be effectively at an end. Or, if it continued to insist on its occupation rights, it would run the risk of creating an explosive incident.

On the other hand, the Soviets offered a "concession" in the prospect of transforming West Berlin into a demilitarized "free city," with a "decent standard of living" assured for the city's population by trade with East and West, free of any foreign interference. But this free city would have to make its own arrangements with the DDR, while East Berlin would become the capital of East Germany. Either way, from the Western point of view, Berlin's status would be transformed and a new reality of two Germanys established.

Underscoring their seriousness, the Soviets concluded with a warning to those who would be willing to risk war for the defense of Berlin: "If such madmen should really appear, there is no doubt that strait jackets could be found for them."[26] Thus began a three-year war of nerves in which the Soviets turned tension on and off like a spigot. With great fanfare they would dramatically announce new deadlines, thereby building up suspense, only to mention casually later that they had been allowed to lapse.

Instead of offering enticements to German unity, as in the past, the Soviets now sought to unmask the official Western policy of unification as a sham. In an interview with SPD leaders in Moscow in 1959, Khrushchev threw cold water on their unification schemes that involved elections, holding that "the majority would win, not the truth" and adding that no one wanted reunification anyway, "not even in the west."[27] He had once told Eisenhower the same thing, that Adenauer's support of unification was "nothing but a show."[28]

The West had been given three basic choices: to accept Soviet terms and admit the hollowness of its German policy; to refuse the Soviet offer, which would likely cause a new blockade and increase dramatically the likelihood of war; or to bargain, which would mean giving up some rights. These were not very desirable options, and, understandably, the Eisenhower administration chose an option labelled "none of the above." Less understandable was the position it adopted: to stand up to the Soviets, but with an obvious reluctance to go to war; to negotiate, but without really giving anything away.

The initial American response was shaky. Though John Foster Dulles had only recently affirmed the United States' determination to defend its rights in Berlin, "if need be by military force," he was sounding less than militant as the crisis began. The day before the Soviet note was received, he had mused publicly about the possibility of accepting the DDR as "agents" of the Soviet Union. Dulles did not believe that Americans could get worked up over who was stamping documents. Instead of girding its loins for battle, the administration did not seriously reconsider its planned troop reductions in the light of the crisis and chose not to respond with limited military force to Soviet harassments of U.S. army convoys on the autobahn. Instead, it decided to stand pat with its increasingly implausible policy of "massive retaliation."

Eisenhower's first reaction to Khrushchev's challenge was decidedly lacking in aggressive enthusiasm. "How, or rather why did the Free World get into this mess?" he wondered. In press conferences and meetings with the congressional leadership, he disavowed any desire for a military showdown over Berlin. The United States "should not look upon this as a Berlin crisis," he said, but as part of a long-range war of nerves that would span decades to come. "You've got to be prepared to live with a series of Berlins for the next forty years."[29] In saying this, Ike was trying to maintain a sense of proportion, but the effect of such comments was to suggest a less than absolute American commitment to the city.

The president, as his biographer makes clear, "let Khrushchev know that although he was standing firm, he was willing to negotiate Berlin's status."[30] Eisenhower was favorably disposed to making all of Berlin a free city, but not West Berlin alone. As a sign of flexibility, early in 1959 Dulles held out the possibility of solutions to the German problem other than those based solely on the unworkable free elections doctrine.

But Adenauer, as usual, was suspicious of any negotiations. During the chancellor's trip to Washington in the spring of 1959, Ike noted that he had "developed almost a psychopathic fear of what he considers to be British weakness."[31] With good reason, too, for the British were showing a disposition to make a deal with the DDR and put an end to the West's constantly being held hostage over the Berlin issue. "Britain will not be atomized over the stamping of papers," was how one Englishman put it.[32] They believed that there was no reason that a deal with the DDR could not be made that would leave Allied rights in Berlin intact.

The initial lack of American vigor sent Adenauer into a state of near shock, but it was not long before Dulles began to offer the desired reassurances. Citing the provocative nature of Soviet diplomacy, Dulles, who was rapidly weakening from terminal cancer, nevertheless sounded once again like the cold warrior of old. "I am now forced to the abyss," he said. "I do not go there of my own volition. But when I am there, I am not willing to retreat."[33] Eisenhower soon expressed similar sentiments. Despite his equivocal press conference remarks on the use of military force, his tone in the National Security Council was deadly serious: "Khrushchev should know that when we act, our whole stack will be in the pot," he said.[34]

By January 1959, American policy was beginning to stiffen, as contingency plans for military escalation were made and quiet measures of military preparation in Europe were taken. In a phone call to Dulles, Ike vented his spleen: "Somewhere along the line we have to find a way to say that we are going to do what we want to do."[35] The administration decided to resist even the most minor displays of East German control over military traffic. And in March, the United States sent a strong signal to Moscow by flying a C-130 transport through the air corridor above the 10,000-foot ceiling unilaterally established by the Soviets.

Still, Eisenhower had concluded that negotiations in this situation were possible. In the 1940s it had been the Americans who believed that deals with the Russians could be made only at the top, but now the Soviets were the ones plainly more eager to play the summit game. Ike was more deliberate, preferring instead a meeting of foreign ministers that, if it showed promise, would lead to a full-scale summit conference. He turned aside British prime minister Harold Macmillan's ardent pleas for a top-level pow-wow by deflating the importance attached to summitry. As he would later tell Khrushchev, he thought that political summits, like mountain peaks, were normally barren.[36] With Macmillan's help, Moscow accepted Eisenhower's two-stage approach to negotiations.

The foreign ministers, with Christian Herter now representing the United States, following Dulles's resignation, met in Geneva from 11 May through 5 August 1959. Both sides trotted out their fusty formulas, but the Allies added a new wrinkle by indicating their willingness to limit their garrisons in the city, to forgo the introduction of nuclear weapons, and to have some clerical duties performed by German personnel—all this pending the holding of free German elections, of course.

Though some observers professed to see a dangerous disposition to soften in the West's positions, the two sides were in truth farther removed than ever from an agreement. In any case, the inconclusive conference proceedings were overshadowed in July by the announcement, after much confusion in Washington regarding the issuance of an invitation, of Khrushchev's acceptance of a long-awaited invitation to visit the United States that autumn.

The Khrushchev visit to the United States in September 1959 gave birth to what was called the "spirit of Camp David." In private talks at the president's retreat in the Maryland mountains, the Soviet boss agreed to remove the Berlin time limit on the understanding that the issue would be resolved through negotiation. Eisenhower's memoirs give the impression that Khrushchev caved in, but records of the meeting reveal a far more ambivalent president. Ike agreed that "the present situation in Berlin is abnormal" and requested a delay, as Khrushchev later reported, "because American prestige was involved."[37] Indeed, at a press conference following Khrushchev's departure, Eisenhower used the word "abnormal," although he emphasized that a solution acceptable to all, including the West Berliners, had to be found. Ike finally agreed to the long-anticipated summit, to be held the following year in Paris, in return for an end to Soviet ultimatums on Berlin.

Whether or not progress would have resulted is impossible to tell. Certainly the West was no longer as dogmatic about Germany or Berlin as it had been. Eisenhower, for one, was increasingly "coming to the view that complete reunification of the two parts of Germany is not going to be achieved early."[38] In his last conversation with Adenauer, Eisenhower noticed a similar realism emerging on reunification from *der Alte*. Adenauer reportedly acknowledged that "the end would have to be achieved in a step-by-step process in which the two sides of Germany would themselves have to exhibit a clear readiness to be conciliatory and reasonable."[39]

The Paris summit never got to address the subjects of Germany and Berlin. Indeed, it broke up before it began as a result of the dramatic U-2 incident (the U-2 was a high-altitude American reconnaissance plane). When Khrushchev revealed that such a plane had been shot down over Soviet territory by anti-aircraft missiles and that the pilot was still alive, Eisenhower took full responsibility but refused to apologize. Khrushchev in turn threw a monumental tantrum and stalked out of the summit. As he said, when Eisenhower "offered us his back end . . . we obliged by kicking it as hard as we could." Fears that he would use the occasion to relight the fuse on Berlin were stilled when he once again pushed back the Berlin deadline pending another summit in six to eight months—that is, following an attempt to strike a deal with a new administration in Washington.

The youthful new U.S. president, John F. Kennedy, came to office as a cold warrior determined to dispel the lethargy of the preceding administration. He was well aware that one of the time bombs that he would inherit from Eisenhower was Berlin, which was, as he later told Acheson, "the most difficult and decisive question of all." He envisioned the possibility of minor changes, perhaps a thinning out of forces and an agreement to end propaganda in return for assured access, but thought that at best "both sides might reach a precarious balance" that was sure to remain for many years.[40]

Though Kennedy, too, was suspicious of the pitfalls of summitry, he agreed to test the political waters in a meeting with Khrushchev in Vienna in June of 1961. In the meantime, Khrushchev launched another campaign for a solution to the German problem. In February, he informed the West Germans that there was no longer any reason for delay. As for Berlin, he continued with his calls for the removal of "this splinter from the heart of

Europe" and urged the West to face the fact that there were now "two German nations in two states."[41]

There was conflicting counsel in the administration. Some, like Senator J. William Fulbright, looked kindly on the idea of establishing Berlin as a free city, somewhat on the pattern of the Vatican. Others, like Dean Acheson, who had been asked by Kennedy to make a special study of the Berlin problem, proposed sterner measures: that in the event of a Soviet provocation, the United States should send an armed column down the autobahn and proceed with military measures as called for. He did not flinch from the consequences: "If the Russians repulsed the probe, then at least the west would know where it stood, and it could rally and rearm as it did during the Korean war."[42]

Kennedy was clearly displeased with this option, since the local superiority of Russian forces meant that there would be little time available before the United States would be forced to swing its nuclear club. Nevertheless, he accepted Acheson's argument that the Soviet pressure "had nothing to do with Berlin, Germany or Europe," but was instead designed "to test the general American will to resist."[43] Redefining the domino theory to fit his administration's virile self-image, Kennedy chose to view Berlin as an all-absorbing battle of wills. As in an arm-wrestling match, the slightest lapse in concentration would bring total defeat.

The meeting at Vienna was a communications disaster. Kennedy had hoped to warn Khrushchev, as he informed General de Gaulle, that "if necessary, we would go to nuclear war" over Berlin. Instead, it appears that Khrushchev sent most of the messages at the meeting, and it is unclear how Kennedy's warnings were taken. Published reports described Kennedy as "shaken and angry" at having been bullied and threatened. According to Kennan, he had been "a tongue-tied young man."

At Vienna, Khrushchev set a new deadline of December 1961, following which he would proceed unilaterally with a peace treaty. If the West challenged it, there would be war. Kennedy could do little but restate his determination to safeguard the West's right of access to Berlin and, in response to Khrushchev's repeated thrusts, inform him that it would be "a cold winter." To demonstrate their seriousness and put Kennedy on the spot, a few days following the meeting the Soviets published the aide-memoire that Khrushchev had used as his talking paper.

Unlike the Eisenhower administration's quiet response in 1958, Kennedy went on national television following his return home to report the total lack of agreement. On 25 July, he used television once again to deliver a dramatic speech designed to mobilize American public opinion for the upcoming test of wills (he was so successful that he started a fallout-shelter scare). He announced stepped-up draft calls and the calling up of reserves, and requested a sizable increase in military appropriations. These measures were intended to increase American credibility in a crisis and to expand the amount of time available for talks before the flare-up would go nuclear. Kennedy reasoned that "if Mr. Khrushchev believes that all we have is the atomic bomb, he is going to feel that we are . . . somewhat unlikely to use it."[44]

In the televised speech, he argued that Berlin was "the great testing place of Western courage and will." The city was "essential to the morale and security of Western Germany, to the unity of Western Europe, and to the faith of the entire free world." It was "the focal point where our solemn commitments . . . and Soviet ambitions now meet in basic confrontation." Everything was reduced to this one single issue: Berlin was "the touchstone of American honor and resolve." "If we do not meet our commitments in Berlin, where will we later stand?" he asked. It was also a personal test. As Robert Kennedy recalled, in the wake of the Bay of Pigs fiasco JFK was anxious to dispel Khrushchev's belief that "the President was not going to be a strong figure."

Kennedy was particularly concerned to combat the impression, as a remark attributed to the outgoing Soviet ambassador had it, that "when the chips are down, the American people won't fight." Khrushchev's rhetoric had been extraordinarily bellicose, adverting repeatedly to the horrible prospect of all-out war while he washed his hands of any responsibility. For example, John McCloy, during an audience with Khrushchev at the end of July, was treated to a tirade in which the Russian leader insisted that American policy would lead to war and vowed, when it came, that Kennedy "would be the last president."

When at length the Soviets and East Germans moved, it came as a stunning surprise. Negotiations having failed, and with the flood of refugees who correctly surmised that the status quo was nearing its end approaching 30,000 per month—more than 4,000 crossed over on 12 August alone—the situation for the DDR was becoming intolerable. The DDR had already lost millions of its population through this leaching away of its citizenry during the preceding years. On Sunday, 13 August, the East Germans began erecting a barbed-wire fence around all 104 miles of West Berlin's periphery. This monstrosity, which was later replaced by a permanent concrete structure, quickly became known as the Berlin wall (the East Germans, placing a defensive interpretation on its construction, preferred to call it a rampart).

Early in August, Kennedy had surmised that something of the sort might occur: "Khrushchev is losing East Germany. He cannot let that happen. If East Germany goes, so will Poland and all of eastern Europe. He will have to do something to stop the flow of refugees—perhaps a wall. And we won't be able to prevent it."[45] But this had been only speculation. Despite a variety of signs that West Berlin would be sealed off, Western expectations and planning were geared to a challenge of their access rights.

The Berlin wall was technically a violation of the four-power agreement, but the Soviets gambled that the West would not view it as a fundamental challenge to West Berlin's existence or to the Western right of access.

Kennedy's concern, as Berliners discovered to their sorrow, was focused mainly on West Berlin. As for access rights to the East, those were Allied rights, which did not extend to Berliners and therefore did not apply to the severance of human contacts.

Furious but impotent, Kennedy chose not to challenge the barrier and settled for reaffirming his intention of staying in Berlin by sending an armored column of 1,500 soldiers down the autobahn and through the checkpoints. Much to his relief, it went through unchallenged. At the same time, he sent Vice President Lyndon B. Johnson to rally the Berliners and, as a more permanent reassuring presence, Lucius Clay as his personal emissary.

If the point of the crisis was to demonstrate the resolve of the alliance, the unhappy truth was that the West staggered through the Berlin affair in considerable disarray. In a discussion with Vice President Johnson, Adenauer suggested economic sanctions and promised in return to extend the period of West German conscription. Johnson intimated that that was hardly enough. American determination, he said, "would be impaired only by [the] conviction that the United States was being asked to bear a disproportionate burden relative to others." Johnson also played down the relative importance of the wall by pointing out that Berlin was "only one battle, although an important one, in the worldwide struggle between communism and freedom."[46]

In response to impassioned requests for a stiffer American response, the comment of Charles Bohlen to West Berlin mayor Willy Brandt was typical of the aloof American attitude: "Other measures would not bring about the unsealing of the city and might indeed lead to a serious reaction by the other side." He opposed economic countermeasures since, once they were imposed, "we would be stuck with them indefinitely." And, perhaps most disheartening of all to Brandt's ears: "This was not the real Berlin crisis," Bohlen argued. "That will come only when the Russians try to interfere with the rights of the Allied powers."[47]

The Germans themselves were at sixes and sevens during the crisis. Adenauer, who reacted with an unexpected lassitude, was accused of caring more for the election campaign then in progress than for Berlin. Anticipating that a rapid appearance would lead to charges that he was using the crisis to electoral advantage, he waited ten days before visiting the city, only to be received without enthusiasm by the townspeople. "You have come too late, Herr Bundeskanzler," taunted the sarcastic hecklers.

The individual who emerged with the greatest credit for his display of energy and concern was the dynamic Mayor Willy Brandt, a Social Democrat. Brandt irritated the Americans by leaking a letter to JFK that demanded stronger action against the "consummate blackmail" of the Soviets. Admittedly at a loss as to how he would deal effectively with the situation, Brandt justified the action as a desperate attempt to get American policy off dead center. The Americans were understandably displeased at being accused of weakness when the whole point of the showdown was to demonstrate national resolve.[48]

The most dangerous event of the crisis was not the erection of the wall, but a tank confrontation at "Checkpoint Charlie," the Friedrichstrasse crossing point in the American sector. In October, East German border police began to demand identity papers from American personnel in civilian clothes. Fed up with the constant "salami tactics" by which the East Germans attempted to shave away American rights, Clay had American tanks rumble up to the wall, only to be matched by Soviet tanks in an eyeball-to-eyeball confrontation that lasted for a few days before the Soviets decided to withdraw their units.

The outcome of the Berlin crisis was a split decision in favor of the Soviets. The wall was in place, but the United States retained its rights in Berlin and demonstrated its determination to stay. Accentuating the positive, Walt Rostow of the National Security Council argued that "this crisis came about because of the extraordinary success of West Germany and West Berlin as compared to East Germany. This is the historical fact on which we should fasten our eyes."[49] Nevertheless, the American contention that the erection of the Berlin wall was a propaganda debacle for the Soviets and an embarrassing admission of the failure of a system that had to keep its people locked up—while certainly true—had a lame ring to it.

All eyes kept returning to the wall, which was, above all, an unwelcome monument to the fact of a division that was the main theme of Soviet diplomacy. No amount of forced good cheer could conceal the fact that Khrushchev had won a major victory in his battle to force the permanent acceptance of two Germanys. From this point onward, the DDR would be able to proceed with the building of socialism with a population resigned to the inevitable. As Khrushchev put it, without any humor intended, the wall "had a very positive effect on the consciousness of the people."[50] In a more thoughtful mode, he would later tell the German ambassador to Moscow that "I know that the Wall is an ugly thing. One day it will disappear again. Though not before the reasons that have led to its construction cease to apply."[51]

Thenceforth escapes from the East, by tunneling, balloon, and all sorts of ingenious methods, would inspire novels, films, and TV dramas, but desperate and courageous attempts at foiling the wall by would-be escapees from East Germany quickly slowed to a trickle and soon were shut off almost entirely by improved security measures. Moreover, American passivity soon made it distressingly clear that the United States accepted the wall. The Peter Fechter affair in August 1962, in which a young escapee was shot near the wall and lay bleeding to death for hours while Western authorities refused to help, was a shocking reminder of the new realities in Berlin.

Though assuring the continued economic viability of West Berlin would now become a major Western concern, economic collapse was less a threat than was psychological depression among the Berliners. Kennedy decided to pitch in by flying to Berlin in 1963 to offer some inspiring words. In a memorable open-air speech before an eager throng of West Berliners, Kennedy drew a thrilling picture of a free and united Germany and identified himself with German aspirations: "All free men, wherever they may live, are citizens of Berlin, and, therefore, as a free man, I take pride in the words *Ich bin ein Berliner*." Understandably, the words were met with a hungry roar of appreciation from the crowd. But the mistaken inclusion of the German article *ein*, which meant that the phrase translated literally as "I am a doughnut" (a *Berliner* being a local variant of the species), only proved what the phrase was intended to obscure: that Kennedy was not a Berliner and that his policies on Berlin and the issue of German unification would be made from an American perspective.

Kennedy was evoking passionate yearnings that he was not prepared to satisfy, for he was in reality quite content to live with a de facto two Germanys policy as the most sensible approach to the problem. In a speech at the Free University of Berlin, he indicated that enthusiastic American support for German unification, as provided in the past, could no longer be expected. The rationale behind this diminished ardor was revealing. To Kennedy's way of thinking, the Berlin confrontation had been harrowing enough, but the continued deterioration of the DDR would in all likelihood have set up a far more explosive situation in which the Soviet Union might have been faced with the crumbling of its entire Eastern European imperium. What ghastly sequence of events would have been played out then? The times certainly had changed. Whereas the Eisenhower administration had looked forward to the disintegration of the Eastern European empire, Kennedy shivered at its implications.

For the United States, Berlin had become a symbol without any Germanic content. The symbolism was about American determination to maintain the global order, not about German interests. It may at first seem ironic that as the symbolic value of Berlin in the cold war mushroomed to the point of U.S. willingness to go to war, its heightened significance was accompanied by a corresponding decline in the urgency attached to the German question. Actually, one was the cause of the other. As the Berlin crisis showed, the prospect of superpower confrontation made change too frightening to contemplate. The result was that any millennial illusions as to reunification were shattered. As General Clay said in September, the Germans would have to "accept reality."[52]

Although officials who were concerned with cold war credibility, like McGeorge Bundy, had argued successfully that "Berlin is no place for compromise," the Kennedy administration was much softer on Berlin and on German issues generally than its public rhetoric indicated. Shortly following the wall's erection, National Security Council staffer Carl Kaysen boldly suggested that, in return for suitable guarantees on Berlin and mutual security, the United States should recognize the DDR, accept the Oder-Neisse line, and negotiate an agreement that recognized that "reunification can come about only by discussion between the two German governments." Averell Harriman saw a similar deal in the offing, noting that "ever since Potsdam, I have been satisfied that Germany will be divided for a long time." Although it was politically impossible for Kennedy to seek an immediate bargain along those lines, his aide Theodore Sorensen recalled the president's later letting Khrushchev know that, following a decent interval of five or ten years, "we might well find that conditions in Germany or in our own country had changed so that a solution was possible which did not seem possible now." And so it would turn out.[53]

Konrad Adenauer signs the Basic Law creating the Federal Republic of
Germany, 23 May 1949. *All photographs in this section courtesy of
the Germany Information Center*

Berlin Wall at Potsdamer Platz

Berlin Wall crossing point

Memorial to a failed attempt to flee over the wall in Berlin

SPD leaders Kurt Schumacher (right) and Erich Ollenhauer in the Bundestag

Secretary of State John Foster Dulles and Vice President Richard Nixon greet Adenauer in Washington

Konrad Adenauer in 1960

Konrad Adenauer and Charles De Gaulle in Reims Cathedral, 1962:
American suspicions were aroused

President John F. Kennedy in Berlin, June 1963: his German was mangled, but they knew what he meant

Adenauer gives some pointers to his successor, Ludwig Erhard

Chancellor Willy Brandt drops to his knees at the Warsaw Ghetto
memorial, Warsaw, 1970

Helmut Schmidt and Jimmy Carter: a strained relationship

Jimmy Carter and Helmut Schmidt in one of their happier moments

Anti-nuclear rally, 1979

Anti-missile demonstra-
tion, June 1982

George Bush and Helmut Kohl: architects of German unification

Ronald Reagan meets with Helmut Kohl, a man "entirely different than his predecessor"

Petra Kelly of the
"Greens"

Meeting of federal delegates of the Green Party

After 45 years of division, Berliners celebrate a unified and sovereign Germany

Breaches in the Berlin Wall, November 1989

Visitors from East Germany being welcomed by West Berliners, 11 November 1989

Demonstrators in Dresden, East Germany: "We want a new Germany"

Mikhail Gorbachev, who gave the green light to German reunification, visits with President Richard von Weizsäcker in Bonn, November 1990

Demonstration in Berlin against anti-foreign outbreaks, 8 November 1992. The victory column is in background.

"No to racism and hatred of foreigners."—Demonstration in Bonn, 14 November 1992

Germans protesting anti-foreign outbreaks in Rostock

chapter 6

TWO ERAS: FROM DIPLOMACY TO HISTORY

The Berlin crisis of 1961 was the point of no return in the formation of two Germanys. The Berlin wall was an aesthetically repugnant piece of masonry work, but its construction proved to be the keystone to the successful completion of a larger, and artistically more satisfying, diplomatic structure. Like a storm clearing the stagnant air, the crisis finally made possible a postwar settlement of the German problem. With the enforced stability introduced by the wall, the twenty-eight years that followed were less hectic and less eventful, allowing time to work out the solution that had evaded diplomacy since 1945. Finally diplomacy caught up with the facts and reconciled itself to awaiting the creation of new realities.

In the gloomy aftermath of the crisis, relations between Bonn and Washington reached their postwar nadir. In part, this reflected the generation gap between the youthful Kennedy and the octogenarian Adenauer. Kennedy was irritated by Adenauer's constant hand-wringing, by the absence of any innovative ideas from his government, and by Adenauer's endless demands for reassurance of American fidelity to NATO alliance goals. He likened Adenauer to an insecure wife who asked her husband every day, "Do you love me?" and after receiving the required assurances, asked, "But do you really love me?" For his part, der Alte cared little for the presidential youngster, whom he once described as "a cross between a junior naval person and a Roman Catholic boy scout."[1] Clearly, Adenauer was looking back nostalgically to his communion with Dulles, whereas JFK was eagerly anticipating the arrival of a new generation of German politicians.

The substantive cause of the rift, however, was a parting of the ways on German policy, even though on the surface policies appeared to settle into their cold war routines. Berlin faded quickly from world attention following the crisis, but in the city itself tensions continued to simmer at reduced a temperature throughout the decade. In 1962 there was renewed harassment of air traffic in the corridors over Berlin, with Soviet MiG fighters buzzing airliners and dropping metallic chaff to impede navigation through the dense cloud cover that frequently blanketed the city. In addition, the by now routine array of petty annoyances never ceased.

This was, in its own way, reassuring, but diplomatically the situation never did come back to normal. The crisis had jolted Kennedy and Khrushchev into taking up a private correspondence and pursuing a series of talks intended to air formulas that might soothe this chronically inflamed sore spot. Having risked all in Berlin, Kennedy now sought to reduce those risks as much as possible through negotiation, by creating "a new configuration of the status quo." The most innovative of the American proposals called for the creation of an international access authority to deal with disputes between East Germans and those using the routes to Berlin. Although the discussions never got beyond the exploratory stage, they did reduce tensions until the course of developments in the DDR had become clear. In January 1963, Khrushchev informed the East German Party Congress that the problem of an East German peace treaty was no longer urgent. The Berlin thorn was still in the bear's paw, but the pain was no longer unendurable.

Kennedy's eagerness to discuss Berlin was viewed dimly by Adenauer, who suspected that the United States might be giving away the store. After his retirement, Adenauer continued to revile Kennedy. "The stupidity and sentimentality of the Germans," he told Henry Kissinger, "was reflected in the fact that they were naming bridges and streets after someone who did them so much damage."[2] Accustomed to having a veto in any American initiatives involving German interests, Adenauer now found that the United States was acting without the close coordination of policy typical of the preceding decade. Since any change in Berlin's relationship to the Federal Republic might be prejudicial to reunification, Adenauer leaked the international access authority proposal and later, in a fit of pique, made public his opposition. In turn, the Kennedy administration, fed up with Adenauer's obstructionism, made it known that the West German ambassador to Washington, Wilhelm Grewe, was no longer welcome. He was recalled in May 1962.

The forging of closer Franco-German links was another sign that the German-American relationship had entered a new era. The friendship began with Adenauer's 1958 visit to General Charles De Gaulle, newly elected as the first president of the French Fifth Republic, in the course of which the two elder statesmen hit it off surprisingly well. Superficially, there seemed little reason why Adenauer should gravitate toward a Gaullist France. De Gaulle's party had worked earnestly against the European army, in addition to which the general was on record as opposing any change in the de facto frontiers in Eastern Europe. Contrary to Bonn's strong alliance orientation, he also favored an independent French stance between Washington and Moscow. Nevertheless, there were strong points of attraction. Adenauer advocated Franco-German reconciliation not only for friendship's sake, but also out of agreement with De Gaulle's conviction that a new Europe was impossible without close working ties between the two nations.

This geriatric romance was consummated in the Franco-German Treaty of Friendship signed on 22 January 1963, which committed both nations to close cooperation in all questions of foreign policy. The reaction in Washington was disbelieving shock, followed by wild rumors of Bonn's intention, with French connivance, to negotiate an independent settlement with Moscow. As George Ball recalled, the likely result of such a deal would have been a death blow to the policy of double containment, meaning "the end of NATO and the neutralization of Germany."[3]

Even more disturbing to Americans were the German implications of De Gaulle's policy of nuclear independence. With the development in the late 1950s of Soviet missiles capable of reaching the American mainland, De Gaulle concluded that the United States could not be depended on to start a nuclear war to save Europe if that meant exposing the now-vulnerable American homeland to attack. Since, by this logic, the American nuclear guarantee was unreliable, and since negotiations in NATO had failed to break the U.S. nuclear monopoly within the alliance, De Gaulle pushed France down the road to becoming a nuclear power. This policy culminated in his 1964 announcement that France would proceed forthwith to develop an independent nuclear deterrent, the *force de frappe*.

Americans feared that if the West Germans followed the French example, the psychological shock to the Soviets and the Western Europeans might knock the delicate machinery of the entire postwar system off its mountings. In an interview with a Soviet newsman in the fall of 1961, Kennedy openly sympathized with Russian concern over the West German acquisition of nuclear weapons. From the German point of view, however, Kennedy's attitude seemed designed to relegate the Federal Republic to a permanently inferior status within the alliance, something the proud Adenauer had never been willing to accept.

Worse yet, in Bonn's eyes the Kennedy administration's hegemonic desires were further tainted by impaired strategic credibility. Kennedy came into office determined to set in place a system of "graduated deterrence" or "flexible response" in which all America's military eggs would not be placed in one nuclear basket. By building up conventional arms, the West would be able to meet Warsaw Pact provocations without immediate resort to nuclear escalation. On his trip to Europe in June 1961, Kennedy let Adenauer know that the Federal Republic would best fit into this scheme of things through further contributions of manpower. But this emphasis on conventional response seemed only to confirm De Gaulle's arguments, which cast doubt on the American willingness to push the nuclear button when the time came to do so.

All's well that ends well, however, and the Franco-German love affair did not leave the Americans as the jilted lover. Before the treaty was ratified, pro-American figures in Adenauer's administration inserted a clause making it clear that the Federal Republic would not go back on any of the multilateral commitments to which it had become a party. Nevertheless, so strong were the fears aroused by this episode that the United States felt compelled to attempt a solution of the nagging problem of Germany and nuclear weapons.

The result was a complicated plan known as the multilateral force (MLF), which envisioned a sea-based force of ships with nuclear missiles manned by mixed NATO crews. According to this scheme, the United States would retain custody of the warheads until a unanimous vote of the alliance members released them for use. The proposal originally envisaged a fleet of Polaris submarines, but U.S. Navy objections to sharing this technology forced a downgrading of the fleet to more vulnerable surface vessels. This was, as its chief salesman George Ball later admitted, a Rube Goldberg solution, "a manifestly absurd contrivance." It was, in addition, openly detested by navy men the world over. "You don't expect our chaps to share their grog with Turks, do you?" asked British prime minister Harold Macmillan, when the proposal was first put to him.

Though this undrinkable military concoction came to be known in some skeptical circles as "the multilateral farce"[4] and was viewed by others as "an elaborate charade to provide the Bonn government with a sense of control over NATO's nuclear power,"[5] it did have medicinal virtues. By giving the Germans a safe but responsible role in alliance nuclear management, it would satisfy the German desire for nuclear status and quell any urge to become an independent nuclear power. As a side effect, the MLF would kill off the incentive for other alliance members to develop an independent nuclear deterrent.

Not least important, for a dedicated band of European integrationists, MLF was an ersatz substitute for the European Defense Community, and this caused its State Department supporters to take heart from the initially favorable German response. Despite some Francophile sentiment within his party that would have preferred to pursue the French connection, Adenauer looked kindly on the scheme. It was, after all, another step up in status for his country within the alliance. In addition, giving his country operational access to atomic weaponry marked a confirmation of the American nuclear commitment to NATO.

Whatever chance there was that MLF might act as a balm in U.S.-German relations, however, was more than offset by other factors. Kennedy, who was lukewarm to the scheme in the first place (he was said to be "two and a half cheers" in favor), preferred to let the European governments take the lead. Given this mildly cynical attitude, he was genuinely surprised to hear that Adenauer liked the MLF. Still, he was reluctant to ride the proposal too hard for fear that it might snarl negotiations with the USSR.

Following the heart-stopping Cuban missile crisis of October 1962, Kennedy ardently pressed for talks with the Soviets that bore fruit in the Nuclear Test Ban Treaty of August 1963. The treaty was a milestone in tranquilizing the cold war, but it aroused among Germans fears of a deal being made behind their backs, not unlike the misgivings that raced through Washington at the time of the Franco-German treaty. If this relaxation were extended to European security issues generally, the Federal Republic would conceivably be pressed to accept a de jure division of Germany. Adding to German apprehensions was America's disregard for the tradition of consultation established in the 1950s. Though the Federal Republic signed the Test Ban Treaty in short order, it did so only after making sure that its signature did not appear on the same copy as that of the DDR.

Clearly, relations between the United States and West Germany were in a transitional stage. The clumsy shifting of gears was smoothed somewhat in 1963 by the emergence of new leaders who developed a good working relationship. The assassination of Kennedy in November 1963 left Lyndon B. Johnson as president. Known primarily for his mastery of domestic politics, Johnson nevertheless prided himself on an understanding of Germans, as a consequence of having grown up near heavily German communities in the Texas hill country. The more significant change in leadership took place in Germany, where in October Adenauer finally relinquished his stubborn grip on power in favor of the amiable and popular Ludwig Erhard, who would be more deferential toward the Americans than the prickly Rhinelander had been.

People had been waiting for Adenauer to step down since 1959, but he surprised everyone by staying on for another term as chancellor because of his low opinion of his likely successor, Erhard. This mean-spirited decision, along with the failure of the Christian Democrats to win an absolute majority in the elections, followed in turn by further electoral reverses in *Land* elections, were indications that political dissatisfaction was beginning to stir the German electorate.

There was much cause for dissatisfaction. The Berlin crisis had demonstrated the sterility of the foreign policies of both major parties. Not only was Adenauer's policy of reunification through strength discredited, but also the Berlin crisis demonstrated that the endless series of optimistic Social Democratic proposals looking toward reunification were quixotic in the cold war context. Shifting geopolitical tides and Bonn's changing relationship with the Western alliance and the United States during this period further underscored the need for a redefinition of basic policies.

Adenauer's image was further blemished by the *Spiegel* affair of 1962. When the sensationalist news magazine published some articles highly critical of the Bundeswehr, its Hamburg offices were raided by the police and a number of its editorial staff thrown in jail on charges of treason. The government even went so far as to have a staffer tracked down and arrested in Franco's Spain. The affair caused such a commotion that Franz Josef Strauss, its guiding spirit, was forced to resign. Five Free Democratic ministers also quit in protest.

Apart from the governmental crisis it caused, Adenauer's inept handling of the affair clearly indicated that his time had passed. Finally facing the inevitable, he accepted a forced retirement with graceless petulance. In the 1940s, he had been a man in advance of his time, ready to ride the crest of history. Fifteen years later, history had passed him by, giving poignancy to his continued attachment to power. Power had not so much corrupted as given a corrosive quality to what had once been a Midas touch.

On first consideration, Erhard appeared to be the ideal successor to the increasingly irascible Adenauer. Besides continuing his successful economic policies, he would repair the close relationship with the United States that had been the key to his nation's rebirth—something that in his later years Adenauer appeared to forget. Yet the belief that Adenauer had abandoned Adenauerism was based on the assumption that his early policies were still valid, when increasingly they were not. As a result, Erhard was left with Adenauer's policy hand-me-downs when they no longer fit the growing Federal Republic. Erhard's policy of nostalgia, of restoring the good old days, was a guarantee that the forces of change would sweep him aside for his failure to adapt.

His easygoing nature also proved to be a liability. When someone remarked to Adenauer that there was no government under Erhard, the waspish elder statesman responded: "That is quite wrong. There are at least three governments, and he's not in charge of any of them."[6] His personableness was even less of an asset in foreign affairs. Erhard visited the United States often, and was treated with frequent invitations to stay as a guest at the LBJ ranch in Texas. "I love President Johnson and he loves me," he once said, in summing up their mutual admiration society. Unfortunately for Erhard, such goodwill could not be banked.

He came to grief over an issue that generated friction throughout the decade, the perennial question of troop stationing costs. By the end of the 1950s, the United States began to experience balance of payments difficulties. Realizing that troops abroad were one prime source of the financial outflow, American administrations in the 1960s began to ask their allies to take compensatory measures. Kennedy solved the problem of offsetting American military costs in Germany by getting the Federal Republic to purchase American military equipment to outfit the expanding Bundeswehr.

By 1966, however, this arrangement was out of date. For one thing, the Bundeswehr was fully equipped, and the Germans felt it was silly to continue with unnecessary purchases. More important, however, was the mood of the West German government. For the first time in the postwar period, the economy had stalled, producing a 1965 trade deficit that made fiscal economy a major concern among skittish politicians in Bonn. The government now sought relief from its burdens, while Washington believed that German alarms were premature and largely imaginary.

Since each party sported the same set of economic horns, some head butting was inevitable. Defense Secretary Robert McNamara took a hard-nosed approach to this issue by publicly warning Bonn that failure to offset American costs would result in a reduction of troop levels. Congress pitched in, too, with the neo-isolationist Mansfield Amendment. As it came up for a vote each year in the late 1960s, increasing numbers of senators jumped on board with votes for substantial reductions of American forces in Europe. Combined with the growing American commitment of manpower to Vietnam, these votes stood as a blunt reminder to the Germans of what could happen if the issue were not satisfactorily resolved.

On this issue of meeting German commitments, Erhard's close relationship with Johnson could not be cashed in. On an earlier occasion, LBJ had gone into a meeting on the issue with the intention that Erhard "should be left in no doubt that performance under offset agreement is indispensable for our continued six division presence."[7] Besides, the president believed that personal experience had given him some insights into the German mentality—"great people," he said, but also "stingy as hell."[8] Erhard attempted to convince LBJ that the Germans were not seeking to renege on their commitment, but were trying to stretch out their payment obligations the way any overextended debtor would do. But Johnson would not budge. "Now we're going to find out who our friends are," he had told the obviously uncomfortable chancellor in December 1965. Prior to their climactic White House meeting in September 1966, Ambassador George McGhee predicted that Erhard would "throw himself on the President's mercy" in seeking relief for his budgetary difficulties. But, following another nose-to-nose discussion with LBJ, Erhard left the meeting empty-handed and "utterly dejected."[9] On returning home, he was forced to request a budget increase, which contributed heavily to his downfall later in the year.

In the hope of averting a rupture, the two allies agreed to a series of offset negotiations that got under way in 1967. These negotiations were about more than money. The potential implications were far more serious. The ante was increased by British participation in the talks, prompted by their threats to begin withdrawals from their Army of the Rhine. As Ambassador George McGhee described the situation: "It looked like the beginning of the end of our strong support for NATO and [like it] might lead to further withdrawals and leave Germany defenseless."[10] Realizing the potential serious-ness of the disagreement, LBJ appointed as his negotiator John McCloy, who took an alarmist view of the stakes involved.

Later in the decade, the problem would be met by a variety of expedients: a modest reduction of American forces, military purchases for reequipment, German purchases of U.S. treasury bonds that would be redeemed only when America's balance of payments difficulties had been resolved, a Bundesbank promise not to convert its dollar holdings into gold, and contributions toward renovation of American base facilities in Germany. Continuing German foreign trade surpluses, which Americans perceived as excessive, were dealt with in a number of upward revaluations of the deutsche mark, but only after strong pressure to do so on the part of the United States and the other allies convinced a reluctant Bonn to give up some of its competi-tive advantage.

The adage that historical tragedy tends to repeat itself as farce was cer-tainly applicable to the MLF. Whereas the end of the EDC had been a stun-ning blow, the demise of the MLF was an Alfonse and Gaston routine between the United States and the Federal Republic, as each backed the plan on the assumption that it was of major importance to the other. Actually, Johnson was even less enthusiastic than Kennedy had been about the MLF, but he decided to go along with it to please the Germans, because he felt they could not afford to be left unhappy on such a major issue. Following an Erhard pilgrimage to the United States in mid 1964, it was agreed that a treaty would be ready for signature by the end of the year. Nevertheless, severe opposition to the scheme emerged in Bonn from German Gaullists and supporters of Adenauer and Strauss, who had decided to become spoilers. This lack of German enthusiasm was matched by a cool to frosty reception in the other NATO countries, especially France, which were pressuring Bonn to decline the American offer.

Meanwhile, Johnson took soundings in the U.S. Senate and discovered that the treaty would stir considerable opposition from both liberal and con-servative circles. These political factors, the resounding silence from across the Atlantic, and the hideously complicated technical issues of manning, control, and nondiscrimination prevented the MLF idea from maturing any further. When Johnson disavowed paternity in December 1964, the MLF was abandoned and allowed to die of neglect. Few cries of mourning were heard, except among the ranks of dedicated Europeanists in the U.S. State Department.

The MLF died, but its root causes lived on. The problem of Germany's nuclear role within the alliance was partially solved by the McNamara Committee, through which the Germans were given a consulting role in NATO's nuclear decisions, but, like a shooting gallery target, the problem immediately popped up again in talks with the Russians. The Soviets had informed the United States that the death of the MLF was a prerequisite to any treaty stopping the spread of nuclear weapons. Solving the so-called "nth country problem" was of great interest to the United States, but as negotiations on a nonproliferation treaty progressed, all the embers of burned out nuclear issues were stirred up, threatening again to ignite the flames of alliance disagreement.

By early 1967, Soviet and American negotiators in Geneva had agreed on the draft text of a nonproliferation treaty. From the standpoint of the two superpowers, the treaty would act as a powerful force for stability by reducing the number of possible fingers on the nuclear trigger, the most worrisome digit of all belonging to the Federal Republic. According to presidential aide Bill Moyers, "The ultimate option [would] be between a nonproliferation treaty and giving the Germans hardware,"[11] and he noted with disapproval that "the German nuklites" in the State Department preferred the latter solution. LBJ also felt that either an alliance solution or a nonproliferation treaty could "keep the Germans locked in."[12] Clearly, however, the United States was more sensitive to Soviet desires on this issue than to the feelings of one of its closest allies.

Naturally, muttering was heard in Bonn about "atomic complicity." It seemed clear that many Germans, as George McGhee noted, "suspected that we had made a deal with the Soviets behind their backs."[13] It was also believed that the Soviets had promised secretly to take a more constructive line in the search for a negotiated settlement to the Vietnam War in return for a West German signature on the nonproliferation treaties. It was not that the Germans actually wanted or expected a nuclear option for themselves, but from Bonn's perspective, West Germany was being asked to forgo developing a capability that her neighbors, England and France, were determined to possess as a matter of prestige. It seemed wrong, also, to practice self-denial and to relegate the country to permanent inferiority within the alliance when no Soviet concessions would be forthcoming on unification. But Bonn had other concerns, too. It did not want to be rushed into a treaty that might inadvertently sign away German rights in the peaceful commercial exploitation of nuclear energy.

In the end, West German objections boiled down to a face-saving opposition to Soviet insistence on the right of direct inspection of nuclear facilities on German soil, which Bonn construed as an insult. The German issue further complicated the accord when the Russians threatened not to sign the pact until Bonn had first done so. The Soviets finally relented, but Bonn did not put its signature to the treaty until 1973, by which time there had been a breakthrough in negotiations on the German problem.

German-American relations during the 1960s were out of phase. The system of double containment established in the 1950s had assured that the German problem and confrontation with the USSR were interconnected and, consequently, that both had to be dealt with simultaneously. Yet in the sixties the United States was clearly pursuing an independent strategy of détente with the Soviets without reference to the German problem. Restoration of German-American harmony and further progress on the German question would require that double containment be replaced by a system of double détente. It was evident that the Germans, still proceeding according to the old assumptions, had not yet adapted themselves to the new facts of life.

Partly this was because domestic politics in the Federal Republic were still in a state of transition. The trend toward internal change was clearly visible following Erhard's exit in the fall of 1966, ironically because of dissatisfaction with his poor management of the economy. The so-called "Grand Coalition" of the two major parties then came to power, with Kurt Kiesinger as chancellor and Social Democratic Party (SPD) leader Willy Brandt as foreign minister. Everyone knew that this was an interim arrangement only. Though the SPD was willing to share its first taste of power as a junior partner, the party was counting on taking over completely in the general elections scheduled for 1969.

In foreign policy, the molting of dead skin had already begun with the de facto abandonment of the Hallstein Doctrine by Erhard's foreign minister, Gerhard Schröder. By 1967, Bonn had established diplomatic relations with Eastern European regimes that recognized the DDR. As another harbinger of change, the Kiesinger government addressed a peace note to the Eastern European satellites, suggesting the renunciation of force. Most significant of all, just beginning to emerge was a willingness, long repressed, to recognize the fact that the DDR actually existed and was not about to disappear.

In part this shift in attitude was conditioned by the changing relationship between the superpowers. In 1966, Johnson made clear that a restored Germany could "only be accomplished through a growing reconciliation. There is no shortcut."[14] Reportedly he made clear to Kiesinger that America was no longer interested in unification. "If you want to live in peace in Europe, you have to look for an alternative," he said.[15] It was now becoming evident that unity could not be the vehicle for East-West détente, but could come only at the end of a long process of peaceful social change. As a corollary to this understanding, the obsessive negotiations on Germany that dominated the diplomacy of the 1950s disappeared from superpower agendas.

It was, however, not only a U.S.-Soviet matter. From the standpoint of intra-alliance relations, too, the pursuit of unification no longer seemed worth the effort. As an intelligence memorandum written in 1965 concluded: "Reunification would upset the present balance of power within the West European half of the Atlantic political system. This question of the balance of power in Europe is not discussed much because the present situation is now so familiar and so much taken for granted . . . the emergence of a united

Germany would upset this system seriously by greatly increasing Germany's 'weight' in proportion to its neighbors'."[16]

Not surprisingly, many commentators at the time suggested that the tensions produced by such changes meant that the close relationship between Germany and the United States was finally coming to an end. Indeed, Kiesinger tried to distance himself from Washington by playing the Gaullist card, but in the end he found the Parisian dalliance to be more suffocating than the American marriage. LBJ acknowledged to some German reporters in 1967 that Kiesinger had "had a little affair with De Gaulle but we let him run off awhile knowing that he would be back."[17]

The readjustment of German thought resulted in equal measure from an acceptance of historical realities and the painful shedding of some cherished illusions. Already in 1960 respected voices were heard arguing that the hallowed cold war policies were little more than useless ideological relics. Philosopher Karl Jaspers and novelist Golo Mann contended that reunification as a practical political goal was unimaginable in the current phase of history. The only conceivable way of reuniting the German nation was one that sought to promote contacts between East and West Germany in the hope that a multiplication of human ties would eventually knit the two sides together.

This logic was picked up and incorporated by the SPD, which had been frustrated by Soviet disdain for its reunification ideas in the 1950s and shocked by the outcome of the Berlin crisis. By this time, the once widely accepted idea that the German problem was the cause and not a symptom of East-West tensions was recognized as a myth. Brandt for one realized that "the German question was not the key to an understanding of the worldwide conflict between East and West."[18] By 1961, he was calling reunification "at present and for an immeasurable time to come, a hopeless issue."[19] In the following year, his party abandoned its outworn advocacy of neutrality as the open-sesame to reunification. The new outlook, no longer bewitched by magical incantations, was fully articulated by SPD spokesman Egon Bahr in 1963 and formalized under the slogan *Wandel durch Annäherung* (Change through contact).

Despite the halting steps toward a conciliatory *Ostpolitik* during the years of the Grand Coalition, further innovation was impossible in any government in which the Christian Democrats played a role. The majority party still claimed to feel the strong pulse of the German people's anger with the continued partition of Germany. Schröder's never-say-die attitude was typical. "We shall not spare efforts to dispel mistrust and fear and thus to relax tension in Europe," he said, "but we cannot achieve this by practicing self-denial."[20]

The CDU's ideological brittleness, complemented by the SPD's suppleness, led to a situation in which the positions of the two parties in their thinking on foreign affairs had been reversed. The CDU was clearly the doctrinaire party. Fogged in by ideas that had outlived their usefulness, it was unable even to think about new departures in its views on such major issues as the eastern frontiers and recognition of the rival regime in the East. In contrast the SPD, formerly a party of starry-eyed dreamers, had shed its idealism and was gamely testing its wings in the changing international environment.

Though the Christian Democrats outpolled the SPD in the 1969 elections, Brandt was able to cement a governing coalition with the Free Democrats largely on the basis of their mutual desire for a new brand of *Ostpolitik*. The new government's desire for far-reaching foreign policy innovations dovetailed with a parallel development in the United States. Earlier in the year, a Republican president, Richard Nixon, had come to office with the avowed intention of opening an "era of negotiation" that would produce a relaxation of tension in the cold war. In the coming years, the Nixon administration would achieve a number of diplomatic breakthroughs, most notably the signature of a strategic arms treaty with the Soviets in 1972 and an agreement to normalize relations with Communist China. More so than any other postwar administration, Nixon's spoke candidly of its desire to forge a stable world balance of power. Conservative in its implications for the United States, Nixon's approach opened up radical possibilities for the Bundesrepublik.

While the new American style was conducive to a frank recognition of German realities and created a favorable environment for the pursuit of *Ostpolitik*, it did not mean that the two governments sang in perfect harmony. Nixon's advisor for national security affairs, Henry Kissinger, whose backstage influence with the president outweighed that of the secretary of state, was at first skeptical of Brandt's intentions. Born in Germany and speaking a heavily accented English, Kissinger nevertheless suffered from traditional American diplomatic phobias. Sounding much like the cold war statesmen who preceded him, he feared that "Brandt's new *Ostpolitik*, which looked to many like a progressive policy of quest for détente, could in less scrupulous hands turn into a new form of classic German nationalism." Moreover, he differed fundamentally with Brandt as to the likely outcome of *Ostpolitik*, believing that it would seal the division of Germany rather than lead to its elimination. This result would have bothered him not at all were it not for his belief that the policy was being fraudulently peddled under the unity label.

Kissinger was the foremost postwar American exponent of realpolitik, but that did not mean he believed that Germany should be allowed to practice it. In a memo to Nixon, he speculated that the new German leaders, though well meaning, might be unleashing forces beyond their control and courting historical tragedy. Once freed from double containment, he wrote, they "could create a momentum that may shake Germany's domestic stability and unhinge its international position."[21] Once the inevitable recognition of failure set in, a neutralist mentality fixated on the dangerous idea of being a bridge between East and West might once again reemerge in Germany, this time in more virulent form. Thus any *Ostpolitik* would have to be carefully monitored by the United States and channeled in the proper direction.

Kissinger was in particular suspicious of Egon Bahr, Brandt's alter ego and the main diplomatic ball carrier for *Ostpolitik*. He considered Bahr to be "above all a German nationalist who wanted to exploit Germany's central position to bargain with both sides." Bahr's eagerness to negotiate with the Soviets in what a distressed Dean Acheson called the "mad race to Moscow" could be destabilizing to the alliance. Yet despite these qualms, the new administration was far less inhibited about undertaking some extensive redecorating than American elder statesmen such as Acheson, McCloy, Ball, and Lucius Clay, who felt secure and content with the old diplomatic design.

Brandt seems to have gotten along well enough with Nixon, although he was somewhat bemused by this emotionally constipated president's strained attempts at bonhomie. (Nixon had committed the gaffe of making a congratulatory phone call to Kiesinger following the election, on the mistaken assumption that he had won. He later jokingly claimed to have dialed the wrong number.) Brandt's dealings with Kissinger went less smoothly. Calling him "arrogant and intolerant," Brandt felt that Kissinger "may sometimes have viewed the old continent with the disdain of the new Roman for Hellenic petty states."[22]

Kissinger's fear of a new Rapallo was matched by Brandt's distrust of excessive Soviet-American collusion. But doubts about mutual intentions were soon laid to rest by Brandt's visits to Washington in 1969 and 1970, where he reaffirmed Bonn's oath of fealty to the West. By this time, however, feudal ceremonies of subordination were clearly passé. There was no question of the United States attempting to restrain its partner, because it was clear that Bonn was dead set on its new course. As Bahr recalled, "I made it clear we'd inform them in advance of what we would do, but we would do it anyway."[23] Washington thus gave Brandt the ball and let him run with it. What differences remained centered on questions of tactics.

In short order the Federal Republic opened the diplomatic equivalent of a three-ring circus by entering into far-reaching negotiations with Moscow, Warsaw, and its next-door neighbor, the DDR. Just as its new policy depended on Washington's prior assent, *Ostpolitik* had no chance of success unless Moscow also smiled upon it. The first step, therefore, was a treaty of friendship, signed with the Soviets in August 1970, that had been negotiated by Bahr. The treaty renounced the use of force and agreed to recognize all existing borders in Europe, the most important being the controversial Oder-Neisse line and the frontier between East and West Germany. Though reunification by force was rejected, a clarifying letter stated that some form of German unity in the future was not ruled out.

Simultaneously, talks began with the Polish government. Again, in a treaty signed in December, the Bundesrepublik accepted the Oder-Neisse line as Poland's western frontier. This was a most difficult pill to swallow, since it killed for those Germans born in the East any chance of exercising the long-cherished "right to the homeland." Forever after, the old *Heimat* would be alien soil. In addition, arrangements were made for normalization of relations, and a start was made on the sensitive question of repatriating Germans still living under Polish rule.

The theme of reconciliation between the two countries received a tremendous symbolic boost when Brandt spontaneously dropped to his knees while laying a wreath before a monument to the victims of the Warsaw ghetto uprising. This unplanned act of contrition did not go over well in West Germany, where strong anti-Polish prejudices still lingered and the sight of their chancellor wearing sackcloth left a bitter aftertaste. But for its effect in restoring the Federal Republic's less than glowing international image, it proved to be a brilliant stroke of inspired statesmanship. Few acts have been as effective as this heartfelt deed in convincing the world that a new Germany, freed from attachment to its Nazi past, had been born. For this reason, despite numerous failings as a politician and a statesman, Brandt attained an international aura of greatness.

Finally, Brandt faced the most touchy question of all: forging a new relationship with East Germany. He arranged first for exploratory meetings with his East German counterparts. The most noteworthy aspect of Brandt's visit to Erfurt, East Germany, in March 1970 was the enthusiastic greeting he received from the East German crowds, whose shouts of "Willy, Willy" were clearly not directed at East German premier Willi Stoph. It was readily apparent, however, that short of acquiring full recognition as an independent state, the East Germans were not very keen on *Ostpolitik*, especially as long-time party leader Walter Ulbricht had made a career of portraying the Bundesrepublik as a monstrous neighbor.

It was here that the opening to Moscow came in handy, for the Soviets had decided that the time had come to strike a bargain that realized most of their diplomatic goals. The Russians were not about to jeopardize their interests by putting up with the surliness of an underling. Thus, once the Moscow treaty was signed, and once four-power talks on Berlin had been set in motion, the East Germans became more accommodating. In May 1971, Ulbricht was kicked upstairs into a largely honorific party post, clearing the way for the more amenable Erich Honecker. Brandt exerted pressure on the Soviets, who in turn prodded their reluctant ally, by letting Foreign Minister Andrei Gromyko know that the Soviet treaty would not be ratified until a satisfactory resolution of the Berlin problem was reached.

Though Brandt had taken the lead, the American-sponsored negotiations on the Berlin problem were central to the success of the entire process. The Soviets since 1969 had indicated a disposition to talk about the city's status, but without betraying any signs of impatience. With the inauguration of *Ostpolitik*, a Berlin agreement became essential to its success. Brandt needed a Berlin solution for domestic reasons, since ratification of the unpalatable Eastern European treaties would be impossible without some sort of compensating Berlin accord as a *digestif*. Given all the unilateral renunciations of long-standing German ambitions, *Ostpolitik* would otherwise have seemed too much of a capitulation. At the same time, the Soviets desired a Berlin accord to get the series of treaties ratified. "The linkage to Berlin was our ace in the hole," Kissinger recalled.[24] The United States could use Berlin talks to regulate the pace and content of *Ostpolitik* while making it clear, if the point needed making, that German problems could be solved only under the umbrella of East-West détente.

Talks that had begun in the old Allied Control Council building in March 1970 were energized the following year when the Soviets, getting the point of the Nixon administration's theme of "linkage," realized how in the case of Germany, and détente generally, everything hung together. The U.S. negotiators to this point, perhaps influenced by State Department fears that an agreement could result only in undesirable concessions, took their time and pressed hard—indeed much harder than the Germans would have preferred. With his domestic position rapidly weakening, Brandt feared he would see his diplomacy go down the drain if no Berlin settlement was reached.

The state of inertia was broken early in 1971 when the White House, tired of State Department "bureaucratic nitpickers" who found it difficult to budge from policies "encrusted with tradition," began deviously to steer the negotiations through back channels. "There was scarcely any topic, from the exact form of a stamp on a pass to the legal status of the city, that had not been squabbled over," Kissinger recalled with distaste.[25] As a result, a bizarre situation developed in which vital backstage negotiations took place, of which the State Department had little knowledge. It was, as Kissinger admitted, "an odd way to run a government."[26] If it was any consolation, it was not the first time U.S. diplomacy had been run this way.

A four-power accord on Berlin was finally signed in September 1971, followed a few months later by supplementary agreements between East and West Germany. The agreements, as one might expect with such an intricate issue, were ambiguous and complicated. The Soviets, not the East Germans, agreed at long last to guarantee unimpeded Western access to Berlin, confirmed Allied rights to enter East Berlin, and allowed West Berliners to visit the eastern half of the city. West Berlin's ties to the Federal Republic were also affirmed, its residents being allowed to travel on West German passports. In exchange, it was agreed that Berlin was not a constituent part of the FRG and that federal elections and other West German political operations would not be conducted in the city. The U.S. negotiators, bypassing the State Department's hard-liners with Nixon's blessing, agreed to make an academic concession by allowing a Soviet consulate in West Berlin (even though this gave weight to the Soviet contention that Berlin was two cities rather than one). The agreements, although incredibly detailed, failed to settle everything, but by finally putting an end to the crisis atmosphere that had plagued the city's existence since 1948, they were another milestone in the evolution of the German issue.

Even with the Berlin accords, ratification of the treaties by the Bundestag was a close call. The CDU and its Bavarian counterpart, the CSU, opposed the treaties, arguing that Brandt had given up all his valuable negotiating cards without receiving anything tangible in return. Meanwhile, Brandt's government had been steadily losing support in by-elections and was plagued by increasing defections among its Free Democrat coalition partners. In April 1972, a vote of constructive no confidence fell just two votes short of passage, amid rumors that some CDU deputies had been bribed by the governing party. The following month, the Soviet and Polish treaties passed with the CDU abstaining.

The Basic Treaty or Grundvertrag negotiated later between the two Germanys proved even rougher sledding politically. Having failed to receive a requested vote of confidence from the Bundestag in September 1972, Brandt ordered its dissolution and gambled on new elections to provide the necessary mandate. The November canvass confirmed his judgment, as the SPD for the first time outpolled the CDU and was able to put together an unambiguous majority for its policies. Following some complicated talks, the Basic Treaty defining relations between the two Germanys was signed the following month. Like the other treaties, it renounced force and sought to create conditions of cooperation, even though the meaning of cooperation would remain a large bone of contention. For the rest, each state respected the other's sovereignty in internal and external affairs, agreed that neither state could represent the other or act in its name, and validated each party's existing treaties and commitments.

The treaty contained some important concessions to the West German desire to leave the door opened symbolically to reunification. Therefore, despite the mutual recognition of sovereignty, it was agreed, in deference to the "special relationship" between the two countries, that they would exchange representatives rather than ambassadors and that they would acknowledge that the two states were not foreign countries. In keeping with *Ostpolitik's* aim of furthering change through contact, the Basic Treaty also called for the continued negotiation of all sorts of agreements designed to improve relations and promote contacts.

The Grundvertrag was shot through with ambiguities, because the goals of the two Germanys were contradictory. West Germany wished to enshrine the ideal of one nation, whereas East Germany sought to confirm its separate identity. The East Germans preferred to see it as the vindication of a long struggle for legitimacy and international recognition, while the West

Germans chose to interpret it as the beginning of a long process of reunion. In any event, it did not constitute a final accounting. The German question was left open by its acknowledgment of Allied responsibility for Berlin and for a general German settlement.

The treaty was also paradoxical. By providing for further negotiations on closer contact between the two Germanys, *Ostpolitik* was a victory for the idea of reunification, yet at the same time it marked the end of the diplomacy of unification by the Federal Republic. *Ostpolitik* was idealistic in that it tried to pave the way for a cultural and historical resolution. On the other hand, it was a realistic approach to diplomacy that realized there was no foreseeable political or military solution to the problem of German unity. Unity would come only through a recognition of division. Culture rather than power, history rather than diplomacy, faith in the future rather than reliance on the present, would settle the matter. Like many diplomatic revolutions, *Ostpolitik* belied its name: it was, in fact, the renunciation of an Eastern policy as it was traditionally understood, born of the recognition that diplomatic maneuvering could only solidify the division of the nation.

Immediately following the signing of the Basic Treaty, the DDR embarked on a path of *Abgrenzung*, or delimitation of differences, in which it tried to frustrate the ultimate aims of *Ostpolitik* while capitalizing on its short-term benefits. Concerned that increased contact might indeed lead to a lessening of differences, the DDR strove to establish its own identity by differentiating itself at every turn from its opposite number. In a more positive attempt to gain cultural legitimacy, the DDR tried to place on its shoulders the mantle of German history. Surprisingly, such ideological villains as Frederick the Great and Martin Luther were rehabilitated and portrayed as forerunners of the East German socialist utopia.

With *Ostpolitik* in place, the Federal Republic possessed a fundamental strategy that was to some degree independent of Washington's views and insulated from the ups and downs of the cold war. Bonn's new-found assurance was accentuated in the 1970s by the emergence of substantial differences within the maturing Atlantic alliance. "As far as European-American relations were concerned," Brandt recalled, "Nixon did not receive on the same wave length I was at pains to broadcast on." Bonn now tended to take the European side of major alliance issues, whereas formerly it had leaned toward the Americans. The result was a marked loosening of the American connection.

The West Germans, like other Europeans, resented the strong-arm tactics of John Connally, Nixon's secretary of the treasury. Connally responded to the continuing weakness of the dollar with a surprise devaluation and by suddenly shutting down the "gold window," that is, by refusing to convert dollars into gold, thereby putting an end to the world financial system in effect since the end of World War II. West Germany reacted coolly to other American initiatives. To Kissinger's annoyance, Brandt followed his

European neighbors by showing little enthusiasm for Kissinger's much-bally-hooed "Year of Europe," an initiative that was supposed to reinvigorate alliance relations long untended as a result of America's obsession with the Vietnam War.

When the United States used its bases in West Germany to resupply Israel in the October 1973 Arab-Israeli war, Bonn, like other European states eager to stay on good terms with the oil-supplying Arab states, complained, in private and public, only to be met by the imperious American response that the Federal Republic "enjoyed only limited sovereignty" in American eyes.[27] Though clearly irked by this desire to put distance between the two governments on Mideast issues, Nixon subsequently expressed regret at these intemperate words and promised in future to consult West Germany before taking such consequential action.

Brandt had little time to savor his triumphs, for no sooner had his policies gained acceptance than a scandal led to his resignation. In April 1974, one of his personal aides, Günther Guillaume, was exposed as an East German spy. Although Brandt was not personally to blame for this embarrassing lapse in security, and though it was widely recognized that the West German government had been deeply penetrated by East German intelligence services, he was tired of political bickering and took the occasion of this revelation to resign his post in favor of the more decorous role of party elder statesman.

Succeeding Brandt as chancellor was Helmut Schmidt. Urbane and almost professorial in style, irascible, and with an impressive colloquial command of English, Schmidt had been recognized since the late 1950s as one of the SPD's most formidable leaders. Whereas his predecessors had been preoccupied with liquidating the legacy of the war, Schmidt was in a position to define assertively the Federal Republic's new identity, free of the encumbrances of the past. With reunification no longer an obsession, he began to pilot the Federal Republic into a new era of relationships. True, his freedom was limited because the basic course had been fixed, but within these limits he was free to tack back and forth. Much of the aura of novelty was a matter of style, but in a deeper sense, it meant that the Federal Republic was pursuing its own version of *Abgrenzung*.

The new West German self-confidence was manifested in ways that in the fifties and sixties would have been inconceivable. Adenauer had been an alliance leader, but there had always been the sense that he was deferred to out of concern for German weakness rather than strength, because a failure to pay him the proper respect would heighten deep-seated German insecurities. Since Adenauer's policies represented a triumph of statesmanlike vision over national feeling, his prestige had largely been personal, whereas Schmidt's character fully embodied that of his country. Schmidt's financial expertise and confident manner, coupled with the Federal Republic's growing economic power in an era when economic issues began to outweigh security concerns on the political agenda of the West, made him one of the dominant figures among Western statesmen. No longer was the Federal Republic an economic giant and a political dwarf.

Schmidt was on generally good terms with President Gerald Ford, whose administration, he later recalled, would be the last to possess a realistic sense of how to pursue détente. But after Ford lost the 1976 election, the stage was set for a squabble between Bonn and Washington over a wide range of issues. The conflicts were exacerbated by Schmidt's inability to get along with the new president, Jimmy Carter. The problem was, at one level, one of personalities, as Schmidt soon sized up the new southern president as "idealistic and fickle."[28] According to Schmidt's account, the president asked him in May 1977: "Helmut, couldn't the two of us remove the Berlin wall?" Dumbfounded, Schmidt asked how this feat might be accomplished. "I thought you might know of a way," responded the earnest Carter.[29]

But incompatible personalities were the least of it. At a deeper level, Schmidt believed that the accession of Carter, and later Ronald Reagan, to the presidency marked an end to the kind of responsible and predictable American leadership provided by the eastern establishment's "wise men," and that thenceforth the Federal Republic and its European allies would be dealing with politicians, who were oriented more to domestic issues, rather than with statesmen. When these new leaders did look overseas, they tended to turn away from the aged dowager of Europe in favor of a flirtation with an Asia still in the youthful phase of political and economic modernization.

One series of disputes revolved around economic policy. With the United States suffering a severe case of "stagflation," a disease that, according to mainstream economic theory, was not supposed to exist, the Carter administration proposed that the Federal Republic act as a "locomotive" for the stalled world economy by providing more fiscal stimulus to the German economy. Bonn initially resisted Washington's suggestion on the predictable grounds that it would be inflationary. Although Schmidt finally agreed to add 1 percent to the German GNP by adjusting taxing and spending, he was never fully reconciled to the idea and would later complain bitterly about having had to swallow this pill. His fears were confirmed when the second oil shock of 1979, a byproduct of the Iranian revolution, worked its inflationary way through the world economy. Schmidt had ample reason to complain in 1979 about "the highest real interest rates since the birth of Christ," as rates skyrocketed throughout the industrialized world.

He was all the more inclined to complain about "American irresolution and neglect of the dollar" as the American currency was allowed to float down to unrealistically low levels vis-à-vis other currencies.[30] Shortly thereafter, the U.S. Federal Reserve's battle against inflation would send the dollar soaring upwards again, but only at the price of even higher interest rates. With the dollar now resembling a yo-yo on the string of the international currency markets, Schmidt believed that the United States had effectively "surrendered the leadership of monetary policy."[31] No less a cause for tongue clucking by the Germans was the fiscal policy of the Reagan administration, which, sanctioned by somewhat dubious economic theory, ran up huge budget and trade deficits. The result of episodes like these was that in future Bonn would ignore American attempts at economic "coordination," hewing instead to its single-minded preoccupation with keeping inflation in check.

Another major flareup was caused by President Carter's decision not to manufacture the enhanced radiation weapon or, as it was popularly called, the neutron bomb. This was actually an atomic bomb whose blast effects were minimized but whose intense radiation would be lethal to humans over large areas. If deployed, it seemed that it would go a long way toward meeting the objections of those Europeans who argued against the stationing of nuclear weapons in Europe on the grounds that atomic war would lay waste to the Continent.

Whatever its actual military value, there was no doubt that the neutron bomb was a public relations disaster. Communist propaganda gleefully labeled it the ultimate capitalist weapon, one that destroyed people and spared property. This theme found a receptive audience in a growing antinuclear movement in Europe (though one may wonder how this weapon was worse than those already in place that killed by both blast and radiation) and particularly in the Federal Republic, where a new "Green" party, a coalition of activists on environmental and nuclear issues, began to register surprising electoral gains. Egon Bahr, speaking for the left wing of the SPD, called the neutron bomb "a symbol for the perversion of human thinking."

Carter himself was not immune to this kind of argument. After taking some soundings, he concluded that there existed no strong European sentiment in favor of deploying this weapon. Moreover, he was irritated to discover in talks with the West German foreign minister, Hans-Dietrich Genscher, that the Germans were, as he said, "playing footsie with us." Taking a more accommodating stance in private than they were willing to do for public consumption, the Germans would have preferred to give the impression that the Americans were twisting their arm to get them to deploy the weapon. Carter refused to play along. Sensing that there was more enthusiasm for the neutron bomb in the Pentagon than in Europe, he decided in April 1978 to defer production, only to hear well-informed rumors that Schmidt was taking him to task for unilaterally changing his mind and leaving him in the lurch after he had already paid the political price of advocating the production of the new weapon.[32]

Increasingly, the Europeans picked up Schmidt's theme and labelled America as an unreliable and mercurial ally—a curious accusation to make against a partner faithfully wed for more than thirty years, most of which had been filled with worries about the inconstancy of the Europeans! Although he refused to make their differences public, Carter was not pleased. As his national security advisor Zbigniew Brzezinski recalled, "relations between Carter and Schmidt took a further turn for the worse and never recovered."[33]

Whatever the justice of the two men's positions, among those in the know Carter was the one sporting the black eye.

The contentiousness surrounding the decision to modernize NATO's intermediate-range nuclear forces (INF) in Europe produced yet another instance of Carter's clumsiness in accommodating the political sensitivities of his German ally. In October 1977, Schmidt delivered a speech warning of the growing strategic imbalance in central Europe resulting from the ongoing Soviet deployment of intermediate-range SS-20 missiles. According to Schmidt, the Carter administration at first seemed unconcerned by this imbalance in missiles, which affected neither the strategic (intercontinental) balance of terror nor the conventional balance. By ignoring this "gray area," the administration appeared to be content, as a matter of policy, to make a nuclear war thinkable for Europe while striving mightily to make it unthinkable in all areas where American lives might be at risk.

Finally goaded to action by Schmidt's persistent prodding, the Carter administration pressed for a NATO decision in December 1979 to deploy in Germany 108 new Pershing II intermediate-range rockets (which could almost reach Moscow) and 464 ground-launched cruise missiles (low-flying, inexpensive jet drones difficult to pick up on radar), as a direct response to the USSR's continued SS-20 deployments. According to prevailing strategic thinking, the continued buildup of the SS-20s, which had the ability to reach any target in Europe, would overshadow the West's nuclear deterrent on the Continent and thus, in a crisis, could well cause a paralysis of Western will power. NATO, however, adopted a "two track" decision according to which the Pershing deployment would not go forward until the fall of 1983. If, in the meantime, negotiations with the Soviets resulted in a satisfactory reduction in the number of the offending SS-20s, the Pershings would not be installed.

Unfortunately, as soon as the decision was announced, Schmidt, the man who was most responsible for raising the issue in the first place, was no longer interested in taking the lead. Following talks in Washington in the spring of 1980, Brzezinski noted that "Schmidt on the whole was positive, but equivocal on concrete support."[34] Although Schmidt was a NATO stalwart who believed fully in the strategic value of modernized forces, he was no longer the unquestioned master of his political house. His delicate political position back home, where his Bundestag majority was dependent on support from the increasingly dovish left wing of his party, prevented him from taking a forthright public stance. To cover his domestic flank, he insisted on a sharing of burdens, which meant that another European nation in addition to the Federal Republic would have to agree to deploy. Caught in the middle of an emotional election campaign in which the INF issue loomed large, Schmidt further suggested in a speech that both sides defer deployments for a period of three years and use the time to discuss mutual limitations.

This idea was firmly rejected by Carter in a private letter to the chancellor. The result was a "nasty confrontation" between the two leaders at a summit meeting in Venice. Carter recalled the session, in which Schmidt was "ranting and raving" at the supposed insult of Carter's letter, as "the most unpleasant personal exchange I ever had with a foreign leader."[35] Schmidt's annoyance with Carter boiled over, and he vented his anger at the American position on a whole host of foreign policy issues, throwing in for good measure the jibe that the Federal Republic was not the fifty-first state of the Union. The unpleasantness passed quickly as both leaders took care to smooth their differences before the public. Nevertheless, such an outburst would have been blasphemous in the old days.

The process of European détente had reached its climax in 1975 at the Helsinki Conference on European Security and Cooperation, where the postwar status quo had received the imprimatur of all concerned. Yet as fate would have it, no sooner had the fabric been woven than it began to unravel. Beginning in 1975, "détente" became a dirty word for President Gerald Ford and other concerned Americans, as a result of Soviet initiatives in Angola, Ethiopia, and Yemen, and finally with the Soviet Union's invasion of Afghanistan in December 1978 to rescue a tottering Marxist regime. By the late seventies, American conservatives feared that the Strategic Arms Limitations Talks (SALT) treaties were providing cover under which the Soviet Union could outstrip the West in overall nuclear capacity. Finally, on assuming office in 1981, President Ronald Reagan would make it clear that he was determined not only to rearm the United States, but also to use America's allies in an all-out effort to drive the "evil empire" into bankruptcy.

For the Federal Republic, however, its counterpart to détente, *Ostpolitik*, was more than a passing diplomatic fad. It represented a long-term national commitment rather than a tactical maneuver in the cold war. This structural disparity in the German-American relationship would be most evident in a series of incidents in the late seventies and early eighties in which Bonn and Washington appeared to be drifting apart. Significantly, this time Washington would do most of the adjusting.

The effect of *Ostpolitik* was, overall, to stabilize the two-Germanys solution arrived at so ponderously in the early postwar period. According to George Ball, "[*Ostpolitik*] relieved the West from a position of some hypocrisy, that actually none of the western countries would have been prepared to accept a unification."[36] As the treaty relationship between the Federal Republic and the DDR got under way and began to build up momentum, both East and West Germans began to view the partition of Germany as, for all practical purposes, a permanent solution. For outside powers also interested in the German problem, the stability introduced by the political landscape of the 1970s made it appear as if the division of Germany were part of the natural order of things. The result would be that when the subterranean tectonic plates finally did shift, the new topography would come as a complete surprise to all observers. Thus the irony of reunification: it would be far less satisfying to many than the stability provided by the cold war system.

In the 1970s, the two German states began to negotiate the details of managing their new cooperative relationship. For the DDR, the signing of the treaties quickly bolstered the international standing of a regime whose legitimacy had long been denied, and, more important, by implication also bolstered the internal legitimacy of a regime that was laboring under a massive inferiority complex. The treaties provided more than a psychological boost, however. For the more than two decades that the regime's political status had been up in the air, its infrastructure had been allowed to deteriorate. Now Honecker's revitalized DDR was in a position to take advantage of the financial benefits derived from its special relationship with the Bundesrepublik.

The new relationship between East and West Germany was equivocal. East German exports to the FRG were treated as "internal trade" by the Common Market and therefore were not subject to European Community tariffs. With this commercial window to the West and with the West's new-found willingness to finance credits for purchases of Western technology and goods, East Germany's dependence on the ramshackle Eastern bloc economic system was lessened. Increasingly, West Germans could take a nationalistic pride in economic improvement across the border. By comparison with other East European economies, the DDR's productivity looked good, a reflection not so much of the benefits of socialism as of the efficiency derived from its being German.

Though agreements were reached on a host of matters, many of them were one-sided, as the Bundesrepublik showed itself willing to bend over backwards to pay for the benefits of contact, while the DDR charged all that the traffic would bear. For example, the West Germans picked up the check for most of the improvements in road, rail, and water communications between the two states. However, the East's eagerness for hard currency led to a situation in which the deutsche mark in some areas became the preferred medium of exchange.

The most visible change came in the number of visits from the West, which rose from 1.3 million in 1971 to 3.6 million in 1979. The "transit fees" collected from the millions of West Germans who were now permitted to make extended visits to the East provided a source of hard currency income to the financially strapped DDR. But the East Germans soon made it clear that visitation was sensitive to fluctuations in the political temperature. Nervous about the possible spread of the revolutionary Solidarity movement that erupted in Poland in 1980, the DDR increased steeply the amount of currency that it required visitors to exchange each day, which resulted in a sharp drop in the number of visits. Meanwhile traffic in the other direction was light, consisting largely of pensioners whose financial support, if they chose to defect, the DDR was cynically willing to entrust to the Federal

Republic. In the mid-1980s, the East Germans would relax their travel regulations; still, this failure to allow free movement in a modern world increasingly defined by the collapse of spatial barriers would remain a sore point with the DDR's citizens.

Nevertheless, from the West's standpoint, too, the treaty had benefits. Postal agreements were signed, as were agreements on cooperation in health care, medicine, and sports. Telephone calls from West Berlin to East Berlin began in 1973. East Germans received exposure to the West as increasing numbers were permitted to visit West Germany for brief periods. The eyes of millions more were opened to the advanced prosperity of the Western lifestyle when the DDR decided to stop jamming Western TV signals.

As the 1980s began, détente between the two Germanys deepened, perhaps a bit too much for the taste of the Americans and even the Russians. The Reagan administration was bent on putting U.S.-Soviet relations back into the deep freeze. Carter had already pressured Schmidt into agreeing to a boycott of the 1980 Moscow Olympic Games in retaliation for the Soviet invasion of Afghanistan—though Schmidt was none too optimistic about forcing the Soviets to reverse course with a policy of what he called a "dozen pinpricks"—and Reagan attempted to go further by trying to convince the Federal Republic to back out of a huge natural gas deal that had earlier been made with Moscow.

Despite Washington's own waffling on the issue, Bonn's soft line seemed to fly in the face of the American desire to pressure the Soviets into relaxing their grip on Eastern Europe. To punish Moscow for the imposition of martial law in Poland, in 1981 and 1982 the Reagan administration moved, without consulting its European allies, to prevent American corporations and their overseas subsidiaries from selling equipment to the Soviet Union that was needed for the construction of a 3,700-mile natural gas pipeline running from Siberia to Western Europe. West Germany already depended on Soviet gas for 17 percent of its domestic usage and was seeking to increase that amount, in part to get away from dependence on volatile Middle Eastern sources of supply. Apart from his skepticism about the effect such sanctions would have on the Soviets, Schmidt was irritated by what he considered to be the hypocrisy involved in Reagan's lifting of the embargo on American grain exports to the USSR. West Germany, therefore, and the other European governments instructed their companies to go ahead with their work on the pipeline project. Realizing that the Europeans would not toe the party line, in November 1983 the Reagan administration announced it was lifting the sanctions against U.S. companies working on the project.

It was just at this time that Helmut Schmidt, pressed by the renewed vigor and strength of his party's neutralist left wing and the heated debate about the INF decision, began to reconsider his former indifference about actively pursuing closer ties with the DDR. For its part, Honecker's DDR suggested none too subtly that the future of relations between the two German states hinged on Bonn's response to the INF treaties. The result was a definite soft-ening of the West German position on INF.

While détente proved to be a delicate bloom, the Germans were now insisting that the German variant, *Entspannung*, was a hardy perennial. In a December 1981 meeting with Honecker, Schmidt attempted to convince his opposite number that the two Germanys should maintain a stable relation-ship regardless of the ups and downs of the cold war. Schmidt talked about the need for "calculability" in FRG-DDR relations and displayed a sensitivity to the East's economic needs; indeed, by the end of the decade West Germany would invest more than 30 billion deutsche marks in the DDR.

In response, Honecker made no attempt to conceal his desire to influence Bonn's foreign policy in the direction of neutralism, emphasizing the need to ensure that "war should never again emerge from German soil." Shortly thereafter, Schmidt's opposition to sanctions against Poland for the imposi-tion of martial law was interpreted in East Berlin as a sign that Bonn's high-est priority was now maintaining good inter-German relations, even if those should conflict with its NATO ties. Predictably, this concern not to rock the boat of *Ostpolitik* would, in short order, make some sizable waves in the West.

With the defection of the Free Democratic Party from the governing coalition in West Germany, the CDU-CSU returned to power after nearly fifteen years in the political wilderness. Despite the fears of some that the growing ties between the two states would once again become strained, the installation of Helmut Kohl as chancellor in October 1982 failed to deflect the trend toward closer relations between the two Germanys. A decade earli-er his party had opposed Brandt's *Ostpolitik* in the most vehement terms imaginable, but behind the scenes its politicians accommodated themselves to the new reality. Although in public the CDU-CSU had continued to cul-tivate a hard-line image, privately its leaders realized that the West Germans had become reconciled to the fruits of *Ostpolitik*. Throughout the 1970s, Christian Democrat leaders travelled in large numbers to the DDR and cre-ated numerous back-channel contacts with the leadership in the East. Beyond that, the FDP coalition partners, with Hans-Dietrich Genscher given the foreign ministry, insisted that *Ostpolitik* be continued. With the hard-line Franz Josef Strauss of the CSU on record as favoring economic aid to the DDR, the conservative parties blithely donned the robes of an *Ostpolitik* they had once contemptuously refused to wear.

Kohl's installation as chancellor marked the emergence of a bipartisan consensus on *Deutschlandpolitik* and a culmination of the trend toward acceptance of the reality of two Germanys that had begun following the Berlin wall crisis. Even though his center-right coalition had promised a change of direction, this did not mean turning the clock back to Adenauer's time. To this point in time, CDU-CSU politicians had only reluctantly accepted the legal obligation to adhere to the treaties. On assuming power, however, they outdid the Social Democrats in their enthusiasm for building bridges to East Germany and "normalizing" relations. Even former hard-liners such as Bavarian party chief Strauss, who earlier had tried to have the Basic Treaty declared unconstitutional, now promoted giving large credits to the DDR, without expecting, or receiving, much in return from West Germany's grasping sibling in the East. With both major parties now in accord, German politics seemed to confirm that the diplomatic odyssey that had begun in 1945 was finally at an end.

Although this closer relationship between the two Germanys would provoke renewed doubts about German fidelity to the Western alliance, these were offset by a variety of factors. For one thing, Kohl and Genscher took care to affirm on every possible occasion the Federal Republic's commitment to continuing integration within the European community. Also conducive to ironing out tensions was a good relationship between Ronald Reagan and Kohl, whom Reagan found to be "entirely different than his predecessor, very warm and outgoing."[37] Although the U.S. and German positions on economic issues remained at odds, the president's chief of staff thought that "the warm spot the President developed in his heart for Kohl had something to do with the fact that the Germans stopped nagging him about taxes and interest rates after the Christian Democrats regained power."[38]

Above all, the dynamics of the situation seemed to favor stability. By comparison with the prima donna Schmidt, Kohl came off as something of a political wallflower. He possessed, in British prime minister Margaret Thatcher's condescending recollection, "the sure touch of a German provincial politician."[39] Clearly a homebody in comparison with his cosmopolitan predecessor, Kohl spoke no English and seemed content to tend his own political garden. Under his care, the issue of reunification seemed finally ready to enter a long period of dormancy. Yet it was into his hands that history thrust the long-awaited opportunity for reunification.

chapter 7

ONE GERMANY, ONE WORLD

During the 1980s, the U.S.-German relationship took contradictory forms. The same differences over cold war policy that had soured relations in the past continued to provoke family spats and brought renewed fears of an imminent breakup. But despite worrisome indications of a trend toward neutralism and nationalism, the West Germans continued their process of cultural modernization and their institutional integration into the larger Western civilization, while their East German cousins, it later became evident, looked on enviously. And while West Germans had become quite weary of the cold war and its incessant demands, they proved quite ready to push for unification on wholly Western terms when the opportunity unexpectedly arose at the decade's end.

Tensions surrounding the modernization of NATO's missiles in Europe carried over into the 1980s and set the stage for a decade-long reemergence of U.S. concern for German fidelity. In an attempt to steal a propaganda march on the Soviets, the Reagan administration proposed in November 1981 a rather implausible "zero-zero" deal in which the Soviets were supposed to remove all their intermediate-range missiles in return for an American promise not to modernize NATO's intermediate-range nuclear forces (INF). The Soviets, however, were not interested in giving up something for nothing and claimed in addition that this arrangement would leave them exposed to French and British missiles, which were not covered by the terms of the bargain.

The Reagan administration's get-tough public relations ploy may have played well in Peoria, but it would not do for Düsseldorf. Reagan faced a shifting political situation in West Germany that was most visible in the sur-

153

prising increase in strength of the so-called Green Party. Reminiscent of the youth movement in the United States in the 1960s, the Greens were less a party in the traditional sense than a spontaneous burst of unfocused political energy. The Greens were a multicolored collage (calling them a coalition would suggest a degree of discipline they did not at first possess) of environmentalists whose opposition to atomic energy plants and the growth dynamic of modern industrial society would have made Henry Morgenthau jump for joy. "Nuclear Power—No Thanks," said the bumper stickers on the jalopies favored by many of these young rebels. In addition, they counted among their number pacifists, food faddists, anarchists, new leftists, lesbians and feminists, and what-not.

The Greens' potential for political growth was limited by their near-anarchic opposition to leadership, organization, and anything approaching party discipline. As a political party, they were even ambivalent about holding power. Moreover their protest against INF was based on apocalyptic expectations, which are notoriously short-lived and incapable of generating sustained interest. Nevertheless, because their nuclear views did have widespread resonance, the Greens managed to coalesce in opposition to emplacement of the missiles and launch a dramatic series of street demonstrations. Surprisingly, too, the Greens managed to capture nearly 6 percent of the vote in the 1983 elections, which made it possible for them to take their lively and irreverent opposition into the Bundestag chamber, where their colorful and unconventional political style attracted further notice to their cause.

The INF crisis came to a head following the national elections of 1983, in which the Christian Democrats returned to power under the leadership of Helmut Kohl. No longer burdened with the responsibility of governing, the Social Democrats became openly hostile to the installation of the missiles. As the date for their emplacement approached, the tempo of protests increased, not only in Germany but throughout Western Europe. At the same time, the Soviets began to increase the diplomatic presssure by attempting, rather heavy-handedly, to capitalize on the unrest in the Federal Republic by threatening a new "Ice Age" in Soviet-German relations. With the failure of U.S.-Soviet negotiators to reach an accord, the Christian Democratic majority in the Bundestag approved missile deployment in November 1983, but only after Kohl had "fought the battle of his political life."[1] Shortly thereafter, the thunderstorm of antimissile protests abated as quickly as it had arisen.

Though the immediate crisis had been weathered, it was generally understood that these political tempests were symptomatic of a deeper change in the country's political climate—a generational change. Despite the fascinating rise of the Greens, more important was a growing radicalization within Social Democratic ranks. The left wing of the SPD had become increasingly restive under Helmut Schmidt's conservative leadership, but by 1983 his moderating hand was no longer at the tiller. Following his departure, the party, the wind of *Ostpolitik* having been stolen from its sails by its conservative rivals, tacked even further left in advocating closer ties with the DDR that would promote a "common security."

With the conservatives now locked into pursuing close relations with the DDR and the Social Democrats once again questioning the Western security connection, the result was a palpable "drifting apart intellectually and emotionally" of Germany and the U.S.[2] A strident anti-Americanism and a radical anticapitalist mentality among German critics of the United States meant that their desire to get out from under the thumb of the superpower was not matched by a corresponding critique of Soviet responsibility for Germany's predicament. The upshot was a worrisome growth of neutralist sentiment as Germans searched for a *Sonderweg*, or third path, between East and West that might somehow bridge the differences between the two superpowers and restore Germany to herself. The most worrisome possibility, recalled Secretary of State Alexander Haig, was that the German consensus on membership in NATO now seemed "in danger of disintegration."[3]

Although such developments triggered the usual nervous reactions among outsiders, in contrast to the aggressive nationalism of the past, this variety was explicitly antimilitarist in its sentiments.[4] Indeed there is some question as to how nationalist it really was. In its preoccupation with Germany, the United States often overlooked the fact that criticism of NATO was even stronger in other important European nations, on the left in Britain for example, and that Americans did not get overly excited about those cases. Moreover, survey after survey showed that public opinion in the Federal Republic was increasingly comfortable with a West German identity and continued to favor the existing, moderate course of policy. Despite many signs that it was in a transitional period, then, Germany was not yet on the threshold of a new geopolitical era.

It soon became clear that despite the superior airs of its young radicals, it was not on the verge of entering a new moral epoch, either. Even though a new generation had come of age in Germany, and though there was justice in the contention that children should not suffer for the sins of their fathers, many Americans and their Allies, however charitably inclined, could not erase the memories of World War II. French president François Mitterrand's refusal to permit the Germans to participate in ceremonies commemorating the fortieth anniversary of the D-Day landings in Normandy suggested the continuing potency of sentiments that were too disturbing to be openly expressed. Partly to mollify Kohl for this snub, Reagan agreed to the chancellor's pleas that he visit a German military cemetery in Bitburg the following year. Following Reagan's commitment to the visit, the press revealed that forty-nine members of the Waffen SS were also buried there, whereupon a powerful geyser of anti-German sentiment erupted. Spurred only in part by the predictable outrage of American Jewish groups, majorities in both the U.S. House and Senate petitioned Reagan not to go.

Reagan revealed in his memoirs that he "didn't think it was right to keep on punishing every German for the Holocaust, including Germans not yet born in the time of Hitler."[5] However, his critics believed the president was confusing forgiveness with forgetfulness. Editors of the *Washington Post* wrote that "Nazi Germany was not, as Mr. Reagan seemed to suggest, the handiwork of 'one man' and his regime or even hundreds of thousands. It remains, in the recollection and understanding of those who dare to recollect and understand, a terrifying—and endlessly instructive—monument to what can happen when a people, for the most part, let it happen."[6] White House suggestions that the SS troops had also been victims of Nazism triggered yet more howls of outrage from a journalistic wolf pack now in full pursuit of the president. Despite considerable pressure from his image-conscious retinue, not to mention the even more formidable suasion of his strong-willed wife, Nancy, Reagan refused to back down. He visited both the Bitburg cemetery and the concentration camp at Bergen-Belsen, and the controversy finally blew itself out in the kind of sentimental photo opportunity at which this actor-turned-president excelled.

It may well be that this episode marked a watershed in the transition from attributions of collective guilt to a more impersonal historical memory of crimes against humanity. Indeed by this time the Germans themselves, many of whom possessed unquestionably pro-Western and democratic credentials, were coming to feel that enough was enough. Kohl suggested as much when he stated that the Germans could not be expected to engage in endless breast-beating and self-abasement. Responding rhetorically to the question of what the Germans wanted, he said: "What do they want? They want to live in peace. They want to live in freedom. They want social justice. They want a good livelihood. They want to find happiness in life. They want to be glad. They don't want to walk around stressed, confronted from morning till evening with the burden of history. There are however people who want to persuade us that we should not be allowed to do this."[7]

Young people in Germany, raised in a democratic climate and well aware of the past, were increasingly impatient with suggestions that some collective taint had been passed down to them, as if cultural transmission somehow obeyed the laws of heredity. "No feeling person expects them to wear a hair shirt merely because they are Germans," said an understanding President Richard von Weizsäcker.[8]

In any case, it was not so clear whether the protests about Bitburg in the United States and elsewhere had been about continuing defects in German culture or whether they had been prompted by a problem that gnawed at non-German consciences. In trying to wrestle with the distinction between forgiving and forgetting, many apparently feared the encroachment of a cultural version of Alzheimer's disease—a forgetfulness that would erode the ethical power rooted in memory. As Kohl's controversial attempt to reintroduce the word *Vaterland* into German political discourse demonstrated, one could not unilaterally put an expiration date on the historical sensibilities of others. For the West, the Bitburg episode demonstrated the uneasy relationship between the political necessity of mollifying the Germans and the moral imperative of not forgetting.

All of this suggests that the revival in the 1980s of Western concern over the German national character was misplaced. To be sure, the noisy and attention-getting *Historikerstreit*, in which a number of revisionist historians were taken to task for engaging in some disturbing rationalizations of the behavior of the Nazi regime, suggested that some Germans were still bent on beautifying an ugly past. But foreign concern over the reemergence of essential antidemocratic traits was misplaced. If culture is learned behavior, then the West Germans' successful transition to democracy—an achievement that only a few were willing to dispute—could only mean that nondemocratic singularities had been correspondingly unlearned.

As a case in point, the fear of German nationalism and neutralism was continuously evaluated from a cold war standpoint, in which the past was the basis for judging contemporaneous German behavior. But it may be that the German outlook emerging in the 1980s was more an anticipation of a *post*–cold war sensibility than it was a recrudescence of old attitudes that no longer possessed cultural resonance. There was indeed a real dissatisfaction with the status quo in Europe and Germany, but this was only the manifestation of a deeper unhappiness at the running down of the cold war's once optimistic historical imagination and the absence of any plausible diplomatic alternatives. And despite the compulsive conjuring up of old bogeys, one senses that American statesmen realized the German cultural question had changed beyond recognition. If one is to judge by the memoirs of those in the government, the few, brief mentions of German matters in their otherwise voluminous recollections suggest that the German problem did not cause any sleepless nights in Washington.

Just as the old ideological wells ran dry, new ideas began to bubble up. The turning point in the cold war came with Mikhail Gorbachev's rise to power in Moscow in March 1985. Faced with a situation in which the USSR was fast losing ground in its economic competition with the West and armed with a growing understanding that the rigid orthodoxies of Marxism no longer commanded unquestioning faith, the new Soviet leadership launched a program of deep reform. The restructuring that came with perestroika and the openness of glasnost, while not intended to do away with communism, at least promised to make the Soviet Union a far more open society.

This new ideology had the potential to cross Soviet borders and carry with it the possibilities for new forms of international life. If the Soviet system were to be restored to health, Gorbachev realized that the bloated

Soviet military establishment, which by some estimates consumed about one quarter of the USSR's GNP annually, would have to be put on a crash diet. This would in turn release capital resources for investment in the emaciated Soviet civilian economy. But military downsizing was impossible without first eliminating the rationale for maintaining a huge defense establishment. An essential part of his program for curbing the military's appetite, therefore, would be to negotiate disarmament agreements. The shrinking of strategic nuclear forces loomed large on Gorbachev's agenda, and so did conventional force reductions in Europe. But all this presupposed a radical restructuring of the USSR's alliance systems, which consumed so much capital.

After Gorbachev finally agreed to sever any linkage between the INF and strategic issues, especially Reagan's so-called Star Wars antimissile defense program, the moribund INF negotiations resumed in 1987 and made rapid progress thereafter. But no sooner was the INF treaty signed on 6 December 1987 than it became clear that the Federal Republic would continue to bear more than its fair share of the alliance's atomic risk. Although the intermediate-range missiles were being removed, more than enough short-range missiles remained on both sides to make a nuclear wasteland of the country in the event of war.

Employing the same logic that earlier had prompted NATO's INF initiative, Kohl now argued that the short-range launchers also needed to be eliminated. At an economic summit in Venice, however, Great Britain's Margaret Thatcher insisted that their removal would effectively rob NATO, long dependent for its credibility on a nuclear strategy, of whatever deterrent force it still possessed. The result was a replay in miniature of the 1978 decisions: a determination by NATO to modernize its short-range Lance missiles, accompanied by all the familiar objections from within West Germany to overnuclearization.

This caused some American diplomats to worry that the West Germans were softening toward the Soviets. Thanks in large measure to the widespread realization that the road leading to the end of the cold war ran through Moscow, Gorbachev was enormously popular in Germany. Outbreaks of "Gorbymania" were not unknown in the United States, too, but in the Federal Republic it was clear that the new Soviet leader was far more popular than Ronald Reagan. This situation was dangerous, for if the new magician from Moscow succeeded in enchanting the Germans, Gorbachev might achieve his goals in central Europe by unraveling the Western security system.

Upstaged for one of the few times in his career as actor-politician, Reagan attempted to recapture the limelight by visiting Berlin in June 1987. Warning that the Soviets might be seeking to "raise false hopes in the West, or to strengthen the Soviet system without changing it," Reagan issued a challenge to his Soviet counterpart. "If you seek peace," he declaimed, "tear down this wall!" The challenge was at this point rhetorical, but it made clear that the Soviets could not expect to get something for nothing in Germany. Little did both sides realize that within the space of a few years, not only the wall but also the cold war's ideological barriers would be dismantled.

Despite Reagan's best efforts, the propaganda advantage continued to shift in favor of the Soviets. Gorbachev's book, *Perestroika,* published in 1987, remained on the German best-seller lists for months. In December 1988, the Soviet leader unilaterally announced significant conventional force reductions. In January 1990, in a notable speech to the United Nations General Assembly, he reiterated one of the book's themes: "freedom of choice" for nations. All of this was eagerly absorbed by an admiring German public. During his visit to the Federal Republic in June 1989, he was greeted in the streets by delirious shouts of "Gorby! Gorby!" "He could be an American . . . the way he does public relations," said one impressed student. Tantalizingly, the Soviet leader suggested that the Berlin wall was not permanent, saying that "the wall can disappear when those conditions that created it fall away." Thoroughly captivated by the Gorbachev mystique, one German newspaper went so far as to declare, "The Russian bear has become a cuddly animal without bloody paws."[9]

Khrushchev in his time had said much the same thing, but there was no mistaking the expectation that Gorbachev was bent on really changing the underlying conditions. Clearly this outpouring of adulation, not unlike that received by Kennedy in the 1960s, was the product of a deep psychological need for change among large segments of the German population. A poll taken in late 1988 found that 75 percent of West Germans no longer believed in a Communist threat from the East. More than 80 percent believed Gorbachev was acting in good faith.[10] The years had taken their toll. Weary of the endless NATO disputes over missile modernization that threatened to make Germany a nuclear battleground, and annoyed by the continued presence of foreign troops as de facto occupiers, the Germans wanted normalization. In Washington, influential figures in the foreign policy establishment, sensitive to these ominous developments, began to worry about the "Finlandization" of the Federal Republic, which the *New York Times* described as "geographically and psychologically vulnerable to the blandishments from the Communist East."[11]

"West Germany is still reliable, but it is becoming increasingly less willing," said one administration source. *New York Times* columnist William Safire, a Cassandra on Germany throughout the decade, was quick to sniff out what he called Gorbachev's "scheme to subvert NATO with a Russo-German entente."[12] The belief that Germany was once again being wooed by the two superpowers appeared to be "heady stuff" for the Germans. Sensing a deep shift in attitudes, the *Times* pointed to the ominous implications of President Richard von Weizsäcker's remark: "We are not a great power. But we are also not a plaything for others."[13]

Although images of German neutralism once again began to dance in the heads of statesmen, German nationalism was no longer its driving force. In 1976, in the immediate afterglow of *Ostpolitik,* only 13 percent of West Germans had believed that reunification would be attained in their lifetime. In 1989, two-thirds of the German population still favored unification, but the numbers were beginning to go down. Whereas in the 1950s and 1960s up to 50 percent of those polled had cited reunification as the central foreign policy task facing the Federal Republic, by the 1980s the figure had fallen to less than 10 percent. It was all the more ironic, then, that reunification would come at the moment in postwar history when people were least prepared for it.[14]

Significantly, only 37 percent of young people surveyed in 1989 said they desired reunification. One pollster predicted that "if a politician just sits and waits it won't be a problem in seven or eight years." Even Egon Bahr, the architect of *Ostpolitik,* said that "reunification is a strange item without any actual relevance." Most assumed that if a breakthrough were to occur, it would take the form of some kind of East German association with the European Community. West Germans had come to think of themselves as good Europeans, something that their politicians reiterated time and again. "Europe is our future," Kohl had said to the Bundestag in March 1987, and he had meant it.[15]

Thus as the 1980s came to a close, the graph of U.S.-German relations showed contradictory trend lines. On the one hand, there was undeniably a growing discontent within the Federal Republic with the endless demands of NATO and a corresponding weakening of the will to resist the siren song of neutrality. At the same time, however, a strong cosmopolitan commitment to Europe and the West had taken the nationalist steam out of the German identity crisis and reduced the pressure for reunification. Gorbymania or no, West German public opinion polls continued to show a strong commitment to the United States as the Federal Republic's closest friend. All of this suggested that changing sentiment within Germany was more the product of a reduced external threat than of an insatiable nationalist drive.

But still, change was in the air, and a new administration was on hand in Washington to greet it. Reagan's Republican successor, George Bush, was an experienced but colorless cold war apparatchik, having served as director of the Central Intelligence Agency, ambassador to China, and representative to the United Nations prior to signing on as Reagan's vice president. His aversion to flamboyance was made clear when he appointed as his secretary of state James Baker, a smooth, behind-the-scenes political operator. Heeding the president's instinct for "prudence," his administration tended instinctively to favor the status quo. However, with the USSR beginning to unravel, top officials realized that the effects on Germany might be swift and dramatic. In an attempt to blunt criticisms that he lacked vision, in May 1989 Bush spoke of moving "beyond containment" and of the need to look forward to a

"Europe whole and free." Inside the State Department, meanwhile, middle-level officials, anticipating further transformations in the Soviet Union, debated their implications for the German question.

While the eyes of all the experts were glued to the drama unfolding within the USSR, quite unexpectedly it was events within the DDR—which by all accounts had achieved extraordinary stabilization over the past fifteen years—that announced the coming drama of reunification. East German citizens were presumed by almost everyone to be the most passive and compliant in the Communist world, so it was all the more startling that they were the ones who kicked off the process that ended an era. The collapse of the DDR came at a time when the West Germans seemed fully reconciled, if not committed, to its survival.

The already close relationship between the two Germanys had deepened further with Erich Honecker's visit to the Federal Republic in September 1987. The visit had originally been scheduled for 1984, but Honecker had been forced to postpone it in the face of Soviet displeasure that the DDR had slipped her leash to go romping about with the Federal Republic. Finally, as the long-delayed INF accord on scrapping intermediate nuclear missiles in Europe at last came within sight, the Soviets allowed the 75-year-old Honecker to return to his homeland in the Saar for the first time since the 1940s, this time with the full honors due to a head of state. He visited the birthplace of Karl Marx in Trier and was feted in great style in Munich by the former 'militarist' Franz Josef Strauss. In a sentimental visit to his hometown of Wiebelskirchen, Honecker took aim at the heart of the prevailing two-Germany sensibility by saying he looked forward "to the day when the border will no longer separate us but unite us."[16]

With reunification no longer a live issue, the relationship between East and West Germany continued to improve as Bonn opened its deep pockets to the DDR's needs and East Berlin became more and more flexible, especially on the all-important issue of loosening border controls and facilitating human contacts between the two countries. Previously the DDR's concessions had been restricted to facilitating West to East visitations. Beginning in 1984, the regime decided that others besides retired pensioners should be allowed to go West. By 1987, more than 1.2 million East Germans under retirement age had travelled into the FRG. With hindsight, it is easy to see that the East German leadership of the mid-1980s, basking in the unaccustomed sunlight of domestic and foreign respectability, was living in a fool's paradise.

However, apart from the obvious economic benefits flowing from this improved relationship, the DDR did have powerful political motives for taking what, for a Communist government, was an uncharacteristic gamble. If freedom to travel were granted—although still with some controls—DDR leaders believed that one of the main complaints about the regime would be undercut and its legitimacy correspondingly buttressed. Internationally, it seemed clear that this new openness would pay dividends, too. Indeed by mid-decade, so seductive was the notion that *Deutschlandpolitik* could be used to bridge differences between East and West, that more and more of the Social Democratic Party's leaders were treating the unification issue as if it no longer mattered. In their eagerness to pursue closer contacts with the SED and to arrive at common positions on security issues and ideological matters, many Social Democrats came to think of the DDR as a full sovereign partner of the Bundesrepublik. Although the governing Christian Democrats were critical of this "shadow foreign policy" being pursued by their parliamentary opposition, it was nevertheless clear that they, too, were so committed to strengthening inter-German contacts that reunification had also disappeared from their working vocabulary.

As it turned out, a treacherous sinkhole of discontent was lurking just beneath the deceptively solid surface of DDR public opinion. Despite copious self-congratulations from the SED on the wonders of industrialization achieved under its leadership, by comparison with its dynamic and well-fed brother in the West, the DDR was an undernourished waif, and the East German people knew it. Years of exposure to Western media and the regime's more relaxed attitude toward travel had allowed the population to size up quite accurately the enormous gap—economic, cultural, political—that had opened up between socialism and the social market society across the border. Thus, when the usual rigged elections were held in May 1989, many people seethed. And when a high party official praised the Chinese government for its repression of the demonstrations in Tienanmen Square, the first bubbles of frustration with the oppressive regime came even nearer to the boiling point.

Nothing, it seemed, became life in the East German paradise like the leaving of it. The first sign that all was not well came in September, when the reformist Hungarian government, having earlier parted the Iron Curtain just a little, now drew it wide open by allowing 7,000 of the large number of East Germans who annually vacationed in Hungary to cross the border into Austria. Condemning this perfidy by her sister state, an outraged DDR attempted to plug the leak, but another quickly burst open in Czechoslovakia, where would-be East German refugees swarmed over the Bundesrepublik's embassy in Prague, all clamoring to be set free. The DDR's decision to allow this group to go West via train backfired when mobs of people frantically tried to get aboard and flee to the Federal Republic. It was fast becoming obvious that the matter would not be ended by simply saying good riddance to a few troublemakers.

The discontent then escalated to outright political protest as demonstrations broke out in October, initially in Leipzig and then throughout East Germany. Crowds who at first chanted, "We are the people" shifted to the more incendiary, "We are the German people." The East German regime was paralyzed by these developments. Although it at first appeared fully prepared to deal harshly with the demonstrators, at the last moment it lost its nerve. When the government failed to imitate the tough Chinese approach, the legs of its authority—legitimacy and power—were knocked out from under it. Neither loved nor feared, the DDR was thenceforth bereft of any ability to influence its citizenry. The belated ouster of the sclerotic Erich Honecker as party chief on 18 October, and his replacement with the younger and somewhat more flexible Egon Krenz, accompanied by a promise of "dialogue" with reform groups, failed to satisfy East Germans, who now harbored revolutionary expectations. Krenz was only the first in a series of relief pitchers who would fail to save the game for the DDR.

The protests spread, toppling not only the regime but also the authoritarian image of German political culture that many people continued to hold. According to historian Robert Darnton, "The peaceful revolution of 1989 did not just free the Germans from the last vestiges of more than a half-century's dictatorial rule. It freed us from what we thought of them."[17] A leader of Neues Forum, one of the more prominent protest groups, explained that the East Germans could "no longer tolerate the kindergarten atmosphere, or constantly being led by the nose on all fronts."[18]

Had a hard-line Soviet regime been in power, to act as head coach of the socialist squad, it would certainly have found a way to quell the unrest. However, at the fortieth-anniversary celebration of the DDR's founding on 7 October, a visiting Gorbachev failed to deliver the much desired halftime pep talk to his dispirited team. If anything, he made things worse by suggesting that the DDR adopt the values of "democratization, openness, socialist equality, and the free development of all peoples" that he was promoting in the USSR. "We have to see and react to the times," he said, "otherwise life will punish us."[19] The Brezhnev Doctrine, which had sanctioned Soviet intervention in Eastern Europe, had been formally repealed in July and replaced by what Gorbachev's spokesman called the "Sinatra (I'll do it my way) Doctrine."[20] Earlier in the year, the Bush administration had doubted the seriousness of Gorbachev's reforming intentions. He had been belittled by a presidential spokesman as a "drugstore cowboy . . . all hat and no cattle, all talk and no delivery." Now he was perceived as "real, real, outrageously for real."[21]

More dramatically yet, on 9 November the Berlin wall was opened in a last desperate attempt to satisfy the East German population by allowing freedom of travel. East German border guards, confused by conflicting signals from a government that was contemplating a more limited relaxation of travel regulations, took the initiative and allowed the swarms of people to pass through. Once the breach was made, there was no plugging it.

The next few days were a political carnival in which conventional behavior was suspended. East German crowds swarmed through West Berlin, marvelling at the sights. Spontaneous acts of generosity and celebrations of brotherhood took place everywhere. Toasts were offered and drunk. People danced with strangers. A group of East Berliners marched to a library in Kreuzberg and returned some books that had been checked out in August 1961, just prior to the erection of the wall (no overdue fine was assessed). Atop the wall roosted people who once would have been shot dead long before reaching it. Indeed before long, the East German government would begin to disassemble the wall, piece by piece, and offer its sections for sale. Already a market was developing, fed by entrepreneurs (*Mauerspechte* or "wall peckers," they were called) who were quick to take hammer and chisel to the structure.

Although in retrospect it seems clear that the time had been coming, these unexpected events proved once again the adage that history is remembered backward but lived forward. Despite the expenditure of enormous amounts of mental candlepower by scholars and policy analysts, the floodlights of the intelligentsia had failed to penetrate the murk of the future. Secretary of State Baker said the day after the wall was opened, "If anybody tells you that they knew this was going to happen yesterday they are smoking something."[22] The West Germans were also ambushed by events, having been committed to a policy of giving face-lifts to an East German regime that was capable of being fitted only for a death mask. Fearful of having to absorb a flood of East German refugees, West Germany had decided that the encouragement of reform in the East was the most convenient course.

The opening of the wall was a symbol of the psychological collapse of the cold war order, but it was out of step with structural realities. Whereas its construction in 1961 had brought symbolic closure to the long-standing de facto division of Germany and Europe, its opening merely anticipated the collapse of a system that was still quite alive, if not exactly well. Although Communism may have lost the will to live, it was still fully capable of dying a violent death and taking others down with it.

After the bacchanal in the streets of Berlin came sober morning-after thoughts in Western capitals. The *New York Times* reported that President Bush "seemed less than elated by the day's events," an unfortunate impression that the president only heightened when he attempted to explain just why he was "not bubbling over." The French, more predictably, were also less than enthused. While the French public seemed remarkably at ease with the idea of reunification, Parisian intellectuals worried openly that a newly reunited German behemoth would turn France into a "marginal power." Former President Valéry Giscard d'Estaing noted with a sense of foreboding that "France's own close relationship with Germany was based on equality."[23] Prime Minister Margaret Thatcher in England, blunt as always, told the Germans, "You are going much too fast." With events rather than diplomats in the saddle, the governments obviously feared that the stampede to unity might crush in its path everything that had been built up since the end of World War II.

Rather than acting as joyful parents at the birth of a new era, the states-men seemed more like fretful physicians determined at all costs to keep a dying patient alive. The emphasis on all sides was on moderation. From East Berlin, Krenz insisted that "reunification is not on the agenda." The willing-ness of the DDR to entertain reforms that would finally bring it into step with *perestroika* led Western officials and commentators to entertain hopes of, at best, some kind of confederation between the two Germanys in the near future. A few observers believed, as did a rather glum Henry Kissinger, that reunification was now "inevitable," but the "Doctor of Diplomacy" esti-mated it would take about three to four years to achieve it. Other old warhorses, however, like Paul Nitze, insisted that "nothing is inevitable," while the aged but still vital George Kennan tried to shush all the "loose talk" of reunification. The consensus within Washington, according to the State Department's director of policy planning, appeared to be that reunifi-cation was "a live, but still very remote possibility."[24] Gorbachev's warning that it was premature to talk about upsetting the postwar order was therefore "received with satisfaction" in Washington.

It was at this point that Helmut Kohl, realizing that his *Deutschlandpolitik* was hopelessly outmoded, began to take control of events. With marvelously poor timing, a *New York Times* analysis found it "almost tempting to pity Helmut Kohl these days. With history being made all around him, the lime-light seems to be everywhere but on the West German Chancellor." The *Times* contrasted the lackluster chancellor unfavorably with his prima donna of a foreign minister, Hans-Dietrich Genscher, who, while putting on his coat during a visit to Washington, had said grandiloquently: "Some touch it only, but I wear the mantle of history."[25] Having served first under Schmidt then under Kohl, it was the Eastern-born Genscher who was widely viewed as the German most anxious to promote unification—too anxious, many believed. However, such analyses seriously underestimated Kohl, who was determined to seize the historic opportunity to become the "reunification chancellor."

Apart from his need to deal with withering criticism at home of his unimaginative policy, Kohl was also concerned that all the talk about con-federation by the major players might, if not challenged, impose an artificial-ly slow speed limit on a situation in which diplomacy, for once, could conceivably approach the unlimited autobahn speeds. Thus, after consulta-tion with a close circle of advisors that excluded Genscher, in a 28 November speech to the Bundestag, Kohl unveiled a surprise ten-point pro-posal for preliminary binational commissions that would lead first to "con-federative structures" and then to a "federation," thereby taking Germany closer to full unity than most anyone else was contemplating at the time.

Despite Bush's earlier reassurance to Kohl that reunification was a "matter for the Germans," there was no turning of handsprings in Washington at the news from Bonn. The United States had no desire to antagonize the West Germans by slamming on the brakes, but, as Stephen Szabo has noted, neither did it wish "to rub the Soviets' noses in their defeat and possibly undermine Gorbachev and his policies."[26] Aware of the need to avoid offending Soviet hard-liners who preferred that their East German trophy remain mounted to the wall, the Bush administration would in the coming year be extraordinarily sensitive to Gorbachev's domestic problems. Should the West overplay its hand, it might among other things, trigger a tough Soviet response in East Germany. "Everyone has this feeling that the way things have gone up to now is just too good to be true," said an obviously nervous policymaker.[27]

Indeed, Gorbachev appears at first to have underestimated the consequences of the wall's opening. In his eagerness to see the transformation of the neo-Stalinist regimes in Eastern Europe, he had failed to realize that reforming Communism was like giving electrical stimuli to a failing heart—the shock could be fatal. Foreign Minister Eduard Shevardnadze in December 1989 sized up the year's events as "the natural collapse of the command-administrative system."[28] But this welcoming attitude toward change was giving the Soviets more to handle than they had bargained for. Taking fright, Moscow soon announced its opposition to "recarving the boundaries of Europe" and tampering with the existing security structure. Unification was "not on the agenda," said Shevardnadze, following a meeting with Genscher on Kohl's ten-point plan. Just to make things perfectly clear, Gorbachev lost no time in letting Bush know that the Soviets continued to have vital interests in Germany. "The guy's really upset, isn't he?" said Bush to his aides.[29]

Others were upset, too. "Western leaders have not been saying what they think about the central problem of a united Germany," reported Craig Whitney of the *New York Times*.[30] The mood in London and Paris was decidedly frosty to Kohl. French president Mitterrand had been quoted as saying, "I am not afraid of German reunification," but that was for public consumption only. Privately, as Margaret Thatcher recalled in her memoirs, he was "driven by a fear of the consequences of German domination." It was no secret that the outspoken Thatcher was herself dismayed by the possibility of a new "German juggernaut" being created in the near future. Thatcher preferred to wait another fifteen years or so until everyone was assured that democracy had taken full root in Eastern Germany. Although he paid for his candor with his job, Thatcher's finance minister, Nicholas Ridley, voiced the deep misgivings of many when he described reunification as "a German racket designed to take over the whole of Europe."[31]

Thatcher and Mitterrand consulted secretly on a number of occasions in an attempt to think up some artful way of slipping a wrench into the works. Offended at not having been consulted prior to Kohl's initiative, Mitterrand tried to deflect Bonn's eastward gaze by talking of "deepening" the European

Community as opposed to "widening" it. An ostentatious visit by Mitterand to the DDR on 20 December and a trip to Moscow also underlined the continuing residual role played in Germany by the Allied powers.

In the end, Mitterrand could not bring himself to go public with his opposition, because he realized that it would summon up the very genie of nationalist sentiment that he wished to keep forever bottled up. The most that he could bring himself to recommend was a four-power meeting in Berlin that would serve as a not-so-subtle reminder to Bonn that it could not afford to ignore the interests of its former occupiers. Some in the United States agreed. Commentator Ronald Steel argued that "Americans and Russians have earned a voice in the coming settlement."[32] Taking note of the discomfiture of their allies, portions of the German press began to grumble about latent anti-Germanism. "They always act as if we want something indecent," said *Der Spiegel*.

Naturally, all this gave rise to the question of whether the West actually wanted the reunification that for decades it had proclaimed was an unshakable goal of policy. Though in some cases accusations of hypocrisy were undoubtedly true, in the case of American public opinion, at least, they were far off the mark. In U.S. opinion polls, two-thirds of those questioned favored reunification, while only 16 percent thought a new Germany would make another bid for domination. Official Washington's view was more nuanced. As an abstract proposition, unity was a good thing for the same reason that an end to the cold war was, in principle, desirable. And even if it were not, it would be difficult if not impossible to renounce decades of policy utterances to the contrary.

Employing a cultural yardstick to measure the German problem, President Bush believed, as Reagan had, that the German national character had changed. "The Germans aren't any kind of threat at all," he was quoted as saying at a state dinner. "They are a totally different country from what they used to be."[33] But in this case structure was at least as important as culture. American advocacy of German unity had never been unconditional. It had always been predicated on the prior integration of Germany into larger European structures. NATO had been only a makeshift organization—long-term, to be sure—but now events were conspiring to diminish NATO's effectiveness before supranational European institutions capable of harnessing national ambitions were fully in place—thus the Bush administration's repeated emphasis in the coming months on the need for a new European "architecture." The new German wing under construction would have to blend stylistically with the rest of the European mansion.

The months following Kohl's proposal were dominated by attempts to regulate the reunification process. While continuing to insist that reunification ought to be worked out as a matter between the two Germanys, at a NATO summit in early December Bush set forth a number of external preconditions for reunification: consultation with allies and neighbors, integration with the

European Community, respect for Soviet security needs, and—most daunting of all—membership of a united Germany in NATO. This latter condition represented a revival of the maximalist American demands of the mid-1950s, this time, however, not so much out of anti-Soviet motives as from a desire to assure Germany's continued anchorage to the West.

Bush insisted publicly that he was not worried about a reunified Germany because Kohl had reassured him that the German "commitment to and recognition of the importance of the alliance is unshakable."[34] Nevertheless it was necessary to insist on continued alliance membership, since some Germans were clearly ready, as a condition of reunification, to shed their NATO suit of armor and don instead the flimsy vest of membership in the unproven Conference on Security and Cooperation in Europe, the unwieldy body established in 1975 in Helsinki. The German insistence that Lance missile modernization, still desired by Thatcher and the NATO high command, was now a dead issue was interpreted by many as a sign of growing disenchantment with the alliance. The Germans, of course, were quite capable of employing a powerful strategic vocabulary to argue their point of view. They pointed out that the short-range missiles could now be used only against an East Germany and Eastern Europe that no longer held the same threatening aspect. "What do we need these missiles for—to bomb Lech Walesa?" asked one German official sardonically.

Despite German protestations of virtue, no one in Washington was in a mood to gamble. Cold war or no, Western statesmen were convinced that continued German membership in a European collective security system was indispensable to continental stability. Amid talk of transforming NATO from a military to a political alliance, Baker insisted that "the new architecture must have a place for old foundations and structures that remain valuable."[35]

Shortly afterward, in a joint press conference following their storm-tossed summit aboard naval vessels off of Malta, Bush and Gorbachev flashed a yellow light. "We for our part, do not want to do anything that is unrealistic," said Bush, and Gorbachev pointed out that the existence of two German states "is the bidding of history."[36] But this view of things assumed a stable situation. Given his commitment to reform and the widespread anticipation that sweeping change was about to engulf Eastern Europe, it was clear that Gorbachev's comment would not be the last word on the issue.

Because the situation in the DDR continued to unravel much faster than anticipated, these caution signals failed to lift Kohl's foot off the accelerator. When Kohl had attempted to take the lead on unification, he had assumed that the DDR would survive for another few years at least. However, with the new year the pace of emigration to West Germany quickened to the point that it was beginning to cause great concern among West Germans fearful of being inundated by needy "Ossis." Indeed, by the end of 1990 about 2 percent of the East German population had migrated westward. At the same time, growing resistance to the now-toothless government in East Berlin mushroomed to the point that Premier Hans Modrow was forced to move parliamentary elections to the Volkskammer from May to March. Early in February, Kohl proposed the immediate adoption of a single German currency based on the deutsche mark. Meeting with Gorbachev in Moscow at about the same time, Modrow announced plans for a German confederation, while the Soviet leader insisted that "no one had ever cast doubt on the unification of the Germans."[37]

In a visit to Moscow in February, Baker agreed with Gorbachev on the need to regulate the external aspects of unification. However, the options he put on the Soviet leader's plate were not very savory: either a united Germany outside NATO, with all its potential for mischief, or "a unified Germany to be tied to NATO, with assurances that NATO's position would not shift one inch eastward from its present position."[38] (Indeed, the idea of a united neutral Germany was beginning to make nervous even the Eastern bloc countries, who soon began openly to voice their preference for a united Germany in NATO.) Shortly thereafter, Kohl arrived in Moscow and began to offer the Soviets various sweeteners to make unification more palatable. Although Kohl took pains to make it clear that the Germans' commitment to NATO was not negotiable, he did offer various compromises, what Baker referred to as "special arrangements," that had been thought up by Genscher.

While neutralism was ruled out for Germany as a whole, Kohl sought to assure the Soviets that NATO forces would not be moved eastward into the territory of the former DDR and suggested that NATO itself would be transformed from an exclusively Western body into a "kinder, gentler" alliance that would look eastward on matters of security cooperation. The Germans also promised to put some cash on the table to help with the withdrawal of Soviet troops, promised to fulfill the GDR's economic obligations to Eastern Europe, and provided reassurances that the new Germany's borders would not disturb the post–World War II status quo. Kohl, quite pleased, announced at the end of the talks that "this is a good day for Germany."

The institutional device for regulating the external aspects of reunification was dreamed up by Secretary of State Baker and his aides. Nicknamed "2 + 4," the approach would leave the internal aspects of unification to the two Germanys, whereas Germany's place in Europe would be settled in discussions with the four occupying powers. In this arithmetical system, the commutative law did not apply. The British and French would have preferred 4 + 0, and the Germans were wary that it not become 4 + 2, while other NATO members were angry at being excluded altogether from the process.

At a meeting of NATO and Warsaw Pact foreign ministers in Ottawa in early February, Baker tried out the 2 + 4 idea on Shevardnadze, who, while not thrilled with the notion, shortly gave the USSR's assent. At the same time, the Soviets accepted the American proposal that they reduce their troops in central Europe, agreeing to an arrangement that would permit the United States to station about 30,000 more soldiers there than the USSR. There would be four formal 2 + 4 meetings in the course of the year. In addition, there were the so-called 1 + 3 meetings, between the directors of the Western foreign offices, that sought to concert positions vis-à-vis the Soviets and the Germans. But all this numerary talk only confused a situation in which basically the Allies would be acting as a board of directors, rubber-stamping the decisions of the chief executive officer, Helmut Kohl.

Later in February, Kohl met with Bush at the Camp David presidential retreat for another survey of joint strategy and a discussion of further incentives for Gorbachev, including a reduction in the size of the Bundeswehr. The only hang-up, created by a concern not to offend Eastern-born Germans in upcoming elections, was Kohl's refusal to guarantee the Polish-German border. The rapid growth in recent years of the right-wing Republikaner party had sensitized Kohl's political antennae to conservative public opinion within the country on Eastern issues. He therefore insisted that the problem had to be settled by an all-German government, which would be the "legally competent sovereign" in this matter. The question was not really whether the Oder-Neisse frontier would be confirmed, but only when, since Kohl made it quite clear that he did "not want to repeat the errors of history." By attempting to delay until elections, however, he left himself open to criticism from those who sensed a renewed German interest in territorial revision.

Although the U.S. government quite correctly sized up the border problem as "small potatoes," the issue nearly turned into a public relations disaster for Kohl. It did not seem unimportant at all to the Poles, who insisted on settling the matter prior to unification, nor was it a small issue in public opinion, as people wondered whether the new Germany, despite all reassurances to the contrary, might be reverting to traditional ways. Foreign Minister Genscher and the Free Democrats also disagreed with Chancellor Kohl to the point of nearly splitting the governing coalition. The border question was taken up at the 2 + 4 meetings and was not settled until mid-June, when the two German parliaments guaranteed the existing Polish borders.

But such crises were only minor speed bumps in what was fast becoming a race to unification. In February Kohl proposed rapid monetary union. On 13 March, he upped the ante by suggesting that the East Germans might be able to exchange their valueless East marks for deutsche marks at a rate of 1-to-1, up to a limit of 4,000 marks. This decision was made in the face of much economic advice to the contrary, which argued that such a move would touch off a severe bout of inflation.

In an area widely considered to be naturally sympathetic to the SPD, nationwide elections held in the DDR on 18 March produced a startling victory for a group called the Alliance for Germany, a bloc of three conservative parties seeking reunification under the West German constitution. Despite criticism of Kohl for trying to buy East German votes, public sentiment was clearly in favor of "deutsche mark imperialism." With this vote, the East German electorate rejected the Social Democratic insistence that unification should be negotiated between the two states. It signaled the people's immediate willingness to have the state completely absorbed into the Bundesrepublik as soon as possible, thereby shelving any ideas of an intermediate period of confederation.

There were those in both East and West critical of this growing pressure for an *Anschluss,* a word that sought deliberately to evoke memories of Germany's bullylike expansionism of the late 1930s. Those who were convinced, like the clergy and intellectuals active in Neues Forum, that the DDR was not all bad and who argued that unification offered a golden opportunity to blend the best of the two Germanys were overwhelmingly and peremptorily rejected by Germans who wanted to throw overboard the failed system and cash in on Western prosperity as quickly as possible. "Those who don't talk about money don't understand how we live," said one woman about the socialists' penchant for theorizing. Thus it seemed likely that the first free election in East German territory might well be the last; that the next vote might come in an all-German election.

Now able to work with the sympathetic government of Lothar de Maizière in the East, Kohl shortened the unification schedule by appealing to the economic interest of East Germans. At the end of April, he confirmed the one-to-one currency exchange ratio. Early in May, the two governments worked out the details of a treaty providing for financial unity, which was to take effect on 2 July. According to its terms, the East German state would adopt West German monetary, economic, and tax policies and dismantle its command economy. Signed on 18 May, Kohl hailed the treaty as "a first decisive step on the path to unity." But the surge of West German investment in the East had actually gotten under way long before this official starter's pistol was fired.

At this point, the two states were ready to consider a state treaty on unification, and on 15 May Kohl called for all-German elections to be held by the end of the year. He was now in more of a hurry, because West Germans, sensing that the festival of reunification would entail enormous costs, were beginning to have second thoughts about footing the bill. Apart from the huge deutsche mark subsidy, a massive reconstruction fund was also in prospect, as were higher expenditures for welfare. Kohl's promises to the electorate that no new taxes would be levied were received with widespread skepticism.

The East Germans did all in their power to push things along by debating in June, with an interested Kohl in attendance, the desirability of being swallowed whole by the python to the West. They agreed to take advantage of Article 34 of the Basic Law, which allowed new states to enter the federation merely by declaration. In July the East German ruling coalition welcomed Kohl's call for December all-German elections. But first the DDR would have to dissolve itself in October into five states, which would then be absorbed by the Bundesrepublik.

Despite this progress and continued expressions of optimism from Kohl, reunification was still far from being a sure thing. Facing tenacious rear-guard resistance from conservatives in Moscow, Gorbachev began to get cold feet. Early in May, Shevardnadze told the Western foreign ministers that reunification and full German membership in NATO were incompatible and, in any case, that numerous security issues needed to be worked out before Moscow would agree to unity. The public Soviet position at this time on a Germany in NATO was, in Shevardnadze's words, that "NATO remains the same as ever—an opposing military bloc."[39]

At the first 2 + 4 meeting in Bonn in May, Shevardnadze had proposed "decoupling" the internal aspects from the external aspects of reunification by allowing Germany to unify while maintaining four-power control pending the creation of a satisfactory new security structure. In a Washington summit at the end of May, Gorbachev repeated public suggestions that Germany be made a member of both NATO and the Warsaw Pact. This unusual proposal was greeted by Bush with incredulity. Even though Bush submitted a list of "nine assurances" on NATO and Germany, many of which had been test-driven earlier, it was clear following this tête-à-tête that the two sides still had some way to go before coming together. "It is not here that the German question will be resolved," Gorbachev told a news conference.[40]

The Soviets made one more attempt at delaying a NATO solution. At the second 2 + 4 meeting, in Berlin on 22 June, Shevardnadze suggested a five-year transition period during which Germany would retain its obligations to both alliances, but with greatly reduced troop strength. However, the Soviet foreign minister indicated privately to his Western colleagues that he was only going through the motions, to show hard-liners in Moscow that resistance to the inevitable was futile. Happy to oblige, the Westerners unanimously rejected this latest Soviet "proposal."

It was now evident to Bush and Baker that the Soviet leader, while personally flexible, was encountering stiff resistance from those in the Politburo still not reconciled to the loss of Eastern Europe. At a Communist Party Congress in early July, Shevardnadze was booed when he tried to explain his German policy. Clearly Gorbachev needed concessions from NATO that he could use in his internal struggle with the diehards. But private discussions between Gorbachev and the West Germans suggested that there were some political levers available to remove the boulder of Soviet opposition from the road, and that economic measures might also prove helpful. A late-May secret meeting in Moscow between Gorbachev and Kohl's national security advisor, Horst Teltschik, indicated that German credits and burden-sharing with regard to expenses of removing Soviet troops from the DDR would be a crucial factor in persuading Moscow to loosen its grip on East Germany.

Eager to please, Bush, in a NATO summit in London on 5 July, pushed a series of proposals that would, symbolically at least, de-fang NATO. The London declaration as adopted sought to redirect the East-West relationship from one of confrontation to cooperation, promised a "reduced forward presence" in Germany, and, abandoning the long-held reliance on first use of nuclear weapons as a deterrent, pledged to make nuclear response a "last resort." The declaration also expressed a desire to strengthen the CSCE. In addition, contrary to previous expressions of an unwillingness to be "singularized," Kohl agreed to accept limits on the new Germany's armed forces. Obviously pleased at hearing of these concessions, a Soviet foreign ministry spokesman said of the hard-liners: "Now we can show them they are wrong."[41]

The final roadblocks to unity were removed in a meeting between Gorbachev and Kohl at Gorbachev's Caucasus home. The German leader did not come bearing all the gifts he had wanted to bring, having been turned down by his fellow Western leaders at an economic summit in Houston where he had requested 15 to 20 billion dollars in aid to Moscow. "One doesn't help his friends by throwing a great deal of money in a hole," British foreign minister Douglas Hurd had said. Nevertheless, on his arrival in the USSR Kohl found himself pushing against an open door as Gorbachev, convinced that reunification would take place with or without him, ignored the hard-liners and gave Kohl everything he wanted. Said one of the Germans present: "The Soviets seemed to come with the general idea to say yes. We filled in the details."[42]

According to the terms of the agreement, a united Germany was free to remain in NATO, and Soviet troops would be withdrawn from East Germany in four years. Allied forces would remain in Berlin until Soviet forces had completed their withdrawal. In return, Germany would compensate the Soviets for the cost of withdrawing their troops. Following their exit, NATO-integrated Bundeswehr troops could be stationed in the new eastern Länder, but not foreign troops or nuclear weapons. The Bundeswehr would be reduced in size to 370,000 troops, including the navy.

Secretary of State Baker, thinking that he was fully on top of things, had been convinced beforehand that the Kohl-Gorbachev meeting would be a "nonevent." Now he was somewhat chagrined to admit that the news from the Caucasus came "a delightful surprise." All that remained was a last 2 + 4 meeting to ratify the results and provide for the termination of Allied rights in Germany.

With all the track signals now running green and East Germany's economy failing quickly, the throttle to unification was opened wide. In late August, the East German Parliament voted to unify with West Germany on 3 October, and a unification treaty was signed on 31 August. On 12 September, the four occupying powers concluded the 2 + 4 negotiations in Moscow by giving their blessing, though the proceedings were accompanied by the usual last-minute snafus and complications. The following day, the

Germans and Soviets signed a treaty of friendship and cooperation. The first all-German elections took place on 2 December, with the Christian Democrats again winning a plurality. Germany was at last unified—and the cold war was definitely over.

The diplomacy of reunification proved to be far less problematic than its economic and social dimensions, as hopes for a relatively rapid and painless transition were soon shattered. The economist Joseph Schumpeter once described capitalism as a process of creative destruction, which suggested that even in a normally functioning market system much painful change was always in process. In the case of the joining of East and West Germany, it soon became clear that, for some time to come, the dismantling of socialism would not be balanced by the creative input of capitalist enterprise. The headaches involved in reconstituting East Germany were enormous. Bureaucrats, soldiers, scholars, and intellectuals would find no ready employment in the new environment. East German farmers would have to learn to compete in an agricultural market where the main problem was oversupply. Inefficient firms would have to be sold off, resulting in massive unemployment. Romantic memories of an unspoiled, preindustrial rural utopia were rudely interrupted by the reality of a horribly polluted environment. The problem of reclaiming property confiscated by the Communists after World War II created enormous legal-bureaucratic tangles.

Added to these were problems of psychological and social readjustment. As was inevitable, the two Germanys had grown apart culturally. Problems of reconciling social policy on such issues as abortion, for example, added to tensions. Westerners complained that easterners were lazy and had forgotten how to work, while easterners resented being treated as country bumpkins. The problems were so daunting and the satisfactions of unification, psychic and material, were so meager that the term "bungled" came readily to mind in describing the way the process of unification was handled.[43]

For the United States, too, the success of its long-term German policy brought little occasion for rejoicing. The end of the cold war saw no victory parades or celebrations, as the American public displayed a ho-hum attitude to the entire business. As the process of German reunification came to a close, the United States cast only occasional sidelong glances toward Europe, its attention being anxiously focused instead on the Persian Gulf and Iraq's invasion of Kuwait. With history refusing to provide a decent intermission, the United States was forced to grapple with the problems of the post–cold war era before the cold war had even come to a close.

It may be that this absence of dramatic interest in the eyes of Americans was a consequence of the fact that the postwar history of the German question was a success story. Success stories are inherently less exciting than diplomatic crises or outright failures; perhaps diplomatic success is even boring. However, there is another reason that the German problem should have ended with a whimper. Despite much melodramatic talk about the explosive dangers embedded in the issue, the transparent news coverage of this story, and the barely stifled yawns with which it was greeted, testify not only to the desire of publicity-seeking statesmen to receive credit, but also to the relatively nonproblematic nature of the process.[44]

The events of 1989 and 1990 flowed from a realization that it remained for the diplomatists only to carry out the verdict of history. The German issue had to come to a peaceful conclusion for the same reason that the cold war had to end peacefully. Because conflict was against the rules and neither side was inclined to gamble, peaceful unification was the only kind conceivable. The anticlimactic ending was due less to the skill of the statesmen in avoiding the dangers—though they surely deserved credit for a job well done—than to the fact that the greatest dangers had already been avoided. Détente and *Ostpolitik*, coming as they did in the wake of war-threatening crises, were the products of a realization that the cold war and German reunification had to be settled historically, which meant that change could take place only if the powers were convinced that the German question in its old guises could no longer arise. In other words, the settlement of the German question presupposed its transformation.

While the culminating events of 1990 produced a satisfying sense of closure so far as diplomacy is concerned, a significant residue of doubt remained as to whether the German problem had in fact been left behind. Just as generals seem always to plan for the last war, diplomats and policy analysts seem determined to continue guarding against a revival of the German problem in forms and contexts long since surpassed. For such pessimists, historical memory tended to confuse historical judgment, clouding the fact that the German question was not a single ongoing problem but a series of problems continually in process of historical transformation.

There was, first, the problem that Germany presented to the United States between 1917 and 1945: the threat of world domination. For American internationalists, Germany was not the historical archenemy, but an enemy of history as American liberals preferred to see it develop. The German roadblock to world order was removed at a cost of two world wars, only to have the problem resurface, this time with the Soviet Union cast in the role of the villain. Germany thus proved to be only incidental to a more comprehensive problem that continued to preoccupy American diplomacy throughout the ensuing cold war. Viewed in this light, the problem was metamorphosed rather than solved; it was superseded and transformed by the cold war and remained unresolved until the collapse of the Soviet Union. Should the problem arise again in future, it is likely that it will have yet another form, just as the Soviet global threat differed significantly from that first posed by Germany.

Second, there was the problem of Germany's being positioned in the center of Europe, which appeared to be one of those uncomfortable facts of geography that everyone was helpless to change. But geography in the modern world has, like much else, been relativized: the globalization of politics during the cold war superseded purely regional logic. Thus the underlying presence of the first problem throughout the cold war helped to resolve the second—by dividing Germany, by linking its respective halves to East and West, and, making assurance doubly sure, by getting the Germans to agree to it. In retrospect the solution of a divided Germany seemed almost preordained, but before it could be achieved Americans had to purge themselves of illusory hopes for cooperation with the Soviets and for a united Europe standing on its own feet.

In turn, however, this solution created a third German problem: that of reunification. A quarter century passed before the West Germans were willing to recognize that Germany would have to remain divided for the foreseeable future. During that time, the German problem was the source of much tension, especially in Berlin. Paradoxically, however, the Germans had to shelve their nationalist aspirations as a precondition to reunification, for which they continued to nurture hopes.

But German self-restraint was not the whole of the story. While *Ostpolitik* laid a foundation for the discontent within East Germany that played such a large role in forcing the pace of reunification, it was hardly a sufficient condition for ending the division of the country or of Europe. Had the Gorbachev revolution in the USSR not removed the repressive controls of Soviet power, the two-Germany solution might have remained viable for a long time to come. Ironically, reunification came at a time when interest in Germany unity was low and waning further and when both German states were preparing to settle down for a long period of separate maintenance. Visitors to East Germany in the 1980s were struck by noticeable differences in culture, language, and appearance between the two states that, had they been allowed to develop, might over time have eroded any sense of national identity.

The end of the cold war finally resolved—with a rapidity no one had dared to imagine and on terms wholly favorable to the West—the problem of German unity. But in so doing, it created a new problem: that of a Germany in a united Europe and a new world order. Western statesmen early in the cold war had anticipated the problems that a united Germany might pose, and rather than regress to a repetition of problem number two, they hoped to embed the new Germany in a European and global matrix from which it could not hope to break free—and, assuming optimal cultural change, from which it would have no desire to break free.

Following the success of unification, it was still open to question whether sufficient capital had been invested in this solution. The insistence upon embedding a united Germany in NATO provided safeguards, of course, but the answer to the German question presupposed the continuing vitality of the alliance. In the absence of a Soviet threat, many observers came to believe that NATO was an alliance without a mission. If NATO's task had once been double containment, should a tame Russia replace the feral USSR, its only conceivable raison d'être would be the containment of Germany. "A united Germany is not likely to accept for very long a structure that rests on this premise," said one hard-boiled observer of affairs.[45] NATO's inability to deal with the dissolution of Yugoslavia was not an encouraging sign of the organization's capacity to deal with post–cold war security issues. Indeed, many were quick to identify Kohl's precipitate recognition of Croatia—historically linked to Germany in some unsavory ways— as the diplomatic signal that began the slide into chaos in the Balkans.

Another essential precondition of German reunification was that nation's integration into larger, federative European structures, such as the European Community. Indeed, Kohl and Genscher themselves made sure to play up on every occasion Germany's role as a good European. "Germany is our fatherland, Europe our future," said the Christian Democratic Union's 1990 electoral program.[46] Following the conclusion of the reunification drama, leaders of the European Community reached agreement in Maastricht, Belgium, in late 1991 on the desirability of monetary union as a prelude to political union. Had their schedule been followed, the Europeanization of Germany would soon have been well on the way to completion. However, events showed quickly that the proponents of European unity had been overly optimistic. Not only did popular resistance to a loss of national sovereignty remain strong throughout the Continent, but in Germany the policies of the Bundesbank made it clear that the financing of German unification conflicted with the economics of Europeanization.

Pushed into maintaining high interest rates by the inflationary pressures of paying for the integration of former East Germany, the Bundesbank forced other nations to follow suit to defend the value of their currencies on international exchanges and keep them within a pre-agreed common range. However, since these countries were in economic recession, the commitment to high interest rates meant that they were unable to open the spigot of credit at a time when an "easy money" approach was indicated as a matter of standard countercyclical policy. Worried as ever about inflation, the independent Bundesbank turned a deaf ear to the pleas of its European neighbors that it relax its monetary policy. Under heavy attack from currency speculators, France and Great Britain were unable, in the end, to avoid devaluation, and thus divergent monetary policies, prompted by German national interests, made a shambles of plans for monetary union and cast into question the prospects for political unity.

There was also a question as to where the new Germany would stand internationally. In the new world order, in which economics appeared to have replaced power politics, Germany, as the world's greatest trading nation, was definitely a world power. Consequently there were calls from many sectors to make Germany a permanent member of the United Nations Security Council. But, as various military interventions by the UN showed, the economistic view of the new world order was far too simple. With the great powers still being called on to take military action in various world situations, membership on the Security Council presupposed Germany's willingness to amend its constitution to allow for participation in peacekeeping missions. Otherwise a Germany on the Security Council, though enjoying the legal status of a major power, would have an anomalous status as a nation that, by choice and necessity, was still "singularized." In July 1994, the Federal Constitutional Court finally ruled that multilateral military missions were legally permissible, but it remained to be seen under what circumstances Germany would agree to send its troops abroad.[47]

Even if one assumes the worst outcome of the situation in the mid-1990s—a breakdown of the European idea and of the liberal international order—there will be no replay of past German problems. Were Germany to fulfill the worst expectations of its critics and become a nuclear power, the constraints of the nuclear era would prevent a repetition of previous adventurism. The "crystal ball" effect of atomic weapons, by which politicians and soldiers can forecast all too well the suicidal consequences of thermonuclear warfare, simply accentuates what the Germans had well learned in World War II. They had, at that time, already seen the future, and it did not work. For all that, diplomatic myths and the memory of Rapallo—now a cliché—have continued to dominate the thinking of statesmen.

However, a willingness to admit that structural change has taken place is not necessarily an admission that the German question, in its fundamentals, has been transformed. Much ink has been spent on yet another apparent constant: the problem of German culture and history that underlies everything else. At one time it was fashionable to fault Germany for her failure to develop a liberal sensibility and for cultivating instead a romantic yearning for national fulfillment that turned her into an enemy of civilization. For many in both world wars, the German problem was not grounded in politics but in the very nature of the German people, the deep structure of German national character. Some American policymakers entertained this notion of a diabolical culture, especially during World War II, but they had clearly abandoned it by the end of the occupation.

To the extent that there was a problem of political culture, it was treated by the Americans, in practical terms, by ideological means. Germany's successful integration into Europe and a liberal world community appeared to many to depend ultimately on whether this aspect of the German problem had been satisfactorily resolved. After a half century, many are still not sure. The Germans abandoned Nazism as a matter of necessity, to be sure, but have they embraced liberal democracy and Western civilization? The external circumstances of geopolitics have changed but have the Germans themselves changed?

As a Germany preoccupied with making a success of unification began to focus on its internal affairs, and as the strain produced by all the sudden changes produced extremist expressions of anger, foreign observers began once again to wonder whether the German problem had been resolved.

Would the East Germans add an element of political immaturity that would undo a half century of progress toward democracy? Attacks on foreigners— gypsies, Turks, Eastern Europeans, even American blacks—stimulated fears that the old demons lurking deep in the German psyche, long repressed, were once again threatening to haunt the rest of the world.

Overall, however, the German cultural problem is neither as grave as it may have seemed to some, nor as unusual. In its external aspects, this antiforeign sentiment is more broadly European than specifically German in character, part of a larger pattern of nativist resentment of a tide of immigration into homogeneous European societies. Its internal dimension, the endless agonizing over German identity, also amounts to less than it has been cracked up to be. Predictably, the vision of unification was so sentimental and melodramatic in its expectations that its achievement failed to provide the catharsis necessary to resolve the endless German identity crisis. But then, one needs to keep in mind that modernity has made *all* national identities and cultural essences problematic—witness the agonized debates within the United States over the implications of multiculturalism.

To be sure, some Americans have continued to harbor misgivings about certain features of the German national character, but in an era dominated by cultural relativism, those qualms are more than offset by a cosmopolitan understanding that unappealing cultural traits are not confined solely to the Germans, and by an awareness that there exists no standard cultural pattern for democracy. In any event, as always there is a ready recognition of the Germans' many outstanding virtues, while the Federal Republic's exemplary transition to good standing in the family of nations and its status as a good European has done much to dispel the notion that the German culture is a cancerous organ in the body of Western civilization.

Getting things back to "normal" for Germany and bringing Germany into harmony with America's image of the world required an amazingly comprehensive set of transformations—of Germany, Europe, the United States, and indeed of the entire structure of world politics. Unlike diplomatic systems of the past, in which balances of power had been like temporary cones on active volcanoes destined once again to erupt, the stability introduced by the policy of double containment allowed time for the process of modernization to do its work, making these peaceful transformations possible. By the time the policy had run its course, the German volcano was extinct.

However, for Americans and Germans caught up in this process of change, what looked like a happy ending was, in fact, only a problematic beginning in an ongoing story of adjustment to new realities. Whatever the successes and failures of the German-American relationship in the future, they will not mechanically echo the past. In the half century since the end of the Second World War, both the world and the German question have been transformed. Any further change in the German question will build on the new structures and processes created out of those transformations.

CHRONOLOGY

1898	Germans observe Dewey's victory at Manila Bay.
	German War Plan.
1903	Venezuela crisis.
	War plan "Black."
1906	Algeciras Conference
1915	Sinking of *Lusitania*.
1916	*Sussex* pledge.
1917	German declaration of unrestricted submarine warfare.
	Zimmermann telegram published.
	United States declares war on Germany.
1918	President Wilson suggests lenient peace if Germans change government.
1921	Treaty of Berlin: United States signs peace treaty with Germany.

1923   Treaty of Commerce and Friendship.

              U.S.-German Claims Commission created.

1924   Dawes Plan.

1929   Young Plan.

1933   Hitler comes to power.

              President Roosevelt's New Deal administration takes office.

1935–1937   Neutrality Acts.

1937–1938   Roosevelt attempts liberal appeasement.

1940   Rainbow Plans adopt "Germany first" strategy.

              Freezing of assets.

              Destroyers for bases deal with Great Britain.

              Tripartite Pact signed between Germany, Japan, and Italy.

              Lend-Lease proposed.

1941   Roosevelt declares unlimited national emergency.

              U.S. Navy begins convoying.

              Roosevelt issues shoot-on-sight order against U-boats.

              Sinkings of *Robin Moor*, *Reuben James*, etc.

              Repeal of Neutrality Acts.

              Lend-Lease extended to USSR.

              Japanese attack Pearl Harbor.

              Hitler declares war on United States.

              United States declares war on Germany.

1942   Roosevelt announces unconditional surrender policy at Casablanca.

1943   Churchill, Stalin, and Roosevelt discuss German dismemberment and partition at Tehran.

1944   European Advisory Commission in London reaches agreement on zonal boundaries for postwar occupation.

Morgenthau Plan discussed.

1945   4–11 February

Yalta Conference discusses postwar partition, borders, and reparations.

May

JCS 1067, occupation directive for Germany issued.

8 May

Germany surrenders.

5 June

First meeting of Allied Control Council in Berlin.

17 July–2 August

Potsdam Conference.

20 November

Nuremberg trials begin.

1946   April

Failure of level-of-industry plan.

21 April

Communists and rump Socialist parties form SED.

June

Council of Foreign Ministers meetings in Paris.

6 September

Secretary of State Byrnes proposes revision of Potsdam and creation of bizonia.

2 December

United States and Britain agree on zonal fusion.

1947 10 March–24 April

Council of Foreign Ministers meetings in Moscow.

12 March

Truman Doctrine announced.

5 June

Marshall Plan proposed.

11 July

JCS 1779, liberalized occupation directive.

25 November–15 December

Council of Foreign Ministers meeting in London.

1948 4 June

London program for a West German state announced.

21 June

Western powers institute currency reform.

24 June

Soviets respond with complete blockade of access routes to Berlin.

26 June

Berlin airlift begins.

1 September

Parliamentary Council meets in Bonn to draft West German constitution.

30 November

Separate city government established in East Berlin.

1949   February–May

Jessup-Malik talks on Berlin.

4 April

United States signs North Atlantic Treaty.

8 April

French zone merges into Bizonia.

Allied High Commission is formed.

4 May

Soviets agree to lift Berlin blockade.

8 May

West German Federal Republic adopts Basic Law.

15 May

McCloy replaces Clay as military governor.

23 May

Council of Foreign Ministers meets in Paris.

30 May

People's Council adopts constitution for DDR.

14 August

First Bundestag elections held.

15 September

Adenauer is elected federal chancellor.

21 September

Federal Republic of Germany comes into being.

Civilianized occupation and Charter of High Commission go into force.

30 September

End of Berlin airlift.

15 October

USSR recognizes DDR.

1950　　　　25 June

North Korea invades South Korea.

September

Acheson proposes German rearmament to Allies.

October

France proposes European army to include German troops.

1951　　　　Pleven Plan conference continues to meet in Paris.

22 November

Western foreign ministers agree on terms for inclusion of West Germany in Europe.

Negotiations with Adenauer on Contractual Agreement to replace occupation statute.

24 October

President Truman announces end of state of war with Germany.

1952   March

Allies adopt Lisbon Program for rearmament.

10 March

Soviets offer peace treaty based on a neutral, united, and rearmed Germany.

25 March

Western powers reply that free all-German elections are pre-condition to reunification.

9 April

Soviets deny entrée to UN electoral commission.

26 May

Contractual Agreements signed.

27 May

EDC treaties signed.

1953   5 March

Death of Stalin.

16–17 June

Berlin uprising starts.

1954   25 January–18 February

Council of Foreign Ministers meeting in Berlin.

29 January

Eden Plan is submitted.

25 March

Soviets announce full transfer of sovereignty to DDR.

30 August

Defeat of EDC by French National Assembly.

23 October

Paris Protocol provides for end of occupation and West Germany's admission to NATO.

1955   5 May

Occupation ends.

9 May

Federal Republic becomes NATO member.

14 May

Warsaw Pact Treaty is signed.

15 May

Austrian State Treaty.

18–24 July

Big Four summit at Geneva.

8–14 September

Adenauer in Moscow, agrees to recognize USSR.

27 October–16 November

Council of Foreign Ministers meeting in Geneva discusses Germany and European security.

9 December

Hallstein Doctrine announced.

1957

1 January

Saar incorporated into Federal Republic of Germany.

25 March

Treaty of Rome provides for European Economic Community.

3 October

Rapacki Plan proposed.

1958

10 November

Khrushchev asserts Allies must leave Berlin.

27 November

Soviet note proposes "free city" solution for West Berlin and presents ultimatum on peace treaty.

1959

May

Foreign ministers meet in Geneva on German question.

24 May

Death of Dulles.

3 August

Eisenhower agrees to Khrushchev visit.

15–28 September

Khrushchev visit to United States.

1960

17 May

Paris summit breaks up because of U-2 affair.

8 November

Kennedy elected president.

1961	3–4 June
	Kennedy and Khrushchev meet in Vienna.
	25 July
	Kennedy TV speech on Berlin.
	13 August
	Construction of Berlin wall begins.
	18 August
	United States announces increase in Berlin garrison.
	19 August
	Johnson and Clay sent to Berlin.
	17 September
	CDU loses absolute majority in West Germany.
	23 October
	Offset agreement on balance of payments.
	27 October
	U.S.-Soviet tank confrontation at Checkpoint Charlie.
1962	2 January
	United States begins diplomatic exploration of Berlin issue.
	14 February
	Soviets harass planes in air corridors.
	May
	Grewe recalled from Washington at United States' request.

17 August

Peter Fechter incident at Berlin wall.

1963   20 January

FRG and France sign treaty of cooperation.

19 April

De Gaulle announces creation of *force de frappe*.

26 June

Kennedy's "Ich bin ein Berliner" speech.

15 October

Adenauer resigns in wake of *Spiegel* affair; replaced by Erhard.

22 November

President Kennedy assassinated in Dallas, Texas.

1964   December

President Johnson announces end of support for multilateral force.

1966   4 April

Grand Coalition formed; Kiesinger is chancellor.

7 October

Johnson speech on "building bridges."

1967   19 April

Adenauer dies.

24 August

United States and USSR agree on Nuclear Nonproliferation Treaty.

1968   12 January

Bonn and Belgrade agree to exchange ambassadors.

1969   21 October

Brandt becomes chancellor.

28 October

Ostpolitik announced.

1970   August

German-Soviet Treaty signed.

December

German-Polish Treaty signed.

1971   August

Four-power accords normalize status of Berlin.

1972   November

Grundvertrag (Basic Treaty) between West and East Germany.

1974   16 May

Brandt resigns; Schmidt becomes chancellor.

1978   April

President Carter defers production of neutron bomb.

1981   October

Antimissile demonstrations begin.

1982   October

Kohl of Christian Democrats becomes chancellor.

1983   March

CDU-CSU wins 48.8 percent of vote in federal election; Kohl reelected; Green Party wins 27 seats in Bundestag.

November

Pershing II missiles begin to arrive in West Germany.

1985   April–May

Bitburg controversy as President Reagan calls SS soldiers "victims."

1989   30 May

President Bush calls the Federal Republic a "partner in leadership" on his visit to the FRG following the NATO summit.

19 August

Seven hundred East German citizens flee to Austria via Hungary.

11 September

Founding of Neues Forum, East German opposition group.

1 October

First trains with East German refugees from West German embassies in Prague and Warsaw enter the FRG.

2 October

First mass demonstrations in Leipzig.

7 October

Gorbachev visit to celebrate the fortieth anniversary of the DDR.

9 October

More than 100,000 people demonstrate on the streets of Leipzig and other cities.

18 October

Honecker resigns. Krenz becomes the new general secretary of DDR.

9 November

Berlin wall opened.

13 November

Modrow becomes minister president in DDR.

17 November

Modrow broaches possible "community of treaties" (*Vertragsgemeinschaft*) between the two Germanys.

28 November

Kohl presents to Bundestag Ten Point Plan for German unity with the goal of establishing a "federation."

2–3 December

Bush-Gorbachev summit at Malta.

3 December

Krenz, the SED Politburo, and Central Committee all resign.

4 December

Bush assures Kohl of U.S. support for unification at meeting in Brussels, but with precondition that a united Germany remain in NATO.

7 December

East German elections scheduled for 6 May 1990.

10 December

Four-power meeting in Berlin at Soviet request.

15 December

De Maizière becomes head of East German CDU.

21 December

1990   Mitterrand meets Modrow in East Berlin.

28 January

Elections moved up to March 18 as Modrow's government loses control.

2 February

Genscher visits Washington and receives support for the Genscher Plan; Baker proposes the 2 + 4 framework.

8 February

Baker proposes 2 + 4 format to Soviet leadership while in Moscow.

10 February

Kohl and Genscher visit Gorbachev in Moscow to discuss unification.

12 February

Ottawa NATO summit. The two Germanys and four powers agree to begin talks on unity under the 2 + 4 framework.

14 February

Modrow visits Bonn; Bonn talks of economic and monetary union.

25 February

Kohl and Bush meet at Camp David.

14 March

Initial meeting of 2 + 4 parties at the ambassadorial level. Agreement to admit Polish representatives to discuss issues affecting Poland.

18 March

CDU wins elections in the five eastern *Länder* (states).

12 April

De Maizière is elected prime minister of the DDR, as head of a conservative ruling coalition.

19 April

Kohl and Mitterrand propose European political and monetary union by 1993.

5 May

Bonn 2 + 4 meeting; Shevardnadze proposes a "decoupling" of internal and external aspects of unification.

15 May

Kohl calls for all-German elections by year's end.

31 May

Bush-Gorbachev summit in Washington; United States offers "nine assurances" to Gorbachev.

8 June

Kohl meets with Bush at Camp David.

21 June

Parliaments of both German states pass resolutions recognizing Poland's western border as final and call for a treaty between Poland and Germany following unification.

22 June

East Berlin 2 + 4 meeting.

1 July

Economic and currency union established.

2 July

Twenty-eighth Soviet CPSU Congress begins in Moscow.

3 July

Shevardnadze favors German unification before Party Congress.

5 July

NATO summit in London.

9–12 July

Houston economic summit of G-7 leaders; $15 billion in aid to USSR is voted down.

15–16 July

Gorbachev and Kohl meet near Stavropol. Gorbachev agrees to Germany's membership in NATO.

17 July

Paris 2 + 4 meeting. Agreement on Polish border reached.

31 August

Unification Treaty signed.

12 September

2 + 4 Treaty signed in Moscow.

13 September

FRG-USSR Treaty on Good Neighborliness, Partnership and Cooperation.

1 October

Signature of agreement on expiration of four-power rights in the Federal Republic and Berlin.

3 October

FRG-GDR union goes into effect.

5 October

Bundestag ratifies 2 + 4 Treaty.

11 October

U.S. Senate ratifies 2 + 4 Treaty.

14 October

German-Polish Treaty confirms Oder-Neisse border.

2 December

First all-German elections; CDU-CSU wins 45.9 percent of votes.

NOTES

PREFACE

1.   From an address on Robert E. Lee delivered at University of North Carolina (19 January 1909), in Arthur S. Link, ed., *The Papers of Woodrow Wilson* (Princeton, N.J.: Princeton University Press, 1966): 638–39.

CHAPTER 1

1.   Quoted in Manfred Jonas, *The United States and Germany* (Ithaca, N.Y.: Cornell University Press, 1984), 29.

2.   John W. Coogan, *The End of Neutrality: The United States, Britain and Maritime Rights 1899–1915* (Ithaca, N.Y.: Cornell University Press, 1981), 180.

3.   Lansing memo of 11 July 1915, quoted in Daniel Smith, *Robert Lansing and American Neutrality 1914–1917* (New York: Da Capo Press, 1972), 60.

4.   Remarks to the National Press Club, 15 May 1916, in Arthur Link, ed., *The Papers of Woodrow Wilson* (Princeton, N.J.: Princeton University Press), 37:48 (hereafter cited as *WWP*).

5.   Address in Pittsburgh on preparedness, 29 January 1916, *WWP* 36:33.

6.   A speech in Long Branch, N.J., accepting the presidential nomination, 2 September 1916, *WWP* 38:136.

7.   An address in Chicago on preparedness, 31 January 1916, *WWP* 36:72.

8.   In a meeting with clergymen, 19 June 1917, *WWP* 42:537.

9.   Letter to the Pope (draft), 23 August 1917, *WWP* 44:34.

10.   An address in Buffalo to the American Federation of Labor, *WWP* 45:13.

11.   Newton D. Baker to Wilson, 2 May 1917, *WWP* 42:194.

12.   In a meeting with clergymen, 19 June 1917, *WWP* 42:537.

13. American exports to Germany, which averaged 400 million dollars annually in the period from 1926 to 1930, shrank to 126 million dollars in 1936, 46 million dollars in 1939, and to virtual insignificance by 1941. While the balance of trade generally favored the United States by a wide margin, imports from Germany followed the same pattern. See the figures in Detlef Junker, *Der unteilbare Weltmarkt: Das ökonomische Interesse in der Aussenpolitik der USA 1933–1941* (Stuttgart: Ernst Klett Verlag, 1975).

14. Gerhard Weinberg, "Germany's Declaration of War on the United States: A New Look," in Hans L. Trefousse, ed. *Germany and America: Essays on Problems of International Relations and Immigration* (New York: Brooklyn College Press, 1980), 54.

15. Andreas Hillgruber, *Germany and the Two World Wars* (Cambridge, Mass.: Harvard University Press, 1981), 49–50.

16. Hillgruber, *Germany*, 93 (quotation); Klaus Hildebrand, *The Foreign Policy of the Third Reich* (Berkeley: University of California Press, 1973), 100; Jochen Thies, *Architekt der Weltherrschaft: Die Endziele Hitlers* (Düsseldorf: Droste Verlag, 1976), 168–82.

17. FDR to John Cudahy, 4 March 1939, in Elliott Roosevelt, ed., *FDR: His Personal Letters* (New York: Duell, Sloan & Pearce, 1947–1950), 4:863.

18. Hopkins quoted in Robert E. Sherwood, *Roosevelt and Hopkins: An Intimate History* (New York: Harper & Brothers, 1948), 160.

19. Beatrice Bishop Berle and Travis Beal Jacobs, eds., *Navigating the Rapids 1918–1971* (New York: Harcourt Brace Jovanovich, 1973), 370.

20. Berle and Jacobs, *Navigating the Rapids*, 224.

21. Kennedy memo of 3 March 1939, quoted in Jonas, *The United States and Germany*, 237.

22. FDR quoted by Wayne Cole, *Roosevelt and the Isolationists* (Lincoln: University of Nebraska Press, 1983), 233.

23. Manfred Jonas, *Isolationism in America 1935–1941* (Ithaca, N.Y.: Cornell University Press, 1966), 274.

24. Bullitt to FDR, 23 March 1939, in Orville Bullitt, ed., *For the President: Personal and Secret* (Boston: Houghton Mifflin, 1972), 233.

25. Gerhard L. Weinberg, *World in the Balance: Behind the Scenes of World War II* (Hanover, N.H.: University Press of New England, 1981), 81–85, 92–93.

26. Quoted in Paul Y. Hammond, "Policy Directives for the Occupation of Germany," in Harold Stein, ed., *American Civil-Military Decisions* (Birmingham: University of Alabama Press, 1963), 355; FDR to Cordell Hull, 1 April 1944, in *FDR: His Personal Letters*, 4:1504.

27. Quoted in Hammond, "Policy Directives," 386.

28. Stimson quoted in Hammond "Policy Directives," 367.

29. Tony Sharp, *The Wartime Alliance and the Zonal Division of Germany* (London: Oxford University Press, 1975).

CHAPTER 2

1. *The Gallup Poll: Public Opinion 1935–1971* (New York: Random House, 1972), 1:460, 470, 485, 506.

2.   James F. Tent, *Mission on the Rhine: Re-education and Denazification in American-Occupied Germany* (Chicago: University of Chicago Press, 1982), 285.

3.   Edward N. Peterson, *The American Occupation of Germany—Retreat to Victory* (Detroit: Wayne State University Press, 1978), 60–61.

4.   George F. Kennan, *Memoirs, 1925–1950* (Boston: Little, Brown, 1967), 428.

5.   Franklin M. Davis, Jr., *Come as a Conqueror* (New York: Macmillan, 1967), 143.

6.   John H. Backer, *The Decision to Divide Germany: American Foreign Policy in Transition* (Durham, N.C.: Duke University Press, 1978), 54.

7.   Backer, *Decision to Divide*, 54.

8.   Richard Mayne, *The Recovery of Europe*, rev. ed. (New York: Anchor Books,1973), 98.

9.   William J. Bosch, *Judgment on Nuremberg: American Attitudes toward the Major War Crime Trials* (Chapel Hill: University of North Carolina Press, 1970), 15.

10.   John H. Hilldring to Eisenhower, 16 January 1946, Pre-Presidential, Box 42, Dwight D. Eisenhower Presidential Library, Abilene, Kansas (hereafter cited as DDEPL).

11.   Stephen Ambrose, *Eisenhower* (New York: Simon and Schuster, 1982), 1:422.

12.   Ambrose, *Eisenhower*, 1:423.

13.   Tom Bower, *The Pledge Betrayed: America and Britain and the Postwar Denazification of Germany* (Garden City, N.Y.: Doubleday, 1982), 154.

14.   Quoted in Hansjorg Gehring, *Amerikanische Literaturpolitik in Deutschland 1945–1973* (Stuttgart: Deutsche Verlags-Anstalt, 1976), 17.

15.   Tent, *Mission*, 77.

16.   Quoted in Tent, *Mission*, 195.

17.   Tent, *Mission*, 93.

18.   Henry J. Kellerman, *Cultural Relations as an Instrument of American Foreign Policy* (Washington, D.C.: Department of State, 1978), 26.

19.   Ambrose, *Eisenhower*, 1:426.

20.   Quoted in Thomas G. Paterson, *On Every Front: The Making of the Cold War* (New York: Norton, 1979), 3.

21.   Tent, *Mission*, 122.

22.   Harold Zink, *The United States in Germany, 1944–1955* (Princeton, N.J.: Princeton University Press, 1957), 259.

23.   Edwin Hartrich, *The Fourth and Richest Reich* (New York: Macmillan, 1980), 127.

24.   Backer, *Decision to Divide*, 13.

25.   Marion Dönhoff, *Foe into Friend: The Makers of the New Germany from Konrad Adenauer to Helmut Schmidt*, trans. Gabriele Annan (New York: St. Martin's Press, 1982), 93.

26.   Hartrich, *The Fourth and Richest Reich*, 60.

27.   Kennan lecture, "Problems of American Foreign Policy after Moscow," 6 May 1947, Box 19, Kennan Papers, Mudd Library, Princeton University.

28.   William Griffith, as quoted in *The New York Times*, 12 November 1989, A:20.

CHAPTER 3

1. Charles Bohlen, *Witness to History 1929–1969* (New York: Norton, 1973), 232–33.

2. Harry S. Truman, *Memoirs*, vol. 1, *Year of Decisions* (New York, Doubleday & Co., Inc., 1955), 230–31.

3. U.S. Department of State, *Foreign Relations of the United States: The Conference of Berlin, 1945* (Washington, D.C.: Government Printing Office, 1960), 2:808–809, 873–76 (hereafter cited as *FRUS*, with appropriate years and volume numbers).

4. Memo to Willard Thorp, 28 July 1945, cited in Bruce Kuklick, *American Policy and the Division of Germany* (Ithaca, N.Y.: Cornell University Press, 1972), 261–62.

5. Robert Murphy, *Diplomat among Warriors* (Garden City, N.Y.: Doubleday, 1964), 227; Dwight D. Eisenhower, *Crusade in Europe* (Garden City, N.Y.: Doubleday, 1948), 444, 458, 475; Walter Bedell Smith, *My Three Years in Moscow* (New York: Lippincott, 1949), 23–24.

6. Clay to General John Hilldring, 7 May 1945, in Jean Edward Smith, ed., *The Papers of General Lucius D. Clay: Germany 1945–1949* (Bloomington: Indiana University Press, 1974), 1:13.

7. W. Averell Harriman and Elie Abel, *Special Envoy to Churchill and Stalin, 1941–1946* (New York: Random House, 1975), 510.

8. Clay to John McCloy, 29 June 1945, *Papers of General Lucius D. Clay*, 1:39.

9. Josiah E. Dubois oral history transcript, p. 32, in Harry S Truman Presidential Library, Independence, Missouri (hereafter cited as HSTPL).

10. Lucius D. Clay, *Decision in Germany* (New York: Doubleday, 1950), 108–109.

11. *FRUS:1946*, 5:416–17; D. U. Ratchford and William B. Ross, *Berlin Reparations Assignment* (Chapel Hill: University of North Carolina Press, 1947), 127–28.

12. *FRUS:1945*, 3:829; John Gimbel, *The American Occupation of Germany* (Stanford, Calif.: Stanford University Press, 1968), 16–18.

13. *FRUS:1945*, 3:829.

14. See *FRUS:1945*, 3:878, 891, 917–19, 907–908; *FRUS:1946*, 5:566.

15. *FRUS:1945*, 3:1040, 1067, 1012–13; Clay, *Decision in Germany*, 119.

16. *FRUS:1946*, 5:505–07; Murphy, *Diplomat among Warriors*, 303, 287.

17. *FRUS:1946*, 2:165–73.

18. George Kennan, "Russia's National Objectives," lecture at Air War College, Maxwell Field, Alabama, 10 April 1947, Box 17, Kennan Papers, Mudd Library, Princeton University.

19. Memo, Clay to Byrnes, November 1946, *The Papers of General Lucius D. Clay*, 1:280–84.

20. *FRUS:1947*, 2:247.

21. Quoted in Edwin Hartrich, *The Fourth and Richest Reich* (New York: Macmillan, 1980), 109.

22. Lucius D. Clay oral history, HSTPL, 21.

23. Quoted in Charles Mee, *The Marshall Plan* (New York: Simon and Schuster, 1984), 90.

24. Quoted in Daniel Yergin, *Shattered Peace* (Boston: Houghton Mifflin, 1977), 298–99.

25. Memorandum, 30 March 1947, summary of discussion in CFM on ACC report, *The Papers of General Lucius D. Clay*, 1:331.

26. Walter Bedell Smith to Dwight D. Eisenhower, 17 November 1947, Pre-Presidential Papers, Box 109, Dwight D. Eisenhower Presidential Library, Abilene, Kansas (hereafter cited as DDEPL).

27. Report by Marshall, 28 April 1947, in *Germany 1947–1949: The Story in Documents* (Washington: Government Printing Office, 1950), 62.

28. *FRUS:1947*, 2:37ff.

29. Kennan, "World Political Situation," address before the Business Advisory Council, Washington, D.C., 24 September 1947, Box 17, Kennan Papers, Mudd Library, Princeton University.

30. *Germany:1947–1949*, 64.

31. U.S. delegation to Truman, 15 December 1947, *FRUS:1947*, 2:771.

32. Walter Bedell Smith to Dwight David Eisenhower, 10 December 1947, Pre-Presidential Papers, Box 109, DDEPL.

33. Memorandum of conversation by Samuel Reber, 18 November 1947, *FRUS:1947*, 2:722.

34. Quoted in Robert J. Donovan, *Conflict and Crisis* (New York: Norton, 1977), 359.

35. Clay, *Decision in Germany*, 367.

36. Quoted in Murphy, *Diplomat among Warriors*, 313.

37. Quoted in Richard Naybe, *Postwar: The Dawn of Today's Europe* (New York: Shocken Books, 1983), 149.

38. CIA 8-48 "Review of the World Situation," 19 Aug 1948, PSF-NSC Meetings, Box 204, HSTPL.

39. Quoted in Donovan, *Conflict and Crisis*, 409.

40. Quoted in Tent, *Mission*, 298–99.

41. *FRUS:1948*, 2:999–1006.

42. Paper prepared by Kennan, 8 March 1949, *FRUS:1949*, 3:96.

43. Kennan, *Memoirs*, 421–26.

44. Kennan, "Foreign Policy and the Marshall Plan," 20 February 1948, Kennan Papers, Box 17, Mudd Library, Princeton University.

45. Paper prepared in the Department of State, undated, *FRUS: 1949*, 3:131–32.

46. Dean Acheson, *Present at the Creation* (New York: Signet, 1970), 386.

47. Quoted in David McLellan, *Dean Acheson: The State Department Years* (New York: Dodd, Mead & Company, 1976), 62.

48. Acheson, *Present at the Creation*, 387–90.

49. In Gordon Craig, *From Bismarck to Adenauer* (Westport, Conn.: Greenwood Press, 1958), 132.

50. Quoted in Terence Prittie, *Konrad Adenauer 1876–1967* (Chicago: Cowles, 1971), 224.

51. Konrad Adenauer, *Memoirs 1945–1953*, trans. Beate Ruhm von Oppen (Chicago: Henry Regnery, 1966), 79.

52. Adenauer, *Memoirs*, 35–36.

53. Quoted in Edward N. Peterson, *The American Occupation of Germany—Retreat to Victory* (Detroit: Wayne State University Press, 1978), 201.

54. Alfred Grosser, *The Colossus Again,* trans. Richard Rees (New York: Praeger, 1955), 202.

55. Leo Lania, "Schumacher: Violent Martyr," *U.N. World* (May 1952):13–14; Dean Acheson, *Sketches from Life of Men I Have Known* (New York: Harper, 1959), 171–72; Acheson, *Present at the Creation,* 447; Lewis J. Edinger, *Kurt Schumacher: A Study in Personality and Political Behavior* (Stanford, Calif.: Stanford University Press, 1966), 144–45, 176, 185.

CHAPTER 4

1. See Alfred Grosser, *The Western Alliance* (New York: Continuum, 1980), 124.

2. Wolfram Hanrieder, "German-American Relations in the Postwar Decades," in Frank Trommler and Joseph McVeigh, eds., *America and the Germans: An Assessment of a Three-hundred Year History* (Philadelphia: University of Pennsylvania Press, 1985), 92–3.

3. Memo, Kennan to Acheson, 6 January 1950, *FRUS:1950,* 1:129.

4. Statement by McCloy, *FRUS:1950,* 3:811, 814.

5. Memo by Henry Byroade, 9 March 1950, *FRUS:1950,* 3:680.

6. McCloy to Acheson, 25 April 1950, *FRUS:1950,* 4:634.

7. Memorandum of conversation, 9 February 1950, *FRUS:1950,* 4:592.

8. NSC-68, in *FRUS:1950,* 1:275.

9. Extracts from NSC-71, *FRUS:1950,* 4:687.

10. Quoted in Donovan, *Tumultuous Years: The Presidency of Harry S Truman, 1949–1953* (New York: Norton, 1982), 178.

11. Memo, Truman to Acheson, 16 June 1950, *FRUS:1950,* 4:687.

12. Department of State (DOS) memo, 16 August 1950, *FRUS:1950,* 3:213.

13. Memo prepared in Bureau of German Affairs, 11 February 1950, *FRUS:1950,* 4:602.

14. DOS paper for CFM meeting, 5 November 1949, *FRUS:1949,* 3:295–96.

15. Acheson circular telegram, 13 March 1950, *FRUS:1950,* 3:30.

16. Quoted in Lawrence Kaplan, *The United States and NATO* (Lexington: University of Kentucky Press, 1984), 154.

17. Eisenhower to Swede Hazlett, 12 September 1950, in Robert Griffith, ed., *Ike's Letters to a Friend* (Lawrence: University of Kansas Press, 1984), 81.

18. Quoted in David McLellan, *Dean Acheson: The State Department Years* (New York: Dodd, Mead & Company, 1976), 328.

19. *FRUS:1950,* 3:187.

20. David Bruce to Acheson, 22 April 1950, *FRUS:1950,* 3:12.

21. Memo of conversation, Marshall and Jules Moch, 16 October 1950, *FRUS:1950,* 3:1415.

22. Ronald Steel, *Walter Lippmann and the American Century* (New York: Vintage Books, 1981), 477.

23. Acheson, memo of conversation, 21 August 1950, *FRUS:1950,* 4:645.

24. Dean Acheson, *Sketches from Life of Men I Have Known* (New York: Harper, 1959), 42.

25. Thomas Alan Schwartz, *America's Germany: John J. McCloy and the Federal Republic of Germany* (Cambridge, Mass.: Harvard University Press, 1991), 103.

26. Ibid., 141.

27. Quoted in Robert McGeehan, *The German Rearmament Question* (Urbana: University of Illinois Press, 1971), 77.

28. Terence Prittie, *The Velvet Chancellors: A History of Postwar Germany* (London: Frederick Muller Limited, 1979), 80.

29. *New York Times*, 20 November, 4 and 10 December, 1949.

30. Konrad Adenauer, *Memoirs 1945–1953*, trans. Beate Ruhm von Oppen (Chicago: Henry Regnery, 1966), 269.

31. Quoted in McGeehan, *German Rearmament*, 141.

32. Quoted in Henry J. Kellerman, "Party Leaders and Foreign Policy," in Hans Speier and W. Phillips Davison, eds., *West German Leadership* (Evanston, Ill.: Row, Peterson, 1957), 80.

33. Dean Acheson, *Present at the Creation* (New York: Signet, 1970), 765. Churchill, as Eisenhower later noted perspicaciously in his diary, may have wanted "to relive the days of World War II."

34. Acheson, circular telegram, 29 January 1951, *FRUS:1951*, 3:761; Acheson to Bruce, 16 July 1951, ibid., 834.

35. McCloy to State, 3 January 1952, *FRUS:1952–1954*, 5:577.

36. *FRUS:1951*, 3:757.

37. Outline for briefing of Eisenhower, 18 November 1952 FRUS: 1952–1954, 1:1502.

38. Eisenhower to George Marshall, 3 August 1951, Pre-Presidential, Box 80, DDEPL; Eisenhower to Robert A. Lovett, 19 December 1987, in Louis Galambos, ed., *The Papers of Dwight David Eisenhower* (Baltimore, Md.: Johns Hopkins University Press, 1989), 12:800.

39. Quoted in McClellan, *Acheson*, 335n.

40. *New York Times*, 5 November 1950.

41. Quoted in Paul Weymar, *Adenauer: His Authorized Biography* (New York: E.P. Dutton & Co., 1957), 385.

42. "Tiger, Burning Bright," *Time*, 9 June 1952, 34.

43. Memo, Kennan to Acheson, 5 September 1951, *FRUS:1951*, 3:1328.

44. Adenauer, *Memoirs*, 368–70.

45. *New York Times*, 5 February 1952.

46. Ibid., 8 February 1952.

47. Ibid., 4 March 1952.

48. Ibid., 10 April 1952.

49. Wilhelm Wolfgang Schutz, *Rethinking German Policy: New Approaches to Reunification* (New York: Frederick A. Praeger, 1967), 116.

50. *Time*, 8 October 1951, 32; 5 November 1951, 38.

51. Acheson, *Present at the Creation*, 803–806; McCloy, "West Germany at the Threshold of Sovereignty," *U.S. Department of State Bulletin* 26 (2 June 1951), 33.

52. McClellan, *Acheson*, 370.

53. Statement by Acheson, 11 May 1950, *Reviews of the World Situation* (Washington, D.C.: Government Printing Office, 1974), 291.

54. Memo by Paul Nitze, 30 July 1952, *FRUS:1952–1954*, National Security Affairs, 68–69.

55. *New York Times,* 23 April and 29 February 1952; Charles Wighton, *Adenauer: Democratic Dictator* (London: Andre Deutsch, 1957), 153.

56. Quoted in Weymar, *Adenauer,* 434.

57. Kurt Schumacher, "Peace Contract Brings No Peace," *Newsweek,* 20 June 1952, 36.

58. *FRUS:1952–1954*, National Security Affairs, 389.

59. Ibid., 406–407.

60. John Foster Dulles, "The Danger in Our Defensive Mood," *Newsweek,* 26 May 1952, 39.

61. Eisenhower to William S. Paley, 29 March 1952, Pre-Presidential File, Box 90, Dwight D. Eisenhower Presidential Library, Abilene, Kansas (hereafter cited as DDEPL).

62. NSC minutes, 1 April 1954, Ann Whitman File, NSC Series, DDEPL.

63. Suggested reply to letter of Field Marshal Bernard Montgomery dated 2 July 1953, in Ann Whitman File, Name series, Box 22, DDEPL.

64. Minutes of NSC meeting, 18 June 1953, Ann Whitman File, NSC Series, DDEPL.

65. Ibid.

66. Quoted in Roger Morgan, *The United States and West Germany 1945–1973* (London: Oxford University Press, 1974), 42.

67. Statement at a press conference, 24 May 1955, *American Foreign Policy 1950–1955* (Washington, D.C.: Government Printing Office, 1957), 2:1885–86.

68. NSC 160/1, 17 August 1953, "United States Position with Respect to Germany," NSC Series, Policy Papers Subseries, DDEPL.

69. *FRUS:1952–1954*, National Security Affairs, 419.

70. Minutes of meeting, 5 December 1953, *FRUS:1952–1954*, 5:1783.

71. Eisenhower to Alfred Gruenther, 2 November 1954, Ann Whitman File, Administration File, Box 54, DDEPL.

72. Memo of State-MSA-JCS meeting, 28 January 1953, *FRUS:1952–1954*, 5:713.

73. Quoted in Ronald W. Pruessen, *John Foster Dulles: The Road to Power* (New York: The Free Press, 1982), 325.

74. Speech to NATO council, 14 December 1953, *FRUS:1952–1954*, 5:461.

75. NSC 160/1, DDEPL.

76. NSC notes, 21 November 1955, *FRUS:1955*, 4:349.

77. John Foster Dulles, *War or Peace* (New York: Macmillan, 1950), 212–14.

78. NSC meeting, 11 February 1953, *FRUS:1952–1954*, 5:1580.

79. Memo of conversation, Dulles and Prime Minister Laniel, 14 April 1954, *FRUS:1952–1954*, 5:938.

80. Dulles to Eisenhower, 6 February 1953, *FRUS: 1952–1954*, 5:1568.

81. Michael A. Guhin, *John Foster Dulles: A Statesman and His Times* (New York: Columbia University Press, 1972), 218–19.

82. Quoted in Dwight D. Eisenhower, *Mandate for Change 1953–1956* (Garden City, N.Y.: Doubleday, 1963), 406.

83. Eisenhower to Swede Hazlett, 21 June 1951, in Griffith, *Ike's Letters to a Friend,* 85.

84. Eisenhower to Alfred Gruenther, 27 October 1953, Ann Whitman File, Administration File, Box 16, DDEPL.

85. Eisenhower to Truman, 24 February 1951, Pre-Presidential, Box 116, DDEPL; Robert Ferrell, ed., *The Eisenhower Diaries* (New York: Norton, 1981), 180.

86. NSC notes, 21 November 1955, *FRUS:1955–1957*, 4:349.

CHAPTER 5

1. Gordon Craig, *The Germans* (New York: Putnam, 1982), 44.

2. Thomas Alan Schwartz, *America's Germany: John J. McCloy and the Federal Republic of Germany* (Cambridge, Mass.: Harvard University Press, 1991), 308.

3. Michael Balfour, *West Germany: A Contemporary History* (New York: St. Martin's Press, 1982), 188.

4. Quoted in Balfour, *West Germany*, 194.

5. Note from the Soviet Union to the United States, 4 August 1953, in Arthur M. Schlesinger, Jr., ed., *The Dynamics of World Power* (New York: Chelsea House, 1983), 1:552.

6. On American views immediately following Stalin's death, see Walt W. Rostow, *Europe after Stalin: Eisenhower's Three Decisions of March 11, 1953* (Austin: University of Texas Press, 1982).

7. Special report prepared by the Psychological Strategy Board, "Reported Decline in U.S. Prestige Abroad," *FRUS, 1952–1954* 1:1485.

8. Stephen Ambrose, *Eisenhower* (New York: Simon and Schuster, 1982), 2:217.

9. Ibid., 2:263.

10. Statement by Molotov, 8 November 1955, quoted in Schlesinger, *The Dynamics of World Power*, 1:591.

11. *New York Times*, 13 June 1955.

12. Charles Bohlen, *Witness to History 1929–1969* (New York: Norton, 1973), 387.

13. Quoted in Gerald Freund, *Germany between Two Worlds* (New York: Harcourt Brace, 1961), 150.

14. Ibid., 155.

15. Quoted in Jacob D. Beam, *Multiple Exposure: An American Ambassador's Unique Perspective on East-West Issues* (New York: Norton, 1978), 37.

16. Dean Acheson, "The Illusion of Disengagement" *Foreign Affairs* 36 (April 1958):371–82.

17. Freund, *Germany between Two Worlds*, 126.

18. Ronald Steel, *Walter Lippmann and the American Century* (New York: Vintage Books, 1981), 508.

19. *New York Herald Tribune*, 1 April 1958.

20. George F. Kennan, *Memoirs 1950–1963* (Boston: Little, Brown, 1972), 253.

21. *American Foreign Policy 1950–1955* (Washington, D.C.: Government Printing Office, 1957), 2:1747–48.

22. Eisenhower phone conversation with Dulles, 1 April 1958, Ann Whitman File, DDE Diary Series, Box 31, DDEPL.

23. Quoted in Warren Cohen, *Dean Rusk* (Totowa, N.J.: Cooper Square Publishers, 1980), 137.

24. Quoted in John Dornberg, *The Two Germanys* (New York: Dial Press, 1974), 16.

25. Strobe Talbott, ed. and trans., *Khrushchev Remembers* (Boston: Little, Brown, 1970), 454.

25. Schlesinger, *The Dynamics of World Power*, 1:616–23.

27. Quoted in Gordon D. Drummond, *The German Social Democrats in Opposition* (Norman: University of Oklahoma Press, 1982), 251.

28. Dwight D. Eisenhower, *Waging Peace 1956–1961* (Garden City, N.Y.: Doubleday, 1965), 351n.

29. Quoted in Blanche Wiesen Cook, *The Declassified Eisenhower* (New York: Penguin Books, 1984), 210.

30. Ambrose, *Eisenhower*, 2:521.

31. Robert Ferrell, ed., *The Eisenhower Diaries* (New York: Norton, 1981), 363.

32. Quoted in Eisenhower, *Waging Peace*, 350.

33. Cited in Townsend Hoopes, *The Devil and John Foster Dulles* (Boston: Little, Brown, 1973), 469.

34. Ibid., 470.

35. Quoted in Cook, *The Declassified Eisenhower*, 209.

36. Eisenhower, *Waging Peace*, 446.

37. Memo of Eisenhower-Khrushchev conversation, 15 September 1959, President's Official Files (POF), Box 126, John F. Kennedy Presidential Library, Boston, Massachusetts (hereafter JFKPL).

38. Ambrose, *Eisenhower*, 2:544.

39. Ferrell, *The Eisenhower Diaries*, 364.

40. Kennedy to Acheson, 14 August 1961, POF, Box 27, JFKPL; Allan Nevins, ed., *The Strategy of Peace* (New York: Popular Library, 1961), 253–54.

41. Quoted in Drummond, *The German Social Democrats in Opposition*, 267.

42. Arthur M. Schlesinger, Jr., *A Thousand Days* (Boston: Houghton, Mifflin, 1965), 380.

43. Schlesinger, *A Thousand Days*, 381–82.

44. Theodore Sorensen, *Kennedy* (New York: Bantam Books, 1963), 662.

45. Walt W. Rostow, *The Diffusion of Power 1957–1972* (New York: Macmillan, 1972), 231.

46. Report by Johnson, 21 August 1961, V-P Security File, Box 2, Lyndon B. Johnson Presidential Library, Austin, Texas (hereafter LBJPL).

47. Memo of conversation with Bohlen, Brandt, and others, 20 August 1961, V-P Security File, Box 2, LBJPL.

48. Memo of conversation between Johnson and Brandt, 19 August 1961, V-P Security File, Box 2, LBJPL.

49. Walt Rostow to Foy Kohler, 18 August 1961, V-P Security File, Box 2, LBJPL.

50. Talbott, *Khrushchev Remembers*, 455.

51. From Hans Kroll, *Memoirs of an Ambassador*, as quoted in Richard von Weizsäcker, *A Voice from Germany* (New York: Weidenfeld and Nicolson, 1985), 5.

52. *New York Times*, 23 and 24 September 1961.

53. Memo, Bundy to Kennedy, 4 April 1961, Box 81, National Security Files, JFKPL; Harriman to Kennedy, 1 September 1961, Box 82, National Security Files, JFKPL; Memo by Carl Kaysen, 22 August 1961, Box WH-3, Arthur Schlesinger, Jr. Papers, JFKPL; Theodore Sorensen oral history interview, p. 94, JFKPL.

CHAPTER 6

1. Quoted in Michael Balfour, *West Germany: A Contemporary History* (New York: St. Martin's Press, 1982), 204; Arthur M. Schlesinger, Jr., *A Thousand Days* (Boston: Houghton, Mifflin, 1965), 403. See also the Robert F. Kennedy oral history interview, p. 996, John F. Kennedy Presidential Library, Boston, Massachusetts.

2. Kissinger memo of conversation with Adenauer, 22 June 1965, Files of McGeorge Bundy, National Security Files, Boxes 15-16, Lyndon B. Johnson Presidential Library, Austin, Texas (hereafter LBJPL).

3. George Ball, *The Past Has Another Pattern* (New York: Norton, 1982), 271.

4. Philip Geyelin, *Lyndon B. Johnson and the World* (New York: Praeger, 1966), 165.

5. Warren Cohen, *Dean Rusk* (Totowa, N.J.: Cooper Square Publishers, 1980), 297.

6. Terence Prittie, *The Velvet Chancellors: A History of Postwar Germany* (London: Frederick Muller Limited, 1979), 127.

7. Memo, Bundy to Johnson, 27 December 1963, Confidential File: CO 52, Papers of LBJ, Box 8, LBJPL.

8. Memo of conversation with Johnson, McCloy, Rostow, Bator, 2 March 1967, NSF: Security Council History, The Trilateral Negotiations and NATO, Box 50, LBJPL.

9. George McGhee, *At the Creation of a New Germany* (New Haven: Yale University Press, 1989), 184–185, 192–193.

10. George McGhee oral history, p. 13, LBJPL.

11. Memo, Moyers to Johnson, Moyers Office File, Box 12, LBJPL.

12. Quoted in Eugene V. Rostow oral interview, p. 15, LBJPL.

13. McGhee oral history, 13.

14. James MacGregor Burns, ed., *To Heal and to Build* (New York: McGraw-Hill, 1968), 142.

15. Quoted in Seymour M. Hersh, *The Price of Power* (New York: Summit Books, 1983), 416.

16. DOS memorandum, "Western Europe Looks at Germany," REU-30, 6 August 1965, Papers of LBJ, NSF: Country File, Germany, Boxes 181–191, LBJPL.

17. Johnson interview with German correspondents, 14 November 1967, Papers of LBJ, Meeting Notes file, Box 3, LBJPL.

18. Willy Brandt, *People and Politics: The Years 1960–1975* (Boston: Little, Brown, 1976), 99.

19. Quoted in Wolfram Hanrieder, *West German Foreign Policy 1949–1963* (Stanford, Calif.: Stanford University Press, 1967), 226.

20. Quoted in Hearings of the Committee on Government Operations, U.S. Senate, 89th Congress, 2d session, 19 May 1966, 99.

21.   Henry Kissinger, *White House Years* (Boston: Little, Brown, 1979), 408–409. See also Kissinger's discussion of Bahr, Brandt, and *Ostpolitik* in the second volume of his memoirs, *Years of Upheaval* (Boston: Little, Brown, 1982), 144–147.

22.   Brandt, *People and Politics*, 282.

23.   Hersh, *The Price of Power*, 417.

24.   Kissinger, *White House Years*, 531.

25.   Ibid., 823.

26.   Ibid., 825.

27.   Brandt, *People and Politics*, 316.

28.   Helmut Schmidt, *Men and Powers* (New York: Random House, 1989), 181.

29.   Ibid., 123–124.

30.   Paul Volcker and Toyo Gyohten, *Changing Fortunes: The World's Money and the Threat to American Leadership* (New York: Times Books, 1992), 168.

31.   Schmidt, *Men and Powers*, 158.

32.   Jimmy Carter, *Keeping Faith* (New York: Bantam, 1982), 227–229.

33.   Zbigniew Brzezinski, *Power and Principle* (New York: Farrar Straus Giroux, 1982), 301.

34.   Ibid., 309.

35.   Carter, *Keeping Faith*, 338.

36.   George Ball oral history, II:26, LBJPL.

37.   Ronald Reagan, *An American Life: The Autobiography* (New York: Simon & Schuster, 1990), 560.

38.   Donald T. Regan, *For the Record: From Wall Street to Washington* (New York: Harcourt Brace Jovanovich, 1988), 259.

39.   *New York Times*, 18 October 1993, A:12.

CHAPTER 7

1.   George P. Shultz, *Turmoil and Triumph: My Years as Secretary of State* (New York: Mamillan, 1993), 767.

2.   Martin J. Hillenbrand, *Germany in an Era of Transition* (Paris: Atlantic Institute for International Affairs, 1983), 44.

3.   Alexander M. Haig, Jr., *Caveat: Realism, Reagan, and Foreign Policy* (New York: Macmillan, 1984), 227.

4.   Walter Laqueur, *Germany Today: A Personal Report* (Boston: Little, Brown, 1985).

5.   Ronald Reagan, *An American Life* (New York: Simon and Schuster, 1990), 380.

6.   Quoted in Geoffrey H. Hartman, ed., *Bitburg in Moral and Political Perspective* (Bloomington: Indiana University Press, 1986), 174–178.

7.   Quoted in David Marsh, *The Germans: Rich, Bothered and Bewildered* (London: Century, 1989), 22–23.

8.   Richard von Weizsäcker, *A Voice From Germany: Speeches by Richard von Weizsäcker*, trans. Karin von Abrams (New York: Weidenfeld and Nicolson, 1985), 48.

9.   *New York Times*, 16 June 1989, A:10.

10. Jeffrey Gedmin, *The Hidden Hand: Gorbachev and the Collapse of Eastern Germany* (Washington, D.C.: The AEI Press, 1992), 44.

11. *New York Times*, 2 August 1987, A:1.

12. Ibid., 15 May 1989, A:19.

13. Ibid., 19 June 1989, A:8.

14. Dirk Verheyen, *The German Question: A Cultural, Historical, and Geopolitical Exploration* (Boulder, Colo.: Westview Press, 1991), 190.

15. *New York Times*, 19 March 1987, A:4.

16. Ibid, 11 September 1987, A:1.

17. Robert Darnton, *Berlin Journal* (New York: Norton, 1991), 36.

18. *New York Times*, 6 October 1989, A:8.

19. Quoted in *New York Times*, 19 October 1989, A:8.

20. Quoted in H. G. Peter Wallach and Ronald A. Francisco, *United Germany: The Past, Politics, Prospects* (Westport, Conn.: Greenwood Press, 1992), 35.

21. *New York Times*, 22 October 1989, A:18.

22. Ibid., 11 November 1989, A:8.

23. Ibid.

24. Ibid., 17 November 1989, A:22

25. Ibid., 27 November 1989, A:12.

26. Stephen Szabo, *The Diplomacy of German Reunification* (New York: St. Martin's Press, 1992), 42.

27. *New York Times*, 30 November 1989, A:20.

28. Quoted in Martin McCauley, "Gorbachev, the GDR and Germany," in Gert-Joachim Glaeßner and Ian Wallace, *The German Revolution of 1989: Causes and Consequences* (Providence, R.I.: Berg Publishers, 1992), 164.

29. Michael R. Beschloss and Strobe Talbott, *At the Highest Levels: The Inside Story of the End of the Cold War* (Boston: Little, Brown, 1993), 136.

30. *New York Times*, 1 December 1989, A:1.

31. Peter Schneider, *The German Comedy: Scenes of Life after the Wall* (New York: Farrar Straus Giroux, 1991), 176.

32. *New York Times*, 1 December 1989, A:35.

33. Beschloss and Talbott, *At the Highest Levels*, 136.

34. *New York Times*, 5 December 1989, A:12.

35. Ibid., 14 December 1989, A:18.

36. Ibid., 4 December 1989, A:13.

37. Quoted in Szabo, *The Diplomacy of German Reunification*, 56.

38. Beschloss and Talbott, *At the Highest Levels*, 186.

39. Quoted in Szabo, *The Diplomacy of German Reunification*, 83.

40. Beschloss and Talbott, *At the Highest Levels*, 221.

41. Ibid., 237.

42. Quoted in Szabo, *The Diplomacy of German Reunification*, 101.

43. See Gordon A. Craig, "United We Fall," *The New York Review of Books* 41 (13 January 1994), 36–40.

44. If one were so inclined, one could even formulate a "law" of foreign policy: that the amount of information leaked varies inversely with the difficulty of the problem.

45. John Mearsheimer, "Back to the Future: Instability in Europe after the Cold

War," in Sean M. Lynn-Jones and Steven E. Miller, eds., *The Cold War and After: Prospects for Peace* (Cambridge, Mass.: MIT Press, 1993), 141–142n.

46. Cited in Renata Fritsch-Bournazel, *Europe and German Unification* (Oxford: Berg, 1992), 215.

47. *New York Times*, 13 July 1994, A:1, 13.

BIBLIOGRAPHIC ESSAY

Far from pretending to be comprehensive, this bibliography is intended only to point out some of the sources that have proved interesting and helpful in this study of U.S.-German relations. Readers seeking detailed bibliographic assistance are encouraged to consult the essays in the Jonas and Gatzke volumes cited below.

The primary source most useful for this study was the U.S. Department of State's documentary series, *Foreign Relations of the United States* (Washington, D.C.: Government Printing Office, annual volumes), which now takes some, though far from all, aspects of German policy into the mid-1950s. Important, too, were materials found in the various presidential libraries, especially the Eisenhower, Kennedy, and Johnson libraries. Special mention must be made of the George F. Kennan Papers housed in the Mudd Library at Princeton University. Kennan's brilliantly crafted speeches and essays, which always penetrate the quotidian and confront the deeper meaning of events, illuminate American thinking on Germany in the late 1940s in a way that pedestrian State Department memos cannot. The same applies to his two volumes of *Memoirs* (Boston: Little, Brown, 1961 and 1972). Right or wrong, Kennan always orients a reader to the larger implications of any issue he addresses.

For those interested in a broad overview of German-American relations, the standard works are Manfred Jonas, *The United States and Germany: A Diplomatic History* (Ithaca, N.Y.: Cornell University Press, 1984), which sticks somewhat closer to the sources and adopts a narrower diplomatic focus than does the more general Hans W. Gatzke, *Germany and the United States: A "Special Relationship"?* (Cambridge, Mass.: Harvard University Press, 1980). Jonas is better on the pre–World War II period, while the bulk of Gatzke's volume deals with events of the past fifty years. These works are engagingly written and grounded in a thorough familiarity with the materials, though their preoccupation with telling the story makes them somewhat flat on the interpretive side. They also contain extensive bibliographic essays (Jonas's includes German-language sources) organized around periods and subthemes of U.S.-German relations that are indispensable starting points for those interested in digging deeper.

An overview of the postwar period may be found in Roger Morgan, *The United States and Germany: A Study in Alliance Politics* (London: Oxford University Press, 1974). This work is full of interesting and informed detail but is weighed down by a rigorous scheme of structural analysis, which, whatever its value as political science, imparts a choppy, multiperspectival quality that detracts from its value as narrative history. On pre–World War I relations, I have relied for general information on Henry M. Adams, *Prussian-American Relations, 1775–1871* (Cleveland: Western Reserve University Press, 1960), and Clara E. Schieber, *The Transformation of American Sentiment toward Germany, 1870–1914* (Boston: Comhill Publishing Co., 1923), a dated but still useful volume. For German military thinking, Holger Herwig, *The Politics of Frustration: The United States in German Naval Planning, 1889–1941* (Boston: Little, Brown, 1976) is informative and interesting. Theodore Roosevelt's approach to Germany is best absorbed firsthand through a reading of his correspondence in William Elting Morison, ed., *The Letters of Theodore Roosevelt* (Cambridge, Mass.: Harvard University Press, 1951). Otherwise, Howard K. Beale, *Theodore Roosevelt and the Rise of the United States to World Power* (Baltimore: Johns Hopkins University Press, 1956) and Frederick W. Marks III, *Velvet on Iron: The Diplomacy of Theodore Roosevelt* (Lincoln: University of Nebraska Press, 1979) are good places to begin, even though in my opinion they overestimate Roosevelt's attachment to realpolitik.

Woodrow Wilson's thinking about Germany and its role in the world is fully documented in the invaluable collection edited by Arthur Link, *The Papers of Woodrow Wilson* (Princeton, N.J.: Princeton University Press, 1966–1994, 69 vols.). John W. Coogan, *The End of Neutrality: The United States, Britain and Maritime Rights 1899–1915* (Ithaca, N.Y.: Cornell University Press, 1981) was helpful in explaining Wilson's attitude toward neutral rights, while Ernest R. May, *The World War and American Isolation 1914–1917* (Cambridge, Mass.: Harvard University Press, 1959) is a classic of diplomatic history unlikely soon to be superseded. Klaus Schwabe, *Woodrow Wilson, Revolutionary Germany, and Peacemaking, 1918–1919: Missionary Diplomacy and the Realities of Power* (Chapel Hill: University of North Carolina Press, 1985) is superb on Wilson's postwar thinking on Germany.

For the 1920s, Werner Link's detailed, challenging, and provocative *Die amerikanische Stabilisierungspolitik in Deutschland 1921–1932* (Düsseldorf: Droste Verlag, 1970), the best work on the period, is unfortunately unavailable in English translation. For non-German readers, Lloyd Ambrosius, *The United States and the Weimar Republic* (Ann Arbor, Mich.: University Microfilms, 1978) is a good survey. On the financial connection during this period, see William C. McNeil, *American Money and the Weimar Republic* (New York: Columbia University Press, 1986).

An understanding of the philosophical and historical nature of the debate between isolationists and internationalists in 1930s America is not possible without first assimilating the analysis and conclusions of Manfred Jonas in his classic *Isolationism in America 1935–1941* (Ithaca, N.Y.: Cornell University Press, 1966). The burgeoning troubles between Hitler's Germany and FDR's America are excellently summarized in the appropriate chapters of Gerhard Weinberg's *The Foreign Policy of Hitler's Germany: Diplomatic Revolution in Europe, 1933–1936* (Chicago: University of Chicago Press, 1971) and *The Foreign Policy of Hitler's Germany: Starting World War II, 1937–1939* (Chicago: University of Chicago Press, 1980). Portions of Robert Dallek's landmark diplomatic biography, *Franklin D. Roosevelt and American Foreign Policy, 1932–1945* (New York: Oxford University Press, 1979), perform the same job from the American perspective.

Hitler's statecraft is analyzed in general terms by Weinberg in *World in the Balance: Behind the Scenes of World War II* (Hanover, N.H.: University Press of New England, 1981) and by Andreas Hillgruber, *Germany and the Two World Wars* (Cambridge, Mass.: Harvard University Press, 1981). Klaus Hildebrand, *The Foreign Policy of the Third Reich* (Berkeley: University of California Press, 1973) and Jochen Thies, *Architekt der Weltherrschaft: Die Endziele Hitlers* (Düsseldorf: Droste Verlag, 1976) have some interesting things to say on this loaded issue. For the immediate prewar years, see Saul Friedländer, *Prelude to Downfall* (New York: Knopf, 1967) and James V. Compton, *The Swastika and the Eagle: Hitler, the United States and the Origins of the Second World War* (London: Bodley Head, 1968).

Arnold Offner, *American Appeasement: United States Foreign Policy and Germany 1933–1938* (Cambridge, Mass.: Harvard University Press, 1969) is well researched, and his argument is still provocative. A revisionist work of high quality from the German side is Detlef Junker, *Der unteilbare Weltmarkt: Das ökonomische Interesse in der Aussenpolitik der USA 1933–1941* (Stuttgart: Ernst Klett Verlag, 1975). Some of Junker's interesting views are available in English, in his essay in Frank Trommler and Joseph McVeigh, eds., *America and the Germans: An Assessment of a Three-Hundred Year History* (Philadelphia: University of Pennsylvania Press, 1985). Of the numerous memoirs and diaries of the Roosevelt administration, the extracts from Adolf Berle's diaries printed in Beatrice Bishop Berle and Travis Beal Jacobs, eds., *Navigating the Rapids, 1918–1971* (New York: Harcourt, Brace, Jovanovich, 1973) provide the greatest insight into the thinking of the president and discussion of the issues in their larger dimensions.

On wartime planning for Germany's future, see John H. Snell, *Wartime Origins of the East-West Dilemma over Germany* (New Orleans: Hauser Press 1959); Tony Sharp, *The Wartime Alliance and the Zonal Division of Germany* (London: Oxford University Press, 1975); Warren F. Kimball, *Swords or*

Ploughshares? The Morgenthau Plan for Defeated Nazi Germany, 1943–1946 (Philadelphia: Lippincott, 1976). Henry Morgenthau, *Germany Is Our Problem* (New York: Harper & Brothers, 1945) is valuable because it minces no words, yet his partisanship lends to his views a short-sighted perspective that fails to capture the subtleties of the German issue. Paul Y. Hammond, "Policy Directives for the Occupation of Germany," in Harold Stein, ed., *American Civil-Military Decisions* (University: University of Alabama Press, 1963) is still an indispensable guide through the tangled bureaucratic politics leading to the drafting of JCS 1076. Wartime thinking on the partition of Germany is discussed in John H. Backer, *The Decision to Divide Germany* (Durham, N.C.: Duke University Press, 1978) and, from the standpoint of American economic ideology, by Bruce Kuklick in *American Policy and the Division of Germany: The Clash with Russia over Reparations* (Ithaca, N.Y.: Cornell University Press, 1972). Despite the high quality of these works, the definitive work on the question of partition remains to be written.

A good introduction to specific problems surrounding the occupation is Robert Wolfe, ed., *Americans as Proconsuls: United States Military Government in Germany and Japan, 1944–1952* (Carbondale: Southern Illinois University Press, 1984). General accounts of the occupation can be found in Eugene Davidson, *The Death and Life of Germany: An Account of the American Occupation* (New York: Knopf, 1959); Franklin M. Davis, *Come as a Conqueror* (New York: Macmillan, 1967); John F. Gimbel, *The American Occupation of Germany: Politics and the Military, 1945–1949* (Stanford, Calif.: Stanford University Press, 1968); Edward N. Peterson, *The American Occupation of Germany—Retreat from Victory* (Detroit: Wayne State University Press, 1978); and Earl F. Ziemke, *The U.S. Army in the Occupation of Germany, 1944–1946* (Washington, D.C.: Office of Military History, 1975). Harold Zink, *The United States in Germany, 1944–1955* (New York: Van Nostrand, 1957) reads like a catalog but has the organizational virtues of a catalog as well. Anne Deighton, *The Impossible Peace: Britain, the Division of Germany and the Origins of the Cold War* (Oxford: Clarendon Press, 1990) offers compelling reminders of the important role played by Britain in shaping U.S. policy during these years. For America's recruitment of ex-Nazis during this period, see Christopher Simpson, *Blowback: America's Recruitment of Nazis and Its Effects on the Cold War* (New York: Macmillan, 1988).

General Lucius D. Clay has told his story in *Decision in Germany* (Garden City, N.Y.: Doubleday, 1950) and *Germany and the Fight for Freedom* (Cambridge, Mass.: Harvard University Press, 1950), while many of his decisions are documented in Jean Edward Smith, *The Papers of Lucius D. Clay: Germany 1945–1949*, 2 vols. (Bloomington: Indiana University Press, 1974). John H. Backer, *Winds of History: The German Years of Lucius DuBignon Clay* (New York: Van Nostrand Reinhold, 1983) and Jean Edward Smith, *Lucius D. Clay: An American Life* (New York: Henry Holt, 1990) are capable biographies of this important figure.

On the Nuremberg trials, the best overall work has been done by Bradley F. Smith in three different volumes: *Reaching Judgment at Nuremberg: The Untold Story of How the Nazi War Criminals Were Judged* (New York: Basic Books, 1977), *The American Road to Nuremberg: The Documentary Record, 1944–1945* (Stanford, Calif.: Hoover Institution Press, 1982), and *The Road to Nuremberg* (New York: Basic Books, 1981). Tom Bower, *The Pledge Betrayed: America and Britain and the Postwar Denazification of Germany* (Garden City, N.Y.: Doubleday, 1982) shows the greatest indignation at what he conceives to be the miscarriage of justice in the war-crimes trials. Other volumes of interest are Wilbourn E. Benton and George Grimm, eds., *Nuremberg: German Views of the War Trials* (Dallas: Southern Methodist University Press, 1955); William J. Bosch, *Judgment on Nuremberg: American Attitudes toward the Major German War-Crime Trials* (Chapel Hill: University of North Carolina Press, 1970); Eugene Davidson, *The Trial of the Germans* (New York: Macmillan, 1966); and Werner Maser, *Nuremberg: A Nation on Trial* (New York: Charles Scribner's Sons, 1979).

The cultural dimension of U.S.-German relations deserves greater attention than it has hitherto received. On the educational ambitions of the American occupiers, James F. Tent, *Mission on the Rhine: Re-education and Denazification in American-Occupied Germany* (Chicago: University of Chicago Press, 1982) is filled with illuminating material; Henry J. Kellerman, *Cultural Relations as an Instrument of American Foreign Policy* (Washington, D.C.: Department of State, 1978) is informative on the details of cultural policy but comes up short analytically. More recently, Ralph Willett, *The Americanization of Germany: Post-War Culture, 1945–1949* (London: Routledge, 1989) provides interesting insights on the transformation of postwar German popular culture. For more in this area, see the essays in Michael Ermarth, ed., *America and the Shaping of German Society, 1945–1955* (Oxford: Berg, 1993). Some items of interest were gleaned from Hansjorg Gehring, *Amerikanische Literaturpolitik in Deutschland 1945–1973* (Stuttgart: Deutsche Verlags-Anstalt, 1976), while Albert Norman, *Our German Policy: Propaganda and Culture* (New York: Vantage Press, 1951) was less helpful.

The complex postwar dispute over reparations was undoubtedly a major source of Soviet-American friction, but its importance as a cause of the division of Germany has been overemphasized. This economic thesis was first advanced as part of a larger revisionist argument by William Appleman Williams in his influential work, *The Tragedy of American Diplomacy* (New York: Delta Books, 1959). In addition to the volumes by Gimbel and Kuklick already cited, see Otto Nubel, *Die amerikanische Reparationspolitik gegenüber Deutschland 1941–1945* (Frankfurt: Alfred Metzner Verlag, 1980) and Manuel Gottlieb, *The German Peace Settlement and the Berlin Crisis* (New

York: Paine-Whitman, 1960). James F. Byrnes, *Speaking Frankly* (New York: Harper & Brothers, 1968) is still useful in recounting the reparations deal at Potsdam.

A far more important economic issue with implications for cold war politics, Germany's role in European recovery, is treated in John Gimbel, *The Origins of the Marshall Plan* (Stanford, Calif.: Stanford University Press, 1976); John Backer, *Priming the German Economy* (Durham, N.C.: Duke University Press, 1971); Herbert C. Mayer, *German Recovery and the Marshall Plan, 1948–1952* (New York: Edition Atlantic Forum, 1969); and Henry C. Wallich, *Mainsprings of German Revival* (New Haven: Yale University Press, 1955). Charles S. Maier, ed., *The Marshall Plan and Germany: West German Development within the Framework of the European Recovery Program* (London: Berg, 1991) offers some essays by first-class scholars. It is useful to step back from immediate German issues and look at the Marshall Plan from a larger perspective. For this purpose, indispensable are Michael Hogan, *The Marshall Plan: America, Britain, and the Reconstruction of Western Europe, 1947–1952* (New York: Cambridge University Press, 1987) and Alan Milward, *The Reconstruction of Western Europe, 1945–51* (Berkeley: University of California Press, 1984); they should if possible be read together. John Gillingham, *Coal, Steel, and the Rebirth of Europe 1945–1955* (New York: Cambridge University Press, 1991) provides a capable overview of the post-war decade.

On the Berlin blockade, see W. Phillips Davison, *The Berlin Blockade: A Study in Cold War Politics* (Princeton, N.J.: Princeton University Press, 1958) and Avi Shlaim *The United States and The Berlin Blockade, 1948–1949* (Berkeley: University of California Press, 1983). On the diplomacy of the period 1945 to 1949, volume I of Kennan's *Memoirs* gets to the meat of the issues most capably. Also helpful are the recollections of Robert Murphy, Clay's political advisor, in *Diplomat among Warriors* (Garden City, N.Y.: Doubleday; 1964). Truman's memoirs (volume 1: *Year of Decisions*; volume 2: *Years of Trial and Hope* [New York: Da Capo Press, 1986, 1987]) are on the whole surprisingly silent on Germany, which leads one to conclude that the German problem played a subsidiary role in the general scheme of things for this forceful president. The mechanics of the creation of the Bundesrepublik are covered in John F. Golay, *The Founding of the Federal Republic of Germany* (Chicago: University of Chicago Press, 1958) and Peter H. Merkl, *The Origins of the West German Republic* (New York: Oxford University Press, 1963).

For German rearmament, Dean Acheson, *Present at the Creation* (New York: Norton, 1969) is chock full of material but needs to be supplemented by David McLellan, *Dean Acheson: The State Department Years* (New York: Dodd, Mead, 1976). Adenauer's *Memoirs, Volume I, 1945–1953* (Chicago: Henry Regnery Co., 1966), the only one of four volumes translated into English, is also important, even though the issues are often muffled by caution. Further information on Adenauer is available in Terence Prittie, *Konrad Adenauer: 1876–1967* (Chicago: Cowles, 1972); Prittie, *The Velvet Chancellors: A History of Postwar Germany* (London: Frederick Muller); and Paul Weymar, *Adenauer: His Authorized Biography* (London: Andre Deutsch, 1957). Hans-Peter Schwarz, *Adenauer: der Aufstieg* (Stuttgart: Deutsche Verlags-Anstalt, 1986) is the first volume of what promises to be the standard German-language biography of Adenauer.

The thinking of John Foster Dulles prior to becoming secretary of state is ably handled in Ronald W. Preussen, *John Foster Dulles: The Road to Power* (New York: Free Press, 1982). Eisenhower's two-volume memoir, *The White House Years* (Garden City, N.Y.: Doubleday, 1963 and 1965), is thin on German issues, aspects of which are better revealed in Robert Griffith, ed., *Ike's Letters to a Friend* (Lawrence: University Press of Kansas, 1984) and Robert Ferrell, ed., *The Eisenhower Diaries* (New York: Norton, 1981). The second volume of Stephen Ambrose's biography, *Eisenhower: The President* (New York: Simon & Schuster, 1984), incorporates a good deal of recently declassified material from the Eisenhower presidential library. Blanche Wiesen Cook's disjointed *The Declassified Eisenhower* (New York: Doubleday, 1981) at least offers some meaty quotes.

A brilliant essay by Wolfram Hanrieder, "German-American Relations in the Postwar Decades," in the volume by Trommler and McVeigh cited above, provides an indispensable conceptual framework for fitting Germany into the larger framework of cold war politics. Hanrieder's more detailed analyses are available in his *West German Foreign Policy 1949–1963* (Stanford, Calif.: Stanford University Press, 1967) and *Germany, America, Europe: Forty Years of German Foreign Policy* (New Haven, Conn.: Yale University Press, 1989). Robert McGeehan, *The German Rearmament Question: American Diplomacy and European Defense after World War II* (Urbana: University of Illinois Press, 1971) is insightful and remarkably comprehensive, given his lack of access to official documentation at the time of writing. For the period to 1955, Thomas Alan Schwartz, *America's Germany: John J. McCloy and the Federal Republic of Germany* (Cambridge, Mass.: Harvard University Press, 1991) is clearly the leading work. Useful also are James Hershberg's recent biography of James Bryan Conant, *James B. Conant: Harvard to Hiroshima and the Making of the Nuclear Age* (New York: Knopf, 1993), and Kai Bird, *The Chairman: John J. McCloy and the Making of the American Establishment* (New York: Simon & Schuster, 1992). For a German view of 1952 as a missed opportunity for reunification, see Rolf Steininger, *Eine vertane Chance: Die Stalin-Note vom 10. März 1952 und die Wiedervereinigung* (Bonn: Dietz, 1985). For a brief but stimulating overview, see Ernest May, "The American Commitment to Germany, 1949–1955," *Diplomatic History* 13 (Fall 1989): 31–60.

The story of U.S.-German relations is closely tied to NATO and its problem-filled history. On this topic, the works of Lawrence S. Kaplan have set the standard.

On the Berlin crisis, see Robert M. Slusser, *The Berlin Crisis of 1961: Soviet-American Relations and the Struggle for Power in the Kremlin, June–November 1961* (Baltimore: Johns Hopkins University Press, 1973); and Jack M. Schick, *The Berlin Crisis, 1958–1962* (Philadelphia: University of Pennsylvania Press, 1971). Honoré M. Catudal, *Kennedy and the Berlin Wall Crisis: A Case Study in U.S. Decision-Making* (Berlin: Berlin Verlag, 1980) argues strongly that the Kennedy administration had foreknowledge of Khrushchev's intention to build a wall. Two works by Michael Beschloss, *Mayday: Eisenhower, Khrushchev, and the U-2 Affair* (New York: Harper & Row, 1986) and *The Crisis Years: Kennedy and Khrushchev 1960–1963* (New York: Edward Burlingame, 1991), are full of interesting detail. Biographies and reminiscences for this tension-filled period are still quite useful. See Arthur Schlesinger, Jr., *A Thousand Days* (Boston: Houghton Mifflin, 1965); Theodore Sorensen, *Kennedy* (New York: Harper & Row, 1963); and *Khrushchev Remembers* (Boston: Little, Brown, 1970).

In the preoccupation with Vietnam, diplomatic historians have tended to assume that European problems and the German question went into remission after the Berlin crisis. A. W. DePorte, *Europe between the Superpowers* (New Haven, Conn.: Yale University Press, 1979) embodies the Whiggish optimism that has tended to characterize analyses of U.S.-German and U.S.-European relations for these years. While the literature in general is large, works on the 1960s and after that are based on primary sources are relatively few in number. George McGhee, *At the Creation of a New Germany* (New Haven, Conn.: Yale University Press, 1989) is a useful firsthand account, though muted by the usual diplomatic caution.

In addition to journalistic sources and various items taken from the social scientific literature on international relations, bits and pieces for the final chapters were gleaned from the following: Warren Cohen, *Dean Rusk* (Totowa, N.J.: Cooper Square, 1980); Willy Brandt, *People and Politics: The Years 1960–1975* (Boston: Little, Brown, 1976); the two volumes of Henry Kissinger's memoirs, *White House Years* and *Years of Upheaval* (Boston: Little, Brown, 1979 and 1982); Seymour Hersh, *The Price of Power* (New York: Summit, 1983); Jimmy Carter, *Keeping Faith* (New York: Bantam, 1982); Zbigniew Brzezinski, *Power and Principle* (New York: Farrar Straus Giroux, 1982); and Alexander M. Haig, Jr., *Inner Circles: How America Changed the World* (New York: Warner Books, 1992). Helmut Schmidt, *Men and Powers* (New York: Random House, 1989) tells his side of the story of the strained alliance.

With the obvious exceptions of the INF and Bitburg controversies, the memoirs thus far published of the Reagan years have relatively little to say about the German question, which suggests a successful cold war transition to preoccupation with other matters. However, for these issues, see Ronald Reagan, *An American Life* (New York: Simon & Schuster, 1990); Alexander M. Haig, Jr., *Caveat: Realism, Reagan, and Foreign Policy* (New York: Macmillan, 1984); George P. Shultz, *Turmoil and Triumph: My Years as Secretary of State* (New York: Macmillan, 1993); and Donald T. Regan, *For the Record: From Wall Street to Washington* (New York: Harcourt Brace Jovanovich, 1988).

The theme of German cultural transformation in the 1970s and 1980s is taken up, inter alia, by Martin J. Hillenbrand, *Germany in an Era of Transition* (Paris: Atlantic Institute for International Affairs, 1983); Dirk Verheyen, *The German Question: A Cultural, Historical, and Geopolitical Exploration* (Boulder, Colo.: Westview Press, 1991); and Walter Laqueur, *Germany Today: A Personal Report* (Boston: Little, Brown, 1985).

During the 1980s a spate of books appeared on East Germany. George McAdams, *Germany Divided: From the Wall to Reunification* (Princeton, N.J.: Princeton University Press, 1993) is a sophisticated analysis from the standpoint of domestic politics in each of the Germanys. Renata Fritz-Bournaschel, *Europe and German Unification* (Oxford: Berg, 1992) is a useful documentary commentary. Gert-Joachim Glaeßner and Ian Wallace, eds., *The German Revolution of 1989: Causes and Consequences* (Oxford: Berg, 1992) and H. G. Peter Wallach and Ronald A. Francisco, *United Germany: The Past, Politics, Prospects* (Westport, Conn.: Greenwood Press, 1992) gaze into the crystal ball.

On the diplomacy of reunification, I have relied heavily on Stephen Szabo, *The Diplomacy of German Unification* (New York: St. Martin's Press, 1992), which is an example of contemporary history at its best. Michael Beschloss and Strobe Talbott, *At the Highest Levels: The Inside Story of the End of the Cold War* (Boston: Little, Brown, 1993) provides the meatiest table scraps from insiders who were willing to speak, but not for attribution. Inside accounts from West Germany are Horst Teltschik, *329 Tage: Innenansichten der Eingung* (Berlin: Siedler, 1991) and Wolfgang Schäuble, *Der Vertrag: Wie ich über die deutsche Einheit verhandelte* (Stuttgart: Deutsche Verlags-Anstalt, 1992). Jeffrey Gedmin, *The Hidden Hand: Gorbachev and the Collapse of East Germany* (Washington, D.C.: The AEI Press, 1992) is a very good analysis of the Soviet role in the DDR's demise. Robert Emmett Long, ed., *The Reunification of Germany* (New York: H. H. Wilson, 1992) offers a useful compendium of article reprints culled from the American periodical press. For readers wishing to go more deeply into recent events, the notes and bibliographic citations in the Szabo and the Glae§ner and Wallace volumes provide good starting points.

INDEX

THE AUTHOR

Frank Ninkovich received his Ph.D. in 1978 from the University of Chicago, where he studied the history of U.S. foreign relations under Akira Iriye. His published work, which includes *The Diplomacy of Ideas: United States Foreign Policy and Culture Relations, 1938–1950, Modernity and Power: A History of the Domino Theory in the Twentieth Century,* and numerous articles in scholarly journals, has explored various aspects of the relationship between culture and foreign policy. He now lives in New York City and teaches at St. John's University.